Chronicle
of the year
1988

Chronicle of the Year 1988

Has been conceived and published by Jacques Legrand

Editor:	**Derrick Mercer**
Assistant Editors:	David Gould *(Research)* Susanna Harrison *(Pictures)*
Specialist Correspondents:	Frank Barber, Robert Carvel, Christopher Dobson, Godfrey Hodgson, Peter Lewis, Louis Nevin, Bryan Silcock, Hugh Stephenson
Writers:	Peter Bently, Liz Gill, Jonathon Green, Robert Jones, Denis Pitts
Editorial Production:	Bronwen Lewis *(Manager)* Ruth Darby, Henrietta Heald, Joan Thomas
Art:	Henry Marganne *(Manager)* Christian Baude
Computer Systems:	Catherine Balouet *(Manager)* Dominique Klutz *(Software Engineer)*

I.S.B.N. 0-582-07740-0
Typesetting: Berger-Levrault, Nancy, France.
Colour process work: Christian Bocquez
Printing & Binding: Brepols, Trunhout, Belgium

Chronicle Communications Ltd.,
C/O Reader's Digest Ltd.,
Berkeley Square House,
14 Berkeley Square,
London W1X 5PD

Longman Group UK Ltd.,
Longman House
Burnt Mill,
Harlow
Essex CM20 2JE

Chronicle
of the year
1988

Longman

Chronicle

January

1. UK: Youth gangs battle the police and each other to celebrate the New Year.

1. Sydney: Aborigine protests mark the start of Australia's bicentennial year.

2. Zimbabwe: Premier Robert Mugabe welcomes his old foe Joshua Nkomo back into the cabinet (→3/4).

2. USSR: Soviet leader Mikhail Gorbachev is reported to be easing control over Eastern Europe (→6).

3. UK: Margaret Thatcher becomes the longest continuously serving Prime Minister this century, with eight years, 244 days.

3. Lebanon: An Israeli air strike kills 21 people.

4. Kenya: Mrs Thatcher arrives for her first state visit to Africa.→

4. UK: Sir Robin Butler replaces Sir Robert Armstrong as cabinet secretary.

5. UK: Eight have now died in an outbreak of meningitis in Gloucestershire.

5. Northern Ireland: Judge Andrew Donaldson resigns in protest at the poor arrangements for his personal safety (→25).

5. London: Rowan Atkinson launches the charity appeal "Comic Relief" (→5/2).

6. USSR: All cities, squares and streets named after ex-leader Leonid Brezhnev are given new names (→10).

7. UK: Labour leader Neil Kinnock calls for £1,300 million more for the NHS.→

8. Manchester: Nurses return to work (→11).

8. UK: House prices are still rising strongly despite the recent shares crash (→28).

9. London: 41 soccer fans are arrested at the Arsenal v Milwall match.

DEATHS

3. British fashion designer William Elphinstone (Bill) Gibb (*23/1/43).

7. British actor Trevor Wallace Howard (*29/9/16).→

Manchester nurses strike for better pay

Jan 7. More than 50 night nurses went on strike today over proposed cuts in "unsocial-hours" payments, which they claim could cost them up to £2,000 a year. As the nurses, all members of the National Union of Public Employees, set up a picket line at North Manchester General Hospital, management brought in agency nurses to ensure cover.

The government plans to replace extra pay for nights, Sundays and bank holidays with a fixed rate "unsocial-hours" payment of £1.20 per hour, in return for a deal which will give more cash to nurses with special skills. Much of the current row over the NHS stems from the plight of desperately ill children unable to have surgery because of the lack of intensive-care nurses.

Elsewhere today a leading geriatrician in east London warned that families were refusing to take their elderly relatives back home because of "enormous holes" in community support services, with the result that patients were having to stay in hospital at a cost of between £500 and £800 each per week.

A Labour Party spokesman claimed that, since Mrs Thatcher came to power in 1979, nearly 19,000 hospital beds in acute specialities had been lost through financial pressures (→8).

No operation yet for hole-in-heart child

Jan 6. The court of appeal today refused to order "desperately needed" surgery for hole-in-the-heart boy Matthew Collier. Four-year-old Matthew's operation has been postponed repeatedly since last September because of a shortage of intensive-care nurses at Birmingham Children's Hospital.

His family lawyers had argued that the health authority had a duty to treat him, but the appeal judges ruled that the courts could not deal with either the philosophy of NHS funding or an authority's decision, unless there was evidence of bad faith or illegality. "We cannot arrange hospital lists," said one.

Doctors have warned that if the boy loses further weight they will be unable to operate (→13).

Still waiting: Matthew Collier.

Windscale cover-up of 1957 revealed

Jan 1. The full report on the 1957 Windscale reactor fire, until Chernobyl the world's most serious nuclear accident, was suppressed for political reasons, according to cabinet papers made public today. Although the inquiry report contains little technical information not released at the time of the fire, it was not published in full because Prime Minister Harold Macmillan feared that it would kill his chances of securing closer Anglo-American cooperation on atomic weapons.

Trevor Howard has his final reel

Howard displaying a stiff upper lip.

Jan 7. Trevor Howard, who died today aged 71, was probably as proud of the six wickets he took before lunch for the MCC as of any of his screen performances. He will always be remembered for the restrained quality of the love duet he played with Celia Johnson in *Brief Encounter*. Nearly 40 years later they found the same moving rapport as the British expatriates left behind in India in *Staying On*.

For all Howard's roistering, he could invest a part, such as the police chief in Graham Greene's *The Heart of the Matter*, with tragic depth of unstated feeling. As his friend Robert Mitchum put it, "You never caught him acting."

These faces ring a bell? They should — it's Princes William and Harry.

Bloodshed worsens in Gaza uprising

Jan 8. The bloodshed continued today in the Israeli-occupied territories of Gaza and the West Bank, when young Palestinians took to the streets after Friday prayers.

One man was killed at Gaza's Bureij refugee camp when protestors stoned army patrols and the soldiers retaliated with automatic rifle fire. Other demonstrators were forced off the streets when helicopters bombed them with tear gas.

Trouble also flared on Temple Mount in Jerusalem, Islam's third holiest site, when a group of Palestinians leaving the Al Aqsa mosque stoned a police station inside the sanctuary walls. Two policemen were injured before the demonstrators were driven off by tear gas.

UN envoy, Mark Goulding, arrived in Israel today to investigate the safety of the 1.5 million Arabs living under Israeli control, but the Israeli Prime Minister, Itzhak Shamir, refused to speak to him.

Mr Goulding's visit follows the highly controversial tour of the troubled areas earlier this week by British Foreign Office Minister David Mellor, who caused a storm by criticising the Israelis for their treatment of the Palestinians.

Today, the Foreign Secretary, Sir Geoffrey Howe, came to Mr Mellor's support, saying that Israel's occupation of the West Bank and Gaza Strip was "bound to have a brutalising influence on events in the area" (→12).

Israeli troops brutally assault Palestinians in the occupied territories.

"This is not good at all," David Mellor tells an Israeli official.

Waldheim's war role faces probe

Jan 5. Six international historians investigating Dr Kurt Waldheim's wartime record with the German army said today they are now ready to begin their interrogation of the Austrian President and former UN Secretary-General. The commission has faced delays because Waldheim and his supporters want the inquiry limited to "personal guilt", with the issue of what he knew about the deportation of Jews and other Nazi atrocities in the Balkans excluded. A spokesman for the right-wing People's Party caused a storm when he defended Waldheim: "So long as it isn't proved he strangled six Jews with his own hands, there is no problem." (→31)

PM's African tour ends in scuffles

Jan 8. Mrs Thatcher ended her tour of Africa today with a visit to the ancient city of Kano, in Nigeria's Moslem north. She was met by drummers, dancers, spear-carrying horsemen, and hundreds of placard-waving anti-apartheid protesters chanting "Thatcher loves apartheid" and "Maggie repent or be damned". Scuffles broke out when security guards from Lagos clashed with Kano guards, both groups trying to protect the British Prime Minister from protesters who had by then been left behind.

Firemen attack lethal foam furniture

Jan 8. Leading firemen today blamed the widespread and avoidable use of polyurethane foam, which burns fiercely and produces toxic fumes, for the deaths of 24 people over the recent holiday period alone. They accused a complacent government and pigheaded manufacturers of ignoring their warnings for 10 years.

Saying they "are sick to their stomachs of going into blackened bedrooms and bringing out charred bodies of men, women and especially children", fire chiefs from across the country asked for tighter regulations to reduce the death toll, now running at one a day. Two

organisations, they said, are preventing the immediate adoption of readily-available, safer "combustion modified foam" — the Department of Trade and Industry (DTI) and the British Furniture Manufacturers' Federation. The DTI wants to phase out standard foam filling over three years, but more than 200 MPs have already signed a Commons motion for a total ban.

While the fire bosses held forth in London, the funeral took place in Merthyr Tydfil of a father and his four children who died pitifully in their beds on New Year's Day, minutes after fire broke out in their house (→11).

North gets poorer, south gets richer

Jan 5. Britain's wealth is growing faster in the south than in the north, dividing the rich and poor halves of the country ever deeper. A report by researchers at Warwick University has applied a range of "prosperity factors" to draw up a list of thriving towns clustered around London. The end of the North Sea oil boom and the 1984 miners' strike have helped accentuate the relative stagnation of the northern economy, says the study. News of a sharpening divide challenges Mrs Thatcher's claim that the north-south divide is a myth (→14).

She's in charge: Mrs Thatcher sets a record for tenancy at No. 10.

January

1988

Su	Mo	Tu	We	Th	Fr	Sa
					1	2
3	4	5	6	7	8	9
10	11	12	13	14	15	16
17	18	19	20	21	22	23
24	25	26	27	28	29	30
31						

10. Moscow: Gorbachev proposes a summit meeting with China. →

10. UK: A doctor suggests prostitutes with the AIDS virus should get a state pension to stop the spread of the disease. →

11. Birmingham: 100 hospital consultants protest against the NHS underfunding (→20).

11. UK: Inflammable foam furniture will be banned from March 1989.

11. Moscow: The Soviet Union agrees to participate in this year's Olympic Games.

12. Israel: Authorities refuse to allow the United Nations to inspect Palestinian refugee camps (→14).

12. UK: Statistics show that one in eight babies was born out of wedlock in 1986 (→14).

12. UK: The "Next Directory" is launched, promising a new approach to shopping by post.

13. Birmingham: Four-year-old Matthew Collier has his long-awaited heart operation (→14/2).

13. West Germany: A major nuclear waste scandal threatens to topple the government.

14. Hastings: John Nunn and Nigel Short draw in the Foreign and Colonial chess tournament final.

14. Jerusalem: Ten Palestinian leaders are detained. →

15. UK: 80 Tory backbenchers rebel to try to save a private member's Bill to reform the Official Secrets Act (→4/2).

15. UK: Television personality and nutritionist, Magnus Pyke, is attacked and tied up by a burglar at his home.

16. UK: 4,500 policemen patrol today's soccer matches at a cost of £450,000.

16. US: New seismic data reveals that the US has conducted 117 secret nuclear tests in the last 25 years.

DEATH

15. Irish politician, international statesman and jurist Sean MacBride (*26/1/04). →

Arabs fight Israelis in heart of Jerusalem

An imam leads Palestinian demonstrators round the Dome of the Rock.

Jan 15. The choking stench of tear-gas drifted through Islam's Noble Sanctuary in the heart of Jerusalem today as Israeli forces battled with demonstrators whipped up by a fiery sermon from Sheik Hamed Beitawi at Friday prayers, which in these troubled times are as political as they are religious.

The troubles, he said, "were the results of Israeli hatred and oppression. They are not satisfied with occupying our land and expelling our people. They ruined our homes and closed our universities. They arrested young people. That is zulm — oppression."

Prayers over, the excited young Palestinians spilled out into the street, but found the Israelis ready for them with assault rifles and tear-gas. Marksmen were posted at vantage points on the rooftops.

The demonstrators burnt Israeli and American flags and flew their own forbidden Palestinian banner. Then came a barrage of stones. The police replied with tear-gas and a baton charge, which scattered the protestors.

Afterwards women, their eyes streaming with tears, accused the Israelis of throwing tear-gas into the Noble Sanctuary: "Those monsters fired into the mosque itself, at women who were praying." (→20)

Ireland mourns peacemaker MacBride

Irishman with international appeal.

Jan 15. Sean MacBride, who progressed from IRA activist to major figure in the quest for world peace, died today in Dublin, aged 83.

MacBride was a key figure in the Irish independence struggle, acting briefly as IRA chief of staff. One of Ireland's top barristers, he founded the Clann na Poblactha Party, which helped defeat de Valera in 1948 and steered Ireland towards full republican status.

His achievements in the international arena were considerable; he was a founder of Amnesty International in 1961 and chairman until 1974. Universally esteemed, he was awarded the Nobel Peace Prize in 1974, the Lenin Prize for Peace in 1977 and the American Medal of Justice in 1978.

Tory stalwart Willie Whitelaw bows out

Jan 10. On doctor's orders Viscount (William) Whitelaw resigned today from his number-two job in the government. He relinquished the official posts of Lord President of the Council and Leader of the House of Lords. He also stepped down from his unofficial ones of deputy prime minister and chief conciliation officer inside the cabinet.

Whitelaw, aged 69, suffered a minor stroke while attending Parliament's annual Christmas carol service. He has recovered well, but reluctantly accepts that nearly 30 years of Tory front-bench service is enough.

Mrs Thatcher spoke of his "unique qualities". She also said that the unofficial deputy prime minister appointment was unique to him and will now lapse.

Lord and Lady Whitelaw step out.

England win shock victory in France

Jan 16. England's rugby players today confounded their critics (and bookmakers who were offering odds on the size of an English defeat) by beating France in the first of the season's matches in the five nations' championship. Playing in Paris the English team won by ten points to nine, while in Dublin, Ireland edged out the Scots by 22 points to 18 (→6/2).

AIDS virus spreads to New York babies

Jan 13. One in every 61 babies born in New York City last month was infected with the AIDS virus, it was revealed today. Just over 9,000 were tested anonymously in a special study and 148 were found to be positive. Medical experts, who describe the rate as alarming, fear that as many as 40 per cent may go on to develop the disease.

Most are the children of poor black or Hispanic drug addicts and their sexual partners — a section of the community difficult to reach or treat.

The total number of AIDS cases in Britain now stands at 1,227, double that of a year ago. There have been 697 deaths (→21).

Royal prerogative cloaks MI5 linetaps

Jan 13. Electronic bugging and burglary by MI5 and other British security services is permitted under the royal prerogative, the *Independent* newspaper claimed today. Senior officers have justified the search and entry of suspects' homes by reference to a 200-year-old precedent, in which a prerogative-based warrant was issued "to seize a man [suspected of sedition] together with his books and papers".

The services' interpretation — based on a 1952 Home Office directive — has never been challenged in the courts (→15).

Finances improve, crime worsens

Jan 14. British people are growing wealthier, but less caring and more violent; society continues to fragment and divisions between rich and poor deepen. These are some of the findings of the government's survey of social trends, published today. The good news is that we are healthier and live longer, and that working households in 1986 were 30 per cent richer in real terms than in 1976. The bad news is that more people are living alone or in one-parent families, and crime and homelessness are increasing (→18).

Dissident Sakharov meets Gorbachev

Dr Andrei Sakharov, who wants Gorbachev to free 200 political prisoners.

Jan 15. Mikhail Gorbachev added a dramatic new dimension to his policy of *glasnost* (openness) when he staged a meeting in the Kremlin today with Dr Andrei Sakharov, the Soviet dissident and Nobel peace laureate. After the two men had shaken hands, Dr Sakharov handed the Soviet leader a list of 200 people still held as political prisoners in labour camps.

Sakharov, who spent seven years in internal exile in the closed city of Gorky until Gorbachev brought him back to Moscow last year, said the country had "the kind of leader needed at this crucial moment in history". Sakharov has agreed to join the board of an international peace and human rights group, which will follow up last year's peace forum in Moscow, attended by Western film stars, novelists and scientists, to publicise Gorbachev's support for human rights. It has been given $1 million by Dr Armand Hammer, the American oil tycoon whose links with the Soviet Union go back to Lenin's time (→5/2).

Liberal MPs quash leaders' blueprint

Jan 14. David Steel and Robert Maclennan, leaders respectively of the Liberal and Social Democratic parties, were involved in a humiliating climbdown today. They tacitly admitted having made asses of themselves as they buried a joint policy statement which they had prepared for the new Social and Liberal Democratic Party (SLD) after its projected merger in the near future.

Through inadequate consultation the document was published before Liberal MPs had studied it and a last-minute attempt to suppress it failed. A joint team was appointed to prepare a different statement for submission to special conferences of the two parties later this month.

The Steel-Maclennan declaration included such controversial proposals as extension of value added tax to food and children's clothing. It was widely seen at Westminster as inept and a recipe for electoral suicide.

Former SDP leader David Owen chortled on the sidelines: "It is all a ghastly mess. The merger should be dead." But it is more likely that the creation of the new party will still go ahead, led by men with self-inflicted injuries.

Britain's fickle husbands think twice about "Fatal Attraction"

Jan 14. *Fatal Attraction*, having galvanised American moviegoers last year, today opened in Britain to a greater flurry of debate about morality than its merits as a stylish, sexy thriller. It proves to have the old message that hell hath no fury like a woman scorned — and that any husband tempted to err would do better to steer clear for fear of falling into her clutches.

The woman in the case, who provokes a married man (played by Michael Douglas) into a one-night affair, takes her revenge not only on him but on his family, right down to his young daughter's pet rabbit. The behaviour of this obsessed Fury (Glenn Close) remains unexplained. Nonetheless, the impact of this suburban parable, directed by Briton Adrian Lyne, cannot be disputed.

Besieged Michael Douglas starts to wonder just what the attraction was.

Su	Mo	Tu	We	Th	Fr	Sa
					1	2
3	4	5	6	7	8	9
10	11	12	13	14	15	16
17	18	19	20	21	22	23
24	25	26	27	28	29	30
31						

17. Haiti: The general election takes place, but is widely boycotted (→7/3).

17. Cairo: British citizen, Maureen Paleschi, is jailed for 25 years for heroin smuggling.

18. UK: Neil Kinnock launches "Labour Listens", a two year policy review (→11/2).

18. Argentina: Aldo Rico, leader of a failed army coup, surrenders to the government.

18. Paris: left-wingers invade Maxim's, planning to turn the smart restaurant into a soup kitchen for the poor.

18. UK: BBC Radio One tells its disc jockeys to talk less and play more music instead.

19. UK: The government is to spend £36 million on making roads skid-proof.

19. UK: Publisher Robert Maxwell concedes defeat in his attempt to buy Watford Football Club.

20. Beirut: Terry Waite has now been missing for a year.

21. Congo: Scientists are predicting that one million Africans will die of AIDS in the next ten years (→24).

21. Paris: The first conference of Nobel prize-winners closes with a list of "conclusions" on the state of the world.

22. London: A judge awards at least £165,000 to each family affected by last March's Zeebrugge ferry disaster (→6/3).

22. Israel: Savage beatings to quash Palestinian protests are now official policy (→24).

23. Zanzibar: President Idris Abdul Wakil dismisses his government after an alleged coup plot.

23. Nicaragua: Internal opposition is hindering President Ortega's peace initiative (→29).

DEATHS

17. South African journalist and anti-apartheid activist Percy Qoboza (*17/1/38).

20. French banker, vintner and entrepreneur Baron Philippe de Rothschild (*13/4/02).

Nolan's clock-watching nets him £20,000

Jan 19. A 22-year-old who has to stab the typewriter with a stick attached to his forehead was today awarded the Whitbread Book of the Year award, worth £20,000. Christopher Nolan, who lives in Ireland, won it with his autobiography, *Under the Eye of the Clock*. Each page took him a day to write.

Nolan, whose brain was starved of oxygen at birth, was left incapable of speech or muscular co-ordination, but his mental muscle is spectacular. He learnt to write from hearing people talk and published a collection of poems when he was 15. He has been compared to James Joyce because his work is rich in words newly minted by himself.

Nolan: a triumph over adversity

Nicaragua offers ceasefire to Contras

Jan 17. Nicaragua's President Daniel Ortega closed the Central American summit in Costa Rica today with a dramatic about-turn. Going against all the pledges he has made to his Sandinista Party, Ortega promised to lift the state of emergency, free all political prisoners, agree a ceasefire and meet the US-backed Contra rebels for direct negotiations.

These concessions are meant to throttle American aid to the rebels at source. On February 4 Congress will vote on President Reagan's key bill asking for $270 million more aid for the Contras, whom he sees as freedom fighters against the Communist Sandinistas. Ortega hopes that his new, conciliatory position will persuade Congress to throw out Reagan's aid bill. If they don't, the peace process which took such a leap forward today will prove stillborn. Ortega has already warned that "one dollar for the Contras will kill the peace effort".

Washington has given the proposals a muted welcome. Ortega must follow his words with swift action if Congress is to believe him and reject the Reagan bill (→23).

Royal Colleges join NHS funding row

Jan 20. Three of the most influential figures in the medical establishment today gave the government a stinging rebuke on NHS cash. Sir Raymond Hoffenberg, president of the Royal College of Physicians, said: "We deprecate the approach of applying Elastoplast to stop a sore to the point where the whole body becomes covered in plasters but new sores keep erupting."

Sir Raymond and his counterparts at the College of Surgeons and at the College of Obstetricians and Gynaecologists told the Commons social services select committee that drip-feeding the NHS with emergency funds was no answer. They called for a fundamental cash review, but stressed there must not be a two-tier system. Good-quality care must be available to all.

Their criticisms came just before nurses at three London hospitals voted for a 24-hour stoppage next month, while in Glasgow health workers marched in protest at the privatisation of hospital cleaning and catering services.

Yesterday a group of children and parents presented a 60,000-name petition at Downing Street, calling for action to ease the Birmingham crisis. All these moves will increase pressure on beleaguered Social Services Secretary John Moore (→25).

Public wins red box reprieve after bout with British Telecom

Jan 18. Despite British Telecom's determination to replace the familiar red telephone box with space-age designs, at least 1,000 of the old type will remain — as listed buildings. BT has already replaced 20,000 of the 50,000 old boxes with a new glass design.

A "delighted" English Heritage have asked the public to nominate boxes for preservation. "It is important that Britain's street furniture is maintained, especially in famous places like Parliament Square and the Law Courts," said its spokesman.

The Gilbert Scott designed boxes are fast becoming collectors' items, some being used as shower cubicles, some even for telephones in private homes (→24/3).

British Telecom's professional vandals root up another red phone kiosk.

Steel quits leadership

Jan 23. David Steel will not stand for the leadership of a merged Social and Liberal Democratic Party. "I have been a leader for 12 years and I have no wish to go on any longer," he told a news conference today.

The Liberal leader clarified his position as his own and SDP officials prepared for membership ballots on whether to merge the two parties or go their separate ways. Merger is likely.

Mr Steel has lately shown signs of exhaustion and loss of patience. His authority was badly dented in the debacle of his sponsorship, and then hurried withdrawal last week, of a policy prospectus which fellow Liberal MPs described as "inept, loopy and ill considered" (→31).

The back benches beckon.

Third World debt to West mounts

Jan 18. The Third World is groaning under an ever larger debt to the West, said the World Bank today in its annual report. The total debt of the developing countries is forecast to reach $1,245 billion this year, and up to 61 per cent of their gross national product goes simply to service the interest payments on existing debts. This makes it almost impossible for the debtor countries to have a viable economy, drawing them deeper into borrowing and more into debt (→19/2).

Bad housing breeds criminal classes

Jan 18. Young people who live in badly-designed housing estates are eight times more likely to commit crimes than those in good ones, a London University study shows. A direct correlation is demonstrated between design and crime. Familiar design features of Britain's worst estates — linked walkways, open layouts, shared corridors, lifts and stairs — are said to make residents feel powerless in their own space and to create an atmosphere of decay and fear.

Jan 22. Mike Tyson knocks out his challenger Larry Holmes, 17 years his senior, in the fourth round, to retain the heavyweight championship.

Gaza rebels face "beatings" says Israel

Jan 20. Itzhak Rabin, Israel's Defence Minister, took a hard line yesterday when confronted by angry Palestinians at Jelazoun refugee camp. He made it clear that there would be no softening in the army's attitude towards demonstrators, who, he said, would be met with "might, power and beatings".

He also imposed a ban on foreign charities sending food and clothing to the occupied Gaza and West Bank, where the commercial strike is biting hard.

"If they want to strike and not supply food," he said, "they should not cry afterwards that there's a food shortage. There is no food shortage. There is an attempt by use of threats to prevent the population from getting food."

The scene of action shifted to the north today when an Israeli patrol intercepted three of Yasser Arafat's Fatah movement shortly after they had cut through the fence separating Israel and Lebanon.

The three men were armed with grenades, AK 47 assault rifles and anti-tank rocket launchers, but the Israelis caught them by surprise and killed all three. One Israeli soldier was wounded.

This action, minor in terms of Middle East guerrilla actions, is important to the Israelis because it wipes out some of the shame of the incident in November when a Palestinian flew a powered hang-glider across the border and killed six Israeli soldiers before being shot.

It shows, nevertheless, that the Israelis are facing problems on all fronts (→22).

A Palestinian, injured in the fighting, screams out his continued defiance.

Alton's abortion bill splits public opinion

Jan 22. The bill to reduce the time limit on abortions from 28 weeks to 18 has split public opinion, according to a new survey. Four out of ten people want the law changed and almost the same number want it left as it is. The poll found, however, that a crucial 12 per cent favour a 22-24 week compromise, a measure the Prime Minister herself is said to support.

The bill, introduced by Liberal MP David Alton, came a step nearer to success today when it won a majority of 45 for a second reading. When the vote was announced at the end of a lengthy and emotio-nal debate, supporters in the public gallery cheered and applauded.

But yesterday 7,000 opponents gathered in London for a series of protests, including a torchlight rally. They fear that the bill, which in its present form would allow late abortions only if the mother's life were at risk or the baby severely physically handicapped, would criminalise desperate women.

There has been mounting disquiet over late abortions at a time when many babies born earlier than 28 weeks are capable of survival. The bill will now go to a Commons committee.

Su	Mo	Tu	We	Th	Fr	Sa
					1	2
3	4	5	6	7	8	9
10	11	12	13	14	15	16
17	18	19	20	21	22	23
24	25	26	27	28	29	30
31						

24. London: Three thousand people march for rights for AIDS sufferers. →

24. Tunis: The Arab League backs the Palestinian uprising with cash for Israeli Arabs (→30).

25. UK: There will be no prosecutions following the alleged "shoot to kill" policy of the Royal Ulster Constabulary (→28).

25. London: Judge Martin Bowley resigns after tabloid press reporting about his private life.

26. London: Financial journalist Jeremy Warner is fined 9c 20,000 for refusing to reveal his sources of information.

27. US: Medical research suggests that aspirin can prevent heart attacks.

27. Cleveland: A judicial inquiry opens into allegations of widespread child sexual abuse.

28. UK: The 1987 balance of payments was 9c 2.7 billion in the red, the worst since 1974 (→1/3).

28. Northern Ireland: Police seize a huge IRA arms dump.

29. UK: Junior Health Minister Edwina Currie tells people to sacrifice holidays to pay for private health care (→31).

29. Costa Rica: Talks between the Sandinistas and Contras end fruitlessly.

30. West Bank: Ten Palestinians are wounded as the Israeli army abandons beatings in favour of gunfire (→1/2).

31. UK: The British Medical Association accuses the government of deliberately running down the NHS (→3/2).

31. West Germany: A telegram is published which seems to implicate Kurt Waldheim in a Nazi mass deportation (→11/2).

DEATHS

28. East German nuclear spy Dr Emil Julius Klaus Fuchs (*29/12/11).

31. Soviet politician Georgi Maximilianovich Malenkov (*8/1/03).

Scargill is re-elected by narrow majority

Jan 24. Arthur Scargill has won his battle for re-election as president of the National Union of Mineworkers — but only just. In a two-man fight he obtained 54 per cent of the vote, compared with the 70.1 per cent of the poll he won in 1982 against three opponents.

His victory this time was thanks to the loyalty of his own members in Yorkshire, which is the biggest mining area. His Yorkshire majority of 6,241 was bigger than the national majority of 5,668. His opponent, John Walsh, won more non-Yorkshire votes and scored massive victories from the white-collar section and power workers.

Mr Scargill campaigned for a continuation of his policies of confrontation with British Coal and the government, opposing more flexible working patterns and the new disciplinary code. Mr Walsh argued for a more conciliatory approach and for an attempt to bring the breakaway Union of

Miners' president once more.

Democratic Mineworkers back into the fold.

Mr Walsh saw the result as showing that the members wanted a change. Mr Scargill, however, said it was "a staggering defeat for 'new realism'".

AIDS experts agree on urgent action

Jan 28. AIDS is a global threat to humanity and urgent international action is needed to combat it. That was the message today at the end of a three-day summit in London on the disease. The declaration from health ministers from 148 countries also stressed the need in prevention programmes to protect human rights and human dignity.

The summit was told that between five and ten million people across the world were now affected by AIDS. There was no cure and a vaccine might not be available before the next century. Figures also released this week suggest that in the UK alone the cost of caring for victims of the disease will be £80 million this year.

The Princess Royal caused a furore when she opened the conference by calling AIDS "a classic own goal scored by the human race against itself". Referring to the tragedy of those, particularly babies, who had been infected unknowingly, Princess Anne added that prevention was the only answer. "We all need to learn. Ignorance in this instance is definitely not bliss." (→27/3)

SDP Council moves closer to merger with Liberal Party

Jan 31. The Council for Social Democracy — the SDP's own parliament — met in Sheffield today and voted overwhelmingly for a full membership ballot on whether the party should merge with the Liberals. This makes merger certain.

Equally certain now is a messy and acrimonious divorce between David Owen's anti-merger supporters and the majority headed by Lord (Roy) Jenkins, Shirley Williams and Robert Maclennan, who took over the SDP leadership when Dr Owen bowed out.

Before the vote Owenites accused Lord Jenkins of betrayal. Jenkinsites advised Dr Owen to take a long holiday. Both sides talked about calling in lawyers. The so-called nice party is now turning quite nasty. Some Liberals are asking: is merger wise? (→3/3)

Aussie soap cleans up over Dirty Den

Jan 24. Fourteen million Britons are now hooked on the daily doings of Madge, Scott, Charlene and Jim in a far away Australian suburb, and the BBC has an unexpected hit on its hands with the new soap opera *Neighbours*.

Originally bought as a cheap filler for its daytime schedules, a switch to teatime has made the series a runaway success. This week's viewing figures show the five-day-a-week teatime serial running a close third to the perennial favourites, *Coronation Street* and *EastEnders*. Fans dismiss critics who purport to see preposterous storylines and acting as artificial as the sets, so the grand soap opera tradition of *Crossroads* lives on. The real lives of blond stars Kylie Minogue and Jason Donovan are also becoming "news" stories for the tabloids.

Charlene and Scott, whose stormy relationship is a national fascination.

IRA pub bombers lose Old Bailey appeal

Jan 28. Anglo-Irish relations reached a new low today with the rejection — after a seven-week hearing — of an appeal by six Irishmen convicted in 1975 for the Birmingham pub bombings when, on November 21 1974, 21 people were killed and 160 injured at two public houses in the city.

The hearing was allowed after the Home Secretary, Douglas Hurd, had decided that there was "sufficient doubt" about the outcome of the original trial.

The court of appeal refused to accept that there had been a "wide-ranging conspiracy" by the policemen involved. Allegations that confessions had been obtained after torture were also rejected, as was supporting evidence by two former police officers.

New scientific evidence — which suggested that positive tests for nitroglycerine on the men's hands could have been caused by chemicals on playing cards — was also produced by the appellants, but dismissed.

Lord Lane, the Lord Chief Justice, said: "The longer this trial has gone on the more convinced this court has been that the verdict was correct."

The Irish Justice Minister, Gerry Collins, said he was "amazed and saddened". British Labour MP, Chris Mullin, who had campaigned for a retrial, described it as "a black day for British justice" (→5/2).

Thatcher sets up radical NHS review

Jan 25. The National Health Service is to get a major shake-up, starting with a top-to-bottom ministerial review, the Prime Minister said today. It will look at "all the possibilities", including an increase in private funding. Mrs Thatcher is against a Royal Commission, which she thinks would take too long. Meanwhile, Royal College of Nursing members at a London hospital want an end to the no-strike rule (→29).

Jan 26. Australia is 200 years old today, and the tall ships in Sydney Harbour are just part of the worldwide celebrations.

Twelve die in new South African riots

Jan 31. At least 12 died in faction fights between radical blacks and their conservative rivals over the weekend. Vigilantes set fire to shanties in the KTC squatter camp near Cape Town airport, leaving five dead and thousands homeless. Squatters say police fuel the violence because they want to clear the camp and resettle people elsewhere. In Natal, Zulu nationalists stormed Edendale shanty town looking for radicals. Seven died (→10/2).

Theatreland stages Clause 28 protest

Jan 25. As the House of Lords considers Clause 28 of the Local Government Bill, which would prevent councils from giving financial support to any work that could be interpreted as "promoting" homosexuality, a protest was staged at London's Playhouse theatre today by actors and showbusiness celebrities to oppose its inclusion.

"This bill could put unprecedented powers in the hands of local authorities," said film director John Schlesinger. In a message Lord Olivier described it as "a dangerous step backwards". Janet Suzman, Ian McKellen, Terry Jones, Lenny Henry and Melvyn Bragg were among those at the protest (→2/2).

"Phantom" arrives to haunt Broadway

Stars of a pop opera: Michael Crawford and Sarah Brightman.

Jan 28. Andrew Lloyd-Webber's *Phantom of the Opera* opened on Broadway last night virtually assured of being as big a hit as *Les Miserables*. The show has cost $8 million, to stage but advance ticket sales will bring in more than twice that figure.

Some of this morning's reviews are, however, less than gushing. Frank Rich in the *New York Times* calls it "impoverished of artistic personality and passion", although praising the mesmeric effect of Michael Crawford's Phantom.

Crawford acquired a hiatus hernia through playing the part. Not prepared to let another actor take over the role he had created, he refused to obey orders to rest.

City crash takes wind out of Porsche sales

Jan 28. As gloom settled over the financial markets and the dollar threatened to sink lower than a Porsche's oil-sump, annual production of the Yuppies' favoured success symbol has slumped from 50,000 cars to 31,000, the German makers revealed today. More than 6,000 workers are on short time after a three-week Christmas lay-off and the company is considering a "one car only" policy. In the USA, Porsche's principal export market, the price of a 944S model — originally $19,990 — has shot to $27,900.

Porsche's sales figures are now as red as this nifty little mover.

February

1988

Su	Mo	Tu	We	Th	Fr	Sa
	1	2	3	4	5	6
7	8	9	10	11	12	13
14	15	16	17	18	19	20
21	22	23	24	25	26	27
28	29					

1. UK: Ex-US Secretary of State, Caspar Weinberger is awarded a knighthood for his support in the Falklands war.

1. London: The inquiry opens into last year's King's Cross tube fire, in which 31 died (→6/4).

2. New Zealand: Zola Budd is banned from the world cross-country championship (→14/3).

2. London: Protestors against Clause 28 of the Local Government Bill abseil into the House of Lords (→8).

2. UK: The National Union of Seamen stages a strike in Northern ports.→

3. London: The government is planning to move 565,000 civil servants to the provinces, leaving just 20,000 in Whitehall.

3. Washington: Congress votes against Reagan's $43 million Contra aid package (→4).

4. Managua: President Ortega says he does not think yesterday's vote will end US aggression in Nicaragua (→21/3).

4. UK: Education Secretary Kenneth Baker announces the abolition of the Inner London Education Authority (→9/2).

4. Israel: Two soldiers are killed by Palestinian raiders from Lebanon (→12).

5. UK: "Comic Relief" fund-raising day brings widespread outbreaks of silliness.→

5. Oslo: President Reagan and Mr Gorbachev are nominated for the Nobel Peace Prize.→

6. Geneva: 30 countries agree a draft treaty on toxic waste disposal (→17).

6. Scotland beat France 23-12 and Wales beat England 11-3 in rugby internationals (→19/3).

6. UK: A survey shows that out-of-order phone boxes and Post Office queues are the top irritants of modern life.

DEATHS

5. British film maker Emeric Pressburger (*5/12/02).

6. British broadcaster and writer Marghanita Laski (*24/10/24).

Panama leader faces US cocaine charges

Feb 5. The Panamanian leader, General Noriega, was charged yesterday by a US Federal Court on twelve counts of smuggling drugs from Colombia into the United States. The Panamanian leader, who is charged among other things with accepting $6.4 million to protect cocaine shipments, could face up to 145 years in prison if convicted on all charges. However extradition proceedings are not expected.

The indictments also allege that President Fidel Castro of Cuba was involved in a dispute between Noriega and the Medellin cocaine cartel when Panamanian soldiers raided drug laboratories Noriega had been paid to protect.

Under suspicion: Noriega.

Learner bikers will have to pass test

Feb 3. Learner motorcyclists will have to take a compulsory one-day training course and pass a test before receiving provisional licences allowing them to drive on the road, Transport Minister Peter Bottomley said today. Hitherto they have been allowed to ride without any training, which is said to be a major cause of the dreadful death and injury toll: motorcyclists account for a quarter of all road casualties, but just two per cent of total road traffic. Bikers' organisations welcomed the initiative.

Air miss was "five feet from disaster"

Feb 6. Over 300 passengers on board a British Airways Tri-Star narrowly avoided death today when their aircraft came within feet of a mid-air collision with a Bulgarian Tupolev 154 over Kent. The Tri-Star swung violently upwards and to the right to avoid the Tupelov, believed to be a Balkan Airways charter flight, which appeared suddenly in a cloud. British Airways claimed the planes were 300 yards apart, although passengers say they were told at the time the distance was five feet.

Nurses start month of strike action

Feb 3. Hundreds of nurses from ten London hospitals marched on Parliament today at the start of a month-long campaign of protests and strikes. Police threw a cordon across Whitehall to stop the demonstration reaching Downing Street. Two nurses were arrested, but six were allowed to present a letter of no-confidence at Number Ten.

Most of the action in support of pay claims and more money for the NHS centred on the capital, but there were also stoppages in other cities across the country. Some were reported to involve Royal College of Nursing members who defied that body's no-strike rule.

The nurses claimed that they had arranged emergency cover, but John Moore, the Social Services Secretary, condemned their actions. "Their first and absolute duty is to patients," he said. The protests coincided with a call by the British Medical Association for an immediate injection of £1.5 billion into the NHS and its continuation as a tax-funded service.

One scheme the government is considering to fund the NHS is a special "health stamp". This could enable individuals to contract out of the NHS, paying lower contributions in return for private insurance. Another idea is for vouchers which could be spent in private or public hospitals (→10/2).

Two Arab youths shot dead in worst West Bank violence so far

Feb 1. Two young Palestinians were shot dead today in the worst outbreak of violence since civil disobedience erupted in the Israeli-occupied territories of Gaza and the West Bank last December.

The most disturbing aspect of the shootings is that they seem to have been carried out by Jewish settlers on the West Bank who were travelling with police and army vehicles and found their way through the village of Anabta blocked by Palestinian demonstrators.

The Israelis are blaming the upsurge of violence on the reopening of the schools and the international impact of the Palestinian campaign of disobedience, now seen to be more effective than terrorism (→4).

Israeli police and troops are stoned by Palestinian youths.

Ferry strike paralyses Britain's ports

Feb 4. Despite a return-to-work call from the general secretary of the National Union of Seamen, Sam McCluskie, most of the 7,000 members working the ferries today continued their strike. Britain's ferry ports are in chaos. At Dover, the biggest of them all, there is a queue of over 1,500 lorries choking the approach roads.

Some people are managing to get away. The French and Belgian ferries, which account for one third of Dover's traffic, are sailing normally. Car drivers can also still use the hovercraft and foot passengers the jetfoil, since these are not affected by the dispute.

The only ferry crossing not disrupted is that to the Isle of Wight, whose crews are members of the National Union of Railwaymen.

The dispute began after the dismissal of 162 ferrymen by the Isle of Man Steam Packet Company. This aroused fears in the union that all the major ferry companies were about to embark on a wave of redundancies. According to NUS research officer Mike Gibson: "It

Striking ferry crewmen picket Dover docks, despite union pleas to return.

is just that the first company in with the proposals was the Isle of Man company, and the dismissal of staff was the catalyst that produced the action."

The two biggest companies, Sealink and P&O, claimed they were not party to the dispute; they won injunctions against the NUS in the courts on Monday and applied to seize the union funds. Mr McCluskie called off the strike, but his members refused to obey, accusing him of a "sellout" (→25/3).

Border pounces to thwart England

Feb 4. Two magnificent catches by rival captains, Allan Border and Mike Gatting, were the highlights as Australia beat England in a one-day match played under floodlights at Melbourne tonight. Border's catch to dismiss Gatting for 37 proved the turning point, with England finishing 22 runs adrift of the Australian total of 235 (→18).

Vice-captain Embury is stumped.

Gorbachev clears leaders shot by Stalin

Feb 5. Old Bolsheviks murdered by Stalin and relegated to the limbo of un-persons 50 years ago, were today officially rehabilitated as part of Mr Gorbachev's campaign to fill in the "blank pages" of Soviet history. Nikolai Bukharin, described by Lenin as the favourite of the Soviet Communist Party, was one of 21 tried and shot in 1938 for conspiring with foreign agents. Today, a Soviet spokesman said the trial had been "falsified" and confessions obtained by "unlawful methods" — presumably torture. Bukharin's widow said the rehabilitation was "a big event".

Alexei Rykov, once Stalin's Prime Minister and also executed in 1938, was cleared of all crimes. Only one of the 21 was not rehabilitated: Genrikh Yagoda, who, as head of the secret police, had worked with Stalin in earlier purges.

In the power struggle to succeed Lenin, Bukharin backed Stalin, believing Trotsky's policies to be too extreme. But when Stalin began his forced collectivisation of agri-culture and the crash programme of industrialisation, Bukharin pleaded for moderation and a mixed-market economy. Ideas that cost the old Bolshevik his life are today echoed in Gorbachev's bid to reform the Soviet system (→8).

Call for new RUC probe in wake of Stalker affair

Feb 5. Claims by former police chief John Stalker that he was suspended from his inquiry into an alleged cover-up of a possible police "shoot-to-kill" policy in Northern Ireland led tonight to Opposition calls for a judicial inquiry. Stalker says he was suspended just as he was about to interview senior officers in the Royal Ulster Constabulary.

Stalker, a former Deputy Chief Constable of Manchester, is convinced that the decision to take him off the inquiry to face disciplinary charges of which he was later acquitted, must have been cleared at cabinet level. In his forthcoming book he writes: "I was on the threshold of causing a major police scandal and political row that would have resulted in several resignations and general mayhem."

The Stalker inquiry probed claims that Ulster police officers organised "hit squads" which shot dead six unarmed men in late 1982, and then arranged cover-up stories. Stalker says that the incidents showed an inclination, but not an official policy, to shoot rather than arrest suspects. Last week the Attorney General caused a storm by announcing that no prosecutions were to result from the Stalker inquiry. Ironically, Stalker now agrees, saying it is too late to prosecute (→11).

Feb 5. Demand for red noses soars, helping Comic Relief to raise £3 million for Africa. Tonight a BBC telethon hopes to raise even more.

13

February

1988

Su	Mo	Tu	We	Th	Fr	Sa
	1	2	3	4	5	6
7	8	9	10	11	12	13
14	15	16	17	18	19	20
21	22	23	24	25	26	27
28	29					

7. Stafford: CS gas canisters are thrown at the world middleweight bout between Tony Sibson and Frank Tate.

7. Haiti: Leslie Manigat, a former professor of politics, is sworn in as president.

8. UK: Workers at Ford plants strike over a productivity and pay deal (→15).

8. Moscow: Gorbachev announces Afghan concessions to speed up withdrawal negotiations (→13/3).

8. UK: Esther Rantzen is named Woman of the Year.

9. UK: government advisers attack a 9c 100 million shortfall in the national science budget (→7/3).

9. UK: The Attorney General drops a three-year-old court fight to revoke the charitable status of the "Moonies".

10. Birmingham: Doctors publish a dossier alleging that NHS cuts have led to patient deaths (→16).

10. UK: Ten people have died in storms this week, with wind gusts of up to 106 miles per hour.

11. UK: Former police chief John Stalker will not face prosecution under the Official Secrets Act (→12).

11. UK: A poll of Labour MPs shows that 40 per cent of them do not trust Kinnock's policy review.

12. Dublin: The government bans future meetings of the RUC and Garda as a result of the Stalker affair (→16).

12. West Bank: Israeli troops shoot dead two Palestinian youths aged 14 and 17 (→9/9).

13. Canada: The 15th Winter Olympic Games open at Calgary, Alberta (→15).

13. London: Starlite Express of Valsett, an English Setter, is judged Best in Show at Cruft's.

DEATHS

11. British nanny, ex-Royal governess Marion Crawford (*5/6/09).

12. British oboist Leon Goossens (*12/6/1897).

Over 100 die as Rio river bursts its banks

A stranded car bears testimony to the fierceness of the floods.

Feb 7. Torrential rain, floods and mud slides have killed at least 127, injured 1,000 and left 6,000 or more homeless in the Rio de Janeiro area. Brazilian officials are already putting the death toll as high as 300 as rescue efforts get under way. Disaster struck on Friday, when the swollen Quitandinha River burst its banks with enough force to sweep away cars and knock down tall buildings.

Petropolis, a mountain resort town of some 300,000 people 30 miles north of Rio, has been hardest hit by the torrent of rain and mud. The mayor, Paulo Rattes, said: "I have never seen a tragedy like this." He was able to confirm 102 deaths, 40 building collapses and 1,300 cases of homelessness in the town. Twenty people are still missing and local damage is estimated at $10 million.

The poor suburbs of Nova Iguacu and Duque de Caxias seem to have taken the brunt of the flooding in Rio, where an estimated 3,200 people are homeless there and 11 deaths have been reported. As the floods recede, rescue workers have started to search the rubble. They expect to find many more bodies hidden by the thick mud (→20).

MPs vote to let TV cameras cover the House of Commons

Feb 9. MPs voted tonight for experimental televising of their proceedings. Conditions to be imposed on the broadcasters will be worked out by an all-party committee.

Mrs Thatcher voted against. "What are you afraid of?" asked opposition leader Neil Kinnock. "I am concerned for the good reputation of the House," she replied. Rowdy scenes often accompany the question-time sparring between the party leaders.

"It's an historic night," said John Wakeham, Leader of the House. TV men rejoiced. Others quaked.

Riot deaths disrupt Bangladeshi poll

Feb 10. Eighty people were killed and more than 1,000 injured today in Bangladesh when bitterly contested local elections erupted into fighting. Rival groups rampaged through the streets settling their differences with guns, knives and bombs, rather than through the ballot box. Polling booths were shut at more than 500 centres because of the "unprecedented violence". The police made 300 arrests.

Impersonal brushstrokes of "greatest living realist painter"

Feb 8. An impressively large retrospective exhibition devoted to the painting of Lucian Freud has opened at the Hayward Gallery, after showing in Washington and Paris. Its catalogue claims that Freud, grandson of Sigmund, the father of psychiatry, is "the greatest living realist painter".

His subject matter is the human body, toughly presented in complete detail. Portraits, such as one of his fellow-artist Francis Bacon, give the effect of the face brought unnaturally close, as if by telescope. Every eyelash is a separate brushstroke. His sitters, withdrawn, almost absent-looking, are studied quite impersonally. The same is true of Freud's female nudes, the very opposite of the magazine or advertising version of womanhood.

"Girl with White Dog" is a portrait of the artist's wife Kitty Epstein.

Gielgud is back on the boards at 83

Feb 11. Sir John Gielgud surprised his fans by going back on the stage for the first time in ten years as a bookish, gossipy antiquarian, Sir Sydney Cockerell, in Hugh Whitemore's play *The Best of Friends*. The play is a conversation piece drawn from the letters Cockerell exchanged with Bernard Shaw and the Abbess of Stanbrook.

Gielgud's part is mostly monologue, garrulous, rambling, absent-minded, but mischievous and twinklingly shrewd. He ends with a long, taxing soliloquy. "The great thing is to keep one's memory going and that is really why I came back," said the 83-year-old actor.

Gielgud plays Cockerell.

Waldheim refuses to go

Austrian public opinion helps ex-Nazi officer Waldheim to ride the storm.

Feb 11. Despite a highly critical report by an international panel of historians, Kurt Waldheim today made it clear he is determined to ride out the storm over his Second World War record. He served as a German army intelligence officer in the Balkans when thousands of Jews, Yugoslav partisans and Italian prisoners were murdered.

Tonight an unshaken Austrian President, wearing white tie and tails and clusters of medals, appeared at the Opera ball, the highlight of the pre-Lenten carnival season. "I shall continue putting my knowledge and experience at the service of my country," he said.

The panel of historians, which was appointed by the Austrian government, reported after a six-month investigation that Waldheim "let slip parts of his past into oblivion, and if that was no longer possible made them appear harmless". Waldheim knew of the deportation of 60,000 Jews from Salonika and their extermination, but made no protest about this or any other atrocity. The commission tells of other German officers serving with Waldheim who refused to obey orders.

Waldheim has threatened to sack the shaky coalition government of socialists and the conservative People's Party and force elections. He is in a strong position. Polls show that 70 per cent of Austrians believe he should not resign (→14).

Dole and Gephardt sweep Iowa caucus

Feb 8. In the Iowa caucus, first event of the American presidential election, Senator Robert Dole came first of the Republican candidates, with 37 per cent of the vote. What was more surprising was that the vice-president, George Bush, ran third, behind not only Dole but also the TV evangelist, Pat Robertson.

In the Democratic caucuses in Iowa, the so-called Seven Dwarves were reduced to the Three Musketeers. Missouri Congressman Richard Gephardt came first with 27 per cent of the votes with Senator Paul Simon second and Massachusetts governor Michael Dukakis third (→17).

Robert Dole leads the Republicans.

Pretoria puts down homeland rebellion

Feb 10. Three South African helicopters and a handful of armoured cars today put paid to an attempted military coup in Bophuthatswana, one of the country's "independent" black bantustans. "Bop" became famous overseas for its gambling, spectacular entertainment and lack of racial barriers. President Lucas Mangope, released after being held at gunpoint in a sports stadium, said when he returned to the presidential palace in an armoured car: "I thank the South African Defence Force for helping me to get back to power to serve my people." (→29)

Church of England split on gay priests

Feb 8. The split in the Church of England over homosexual clergy became more evident today when the House of Laity called on the bishops to make a clear statement of their policy. One member, John Selwyn Gummer MP, wanted them to reaffirm traditional morality and to denounce the "condom culture".

The pressure on the leadership has been increasing with the spread of AIDS. The bishops are trying to respond to this pressure without pushing out of the church those clergy who are homosexual in feelings if not in deeds.

Feb 11. The blouse worn by Marilyn Monroe in "Bus Stop" is auctioned to property developer Patrick Mills for a mere £7,150.

Su	Mo	Tu	We	Th	Fr	Sa
	1	2	3	4	5	6
7	8	9	10	11	12	13
14	15	16	17	18	19	20
21	22	23	24	25	26	27
28	29					

14. Birmingham: Matthew Collier, who waited three months for heart surgery, dies.→

14. Cyprus: Three senior officials of the Palestine Liberation Organisation are killed by a bomb blast (→15).

14. Austria: Chancellor Franz Vranitzky threatens to resign because the Waldheim scandal undermines his government (→15).

15. UK: Ford offers strikers a new deal (→16).

15. Austria: Waldheim calls his critics slanderers and vows never to resign (→10/3).

15. Cyprus: An explosion disables a PLO deportee ship bound for Israel.

16. London: An unemployed man commits suicide by setting his car on fire outside Downing Street.

16. UK: Ford strikers accept a 14 per cent pay rise and agree to return to work (→17/3).

17. UK: Northern Ireland Secretary Tom King is to reform the RUC, after the Stalker investigations (→22).

18. Christchurch: England cricketers draw with New Zealand, but Graham Dilley is fined for swearing (→23/3).

18. UK: Midland Bank records a 9c 505 million loss, having written off 9c 1,000 million of Third World debt.→

19. Israel: Neil Kinnock accuses troops of using banned bullets against Arabs (→24).

19. Namibia: A bomb blast kills 14 people near a military base (→5/3).

20. Wales beat Scotland 25-20 and France beat Ireland 25-6 in Rugby internationals (→5/3).

20. Rio de Janeiro: Over 48 people have died and 10,000 are homeless in fresh flooding (→22).

DEATHS

14. American composer Fritz Loewe (*10/6/01).

15. American physicist and Nobel Prize winner Richard Phillips Feynman (*11/5/18).

Yeltsin sacrificed in new Gorbachev move

Feb 18. Mr Gorbachev today called for a more determined fight to implement *perestroika*, his economic and social reform programme. "We are losing ground," he said. "We have failed to release the people's initiative at grass roots."

He also tried to reassure conservatives by denying he was leading a retreat from socialism. He told the 300-member Communist Party Central Committee he was simply striving to revive true Leninism. In another gesture to the disgruntled old guard, he finally abandoned his former protege, Boris Yeltsin, who was sacked as Moscow party boss last year after complaining about the slow pace of reform, but stayed on — until today — as a junior member of the Politburo (→20).

Kicked out: reformer Yeltsin.

Pope slams Third World betrayal

Feb 19. Pope John Paul II slammed both superpowers in a hard-hitting encyclical letter today for not helping the Third World. He attacked the West for "abandoning itself to forms of growing and selfish isolation", and the East for ignoring "its duty to cooperate in the task of alleviating human misery".

The superpowers' attitude amounted to a "betrayal of humanity's legitimate aspirations", and "a real desertion of moral obligation". The Pope called for a reform of the United Nations and the establishment of a genuine international system, "which will rest on a foundation of the equality of all peoples".

Zurbriggen strikes gold, but Eddie steals the hearts in Calgary

Martin Bell, from Harrogate, on his way to glory at the Olympics.

Eddie Edwards tells eager reporters the secret of his skiing "success".

Feb 15. Pirmin Zurbriggen of Switzerland is the new Olympic men's downhill ski champion. The Swiss star today sped down Calgary's Mount Allan to beat his fellow-countryman, Peter Muller, by 0.51 seconds with Frank Piccard of France winning the bronze.

Britain's Martin Bell is also celebrating tonight after finishing eighth, the best-ever finish by a Briton in this, the blue riband event of men's skiing. He was only 1.25 seconds away from a medal. "I'm very surprised," admitted Bell, a 23-year-old from Harrogate who has had a disappointing season until today's 122.49 seconds of glory.

Whether or not Bell's success — or even Zurbriggen's undoubted brilliance — will attract any attention away from the hapless Eddie Edwards seems increasingly unlikely. Edwards, aged 24, finished last in the 70-metre ski jump, yet has found himself feted by the world's media and courted by companies wishing to use his name.

The Canadian public has certainly taken Edwards — he calls himself Eddie the Eagle — to their hearts, after watching the bespectacled plasterer from Cheltenham land 20 metres behind the next worst competitor. Whether it was relief that he survived at all or admiration of courage bordering on lunacy, the cheers were greater than those for many winners (→29).

Nurses picket hospitals

Feb 16. The latest NHS protest action brought thousands of nurses and co-workers out onto the streets and picket lines today in London and south-east England. The campaigners want the money that could be given away in a 2p income tax cut injected into the NHS instead, and plan a national day of action on the eve of next month's Budget.

Protesters have pledged that patients will not suffer and only a minority of today's demonstrators were on strike: most were using their own time off.

A poignant reminder of the crisis came earlier this week with the death of Matthew Collier, four weeks after his much-delayed operation in Birmingham (→ 29).

Defending attacks on the NHS.

It's Bush versus Dole in Republican race

Feb 17. Vice-President George Bush won the New Hampshire primary, the first of the US presidential election, with 38 per cent of the votes. Senator Robert Dole, from Kansas, came second with 29 per cent.

Three other candidates, Congress-man Jack Kemp, with 13 per cent, ex-Governor Pierre DuPont of Delware, and TV evangelist Pat Robertson, all finished far behind. The result, commentators generally agree, is that the Republican contest will now be a two-horse race between the Vice-President and the sharp-tongued Mr Dole.

Bush has now recovered the lead he lost to Dole in Iowa, and defied the New Hampshire pollsters who tipped Bush to lose (→ 23).

Bush wins in New Hampshire.

Ozone-destroying aerosols phased out

Feb 17. Eight British companies manufacturing 65 per cent of the aerosols used for toiletries have agreed to phase out the ozone-destroying propellants by the end of 1989.

Fears that the ozone layer in the earth's upper atmosphere is being damaged by long-lived chloro-fluoro-carbon aerosol propellants have been boosted recently by the discovery of a hole in the layer over Antarctica. The ozone layer screens out most of the harmful ultra-violet radiation from the sun, and one consequence of damage could be an increase in human skin cancers.

Although the major producers of the chlorofluorocarbons dispute some aspects of the scientific evidence, Beecham, Carter-Wallace, Elida Gibbs, L'Oreal, Gillette, Colgate-Palmolive, Cussons and Reckitt and Colman have bowed to public pressure and decided to discontinue them (→ 23).

Douglas Hurd toughens up terrorist laws

Feb 16. The sombre threat from continuing world terrorism makes it essential for Parliament to enshrine the Prevention of Terrorism Act in permanent legislation. So Douglas Hurd, the Home Secretary, told MPs tonight when that five-year Act — originally passed to cope with IRA terrorism — came up for the last time for annual review.

Tougher new anti-terrorism laws will still be subject to annual parliamentary scrutiny and renewal. Mr Hurd rejected Labour charges that the government's plans will make security cooperation with the Irish government more difficult.

"You are playing into the hands of the IRA propaganda machine," shadow Home Secretary Roy Hattersley told him. Nevertheless the use of exclusion orders against suspects will continue. Police powers for extended detention of suspects will be confirmed (→ 17).

Kim Philby appears on Soviet TV show

Feb 18. Against a background of British detective novels — P.D. James a clear favourite — traitor Kim Philby talked to Russian TV viewers from his study tonight. With a Russian "voice over" masking his upper-class British accent, Philby praised the work of his friend Graham Greene in a film eulogy of the pro-Gorbachev novelist.

Philby revealed that, while an intelligence officer in the Second World War, he "controlled" Greene as an agent in West Africa. Greene had turned down an offer to become his deputy, he said, and later "rather dropped out of my life during my troubles". Philby fled to Russia in 1963.

Academic profits as prophet of decline

Feb 15. A 676-page study of world history by an English-born professor at Yale University, Paul Kennedy, is a runaway best-seller, catching the wind of a new mood of concern about American "decline".

Tens of thousands of copies of this book have already been sold in hard-back, and its author is in constant demand on talk shows and magazine covers. Its vogue is surprising because *The Rise and Fall of Great Powers* is an academic study covering over 500 years. It seems readers are flocking to buy it because of the section on the relative decline of US power which asks whether, since the great empires of Rome and Babylon fell, America's time will come.

TV film, showing Israeli soldiers beating Palestinian youths Osama and Wael Judi with batons and rocks, has aroused an international outcry. The victims have denied throwing stones at the soldiers.

February

1988

Su	Mo	Tu	We	Th	Fr	Sa
	1	2	3	4	5	6
7	8	9	10	11	12	13
14	15	16	17	18	19	20
21	22	23	24	25	26	27
28	29					

21. Kenya: General elections start, with voters queuing up behind pictures of their preferred candidates.

22. Rio de Janeiro: The city is now a mass of rubble and mud, with a death toll of 250.

22. UK: British Telecom axes its "Talkabout" chat line after some teenagers run up £3,000 on their parents' phone bills.

23. US: Bob Dole wins Republican backing in primaries; the Democrats are split between Gephardt and Dukakis (→11/3).

23. UK: Prince Charles says he has banned aerosols from his household (→19/3).

24. Seoul: Roh Tae Woo assumes the presidency.

24. Jerusalem: Arabs hang a man alleged to be an Israeli collaborator.→

25. UK: The government reveals its plans for electricity privatisation (→5/3).

25. UK: A study concludes that a less green diet makes the working classes more vulnerable to cancers.

26. London: Railway rapist and multiple murderer John Duffy receives seven life sentences.

27. UK: Luton Town beat Oxford United to meet Arsenal in the Littlewoods Cup Final (→9/4).

28. Ireland: The body of Aidan McAnespie, shot by soldiers in Belfast, is exhumed for a second post-mortem (→7/3).

28. Cyprus: New President George Vassiliou is sworn in, and invites Turkey for talks on reunification of the island.

29. UK: Prescription charges are to rise 20p to £2.60 per item from April 1 (→5/3).

29. UK: British Aerospace asks for public funds to help develop the Hotol space craft.

DEATHS

24. American blues singer Memphis Slim (*3/9/15).

27. British humourist John Basil Boothroyd (*4/3/10).

West Bank violence greets George Shultz

The pleas of the Palestinians are met with machine-guns and riot gear.

Feb 26. US Secretary of State George Shultz's peace mission to the Middle East got off to a bad start today. Palestinian notables refused his invitation to a meeting, and his proposal for a period of autonomy for the West Bank and Gaza was flatly rejected by Israeli Prime Minister Itzhak Shamir.

These diplomatic failures took place against a background of increased violence. The unrest, deliberately whipped up to coincide with his mission, was met with harsh action by the Israeli security forces. The day's total of casualties was four Palestinians shot dead, several wounded and a number of soldiers injured by stones hurled by gangs of often very young Palestinians.

The day was also marked by the arrest of four soldiers, following the notorious TV film of them trying to break the arms of Palestinians in the West Bank city of Nablus.

The film, which showed the soldiers battering their captives' arms with rocks, shocked Israelis, many of whom have little idea of the viciousness of the fighting in the occupied territories (→4/3).

Tearful US preacher falls from grace

Feb 21. A tearful Jimmy Swaggart — America's leading television evangelist — told 7,000 admirers about his downfall today and admitted the "past sin" of consorting with a prostitute. "I beg your forgiveness," he cried as he announced his retirement from the pulpit for "an indeterminate period of time".

Swaggart's disgrace follows his own exposure of similar activities by fellow TV evangelists Jim Bakker and Marvin Gorman, who sued him last year and lost. The triple scandals are threatening to erode the multi-million-dollar religious television industry.

Sinful Swaggart confesses his crimes.

Royalty, traders and pop stars: Britain's new multimillionaires

Feb 24. The country may be governed by a grammar school girl, but royalty and aristocracy have kept a grip on the nation's wealth, according to *Money* magazine's list of Britain's richest 200 people.

Richest of all is the Queen, with a personal fortune estimated at £3,340 million; Littlewoods founder, Sir John Moores, is one of her wealthiest subject, with £1,700 million. But old money still dominates the list, with the Duke of Westminster (£1,400m), Viscount Chelsea (£400m), Prince Charles (£340m) and the Duke of Buccleuch (£309m) in the top 20.

Enterprise, however, also pays off. Financier Sir James Goldsmith joins the Vestey family (owners of Dewhurst and West butchers) and supergrocers the Sainsburys, with £1,000 million. Amstrad's Alan Sugar is worth £280 million, Virgin's Richard Branson £130 million and turkeyburger guru Bernard Matthews £58 million.

Ex-Beatle Paul McCartney has £79 million, and Phil Collins £22 million. Writer Catherine Cookson (£10m) and Sock Shop founder Sophie Mirman (£30m) have also done well.

Rich: The Queen, Alan Sugar, Bernard Matthews, Catherine Cookson, Phil Collins, and Sophie Mirman.

Tutu is arrested on apartheid protest

Feb 29. South Africa's two Anglican archbishops, Desmond Tutu of Johannesburg and Stephen Naidoo of Cape Town, were arrested today and held for several hours after they defied the law banning demonstrations outside parliament. They and other religious leaders were protesting at the government crackdown on anti-apartheid groups.

As the clergymen were led away, water cannons were turned on remaining demonstrators, who knelt in the road and prayed. A government statement said police had been "forced" to make arrests after "showing all possible reasonableness" to the archbishops. After his release, Archbishop Tutu said the demonstrators had simply been "obeying God" (→1/3).

Archbishop Tutu (centre) and other leading clerics pray for change.

Coup sends Panama president into hiding

Feb 27. President Eric Arturo Delvalle of Panama went into hiding last night just before army officers, sent by the army chief and de facto dictator, General Noriega, arrived to arrest him.

His wife Mariella kept the soldiers talking at the front door while her husband slipped out of a back door into the dark.

The National Assembly, controlled by General Noriega, chose Manuel Solis Palma president after Delvalle dismissed Noriega, who has been indicted in the United States for drug trafficking.

Delvalle said in a radio interview after the assembly vote: "The people of Panama know that this is all a farce. I am the President of Panama". Recently Panama's consul in New York resigned and gave evidence to the US Senate that Noriega had been protected by the US government in return for intelligence (→28).

Dublin launches its own Stalker inquiry

Feb 22. The Irish government demonstrated its lack of confidence in the Royal Ulster Constabulary tonight by ordering its own inquiry into a shooting at a border checkpoint. The victim, 24-year-old Aidan McAnespie, a lorry driver, was killed by machine-gun fire from a security post 200 yards away. A soldier is being held in custody.

Despite claims that he was hit by an accidental ricochet — from a shot fired by a Grenadier Guardsman — Dublin authorities insist that McAnespie had been given "special attention" by the RUC and had been described as "Ireland's most searched driver" (→28).

Britain's top towns identified by survey

Feb 22. West Midlanders have the most dismal towns in Britain,: today a study rates Wolverhampton, Walsall, Coventry and Birmingham as having the worst facilities, rivalled only by London. The best-off townspeople are in Aberdeen, Cardiff, Plymouth and Motherwell. The Glasgow-based researchers are honest enough to admit that Britain's best city is...Edinburgh.

Territorial disputes grow in Armenian enclaves of Russia

Feb 28. A territorial dispute on the fringes of the Soviet empire today confronts Mr Gorbachev with the most serious challenge to his authority since he came to power three years ago. In Yerevan, capital of the Soviet republic of Armenia, thousands daily assemble outside the opera house to proclaim solidarity with fellow Armenians in the enclave of Nagorny Karabakh, in neighbouring Moslem Azerbaijan. Claiming that Armenians are persecuted by the Moslems, they are demanding that the enclave become part of Soviet Armenia.

The authorities have barred foreign reporters from the region, but phone conversations with local activists provide a glimpse of the upheaval. It is claimed that at times the protesters number a million or more. "People are coming in from villages all over the country," one phone caller said.

Mr Gorbachev sent senior party officials to Yerevan and himself appealed in vain for "maturity and restraint". Now troops have been airlifted to the city. Gorbachev's dilemma is that if he gives in to the Armenians he risks facing similar demands from others among the Soviet Union's 100 non-Russian nationalities (→2/3).

Genuine stars shine amid artificial snow

Feb 29. The Winter Olympics ended today with a spectacular display of ice-skating before a crowd of 70,000 enthusiastic Canadians. After all the worries about artificial snow and events being located far away from Calgary, the XVth Winter Olympiad has been a popular success.

The Soviet Union, predictably, topped the medals table with 11 golds, nine silvers and nine bronzes. The Russian ice hockey team were amongst the stars of the games, while individuals who will be remembered include Finnish ski-jumper Matti Nykanean, East Germany's elegant free skater Katarina Witt and Yvonne van Gennip, a Dutch speed skater who won three gold medals (→3/3).

Katarina Witt ends with a flourish.

Flares are back with a vengeance after ten years away. The Spring collections have London's mannequins swathed in bell bottoms.

March

1988

Su	Mo	Tu	We	Th	Fr	Sa
		1	2	3	4	5
6	7	8	9	10	11	12
13	14	15	16	17	18	19
20	21	22	23	24	25	26
27	28	29	30	31		

1. UK: A January overseas trade deficit of 9c 905 million prompts fears that the economy is overheating (→4).

1. S. Africa: The government launches an inquiry into the extreme right-wing Afrikaner Resistance Movement. →

1. London: Underground passengers hijack a train in protest at the poor service.

2. Brussels: The NATO summit opens with a proposal to cut conventional weapons and modernise nuclear arms.

2. Humberside: A high incidence of childhood cancers is linked with local toxic waste dumps.

2. USSR: the first Soviet credit card is announced.

3. Panama: Threats of a halt in US aid bring a cash crisis, forcing banks to limit their activities (→18).

3. Bedford: Rioting, believed to be caused by overcrowding, hits the prison.

3. Cheltenham: Eddie "The Eagle" Edwards returns from the Winter Olympics to a hero's welcome.

4. India: Sikh gunmen kill 34 people, mainly Hindus, in a raid on a Punjab village (→3/4).

4. West Bank: Israel bans all foreign journalists (→7).

4. UK: House prices have risen by an average of 16.9 per cent in the last 12 months (→13).

5. Pretoria: The government is reported to be ready to enter talks for peace in Angola (→13).

5. London: 100,000 people march for increased NHS funding (→7/3).

5. UK: Fury greets government proposals to sell off Stonehenge and other monuments to private enterprise (→8).

5. Pittsburgh: Prince Charles complains that British planners make fun of his ideas about architecture.

DEATH

3. British circus proprietor Richard Chipperfield (*3/3/04).

Troops impose curfew in Azerbaijan

March 2. Troops have been sent to the industrial city of Sumgait on the Caspian Sea, in Soviet Azerbaijan, and a curfew has been ordered after "hooligans" exploited "ethnic tensions" and set off disturbances that led to "rampage and violence", according to official statements. A number of people have been injured, though no figures have been released, nor is it known whether anyone has been killed.

The reluctance of the authorities to provide a fuller picture is seen as evidence of disquiet at the nationalist unrest in the Transcaucasian republics of Azerbaijan and Armenia. Western reporters at a Soviet foreign ministry briefing were told by government spokesman Gennady Gerasimov of Moscow's "deep concern" over the disturbances. He said the situation in the city was now "calm but tense"; he did not know whether tanks had been sent in to quell the rioting.

Unofficial reports from Sumgait say the unrest began with attacks on Armenians. However, neither — Gerasimov nor the official news agency Tass made a connection between events in Azerbaijan and the recent trouble in the Armenian capital, Yerevan, where thousands have been demanding the return of Nagorny Karabakh, an Armenian enclave in Azerbaijan. The enclave, largely populated by Christian Armenians, was given to Moslem Azerbaijan in 1923 after Stalin, as commissar for nationalities, had tried to force a merger of Armenia, Azerbaijan and Georgia in a single Transcaucasian federation (→18).

Armenian demonstrators demand the return of Nagorny Karabakh.

City stunned by Rover take-over bid

March 1. The government took everyone by surprise today when it announced that British Aerospace has until the end of April to negotiate the takeover of the state-owned Rover Group. Some Tory MPs joined the opposition in questioning the wisdom of talking to only one bidder.

Lord Young, the Trade and Industry Secretary, emphatically denied that the government was rushing to sell Rover Group "at any price". But BAe's chairman, Professor Roland Smith, will want to drive a hard bargain.

City analysts this evening could see little logic in the deal for BAe, itself privatised in 1984, unless it bought the Rover assets cheap and forced the government to write off the group's current borrowings of almost 9c 1 billion. The government has been desperate to find a British buyer since plans to sell Austin-Rover to Ford and Land-Rover to General Motors were thwarted in 1986 by backbench jingoism (→29).

Wales battle back to beat the Irish

March 5. Wales went top of the five nations' rugby championship today by beating Ireland in Dublin. In a solid, if uninspiring, performance the Welsh team fought their way back to overturn a 9-3 deficit at half-time to win by 12 points to nine. The win makes Wales favourites to clinch their first title since 1979. Also today England battled to their first win of the season, a 9-6 victory over Scotland (→19).

Owen goes it alone as new party forms

March 3. The centre-ground Social and Liberal Democratic party (SLD) had a difficult birth today.

Bitter wrangling began immediately between it and the Social Democrats led by David Owen, who had earlier refused to merge his faction with the Liberals. Each side accused the other of name-stealing and they swopped insults.

The SLD's interim leaders — David Steel and Robert Maclennan — hit out. Mr Steel told the Owenites: "You are a small rump making bombastic claims." Dr Owen retorted: "The merger is a fiasco."

A majority of Liberal and SDP paid-up members voted for it.

Steel: familiar face, new party.

Iraq and Iran locked in capital warfare

Iran's women help fire the missiles in the deadly "war of the cities".

March 1. "Iraq possesses gigantic strategic capabilities to destroy Tehran, the nest of evil," said Baghdad's Information Minister, Latif Jassim, on the day that the Iraqis fired 17 missiles into the heart of the Iranian capital.

Tehran has been bombed a number of times during the seven-year-old Gulf War, but this is the first time it has been subjected to a barrage of rockets from nearly 300 miles away. Reports emerging from Tehran give the official casualty figures of 27 civilians dead and 100 wounded.

Unofficial reports speak of the terror brought by the rockets, which landed without warning over a period of 28 hours. Many people are now refusing to emerge from their cellars and there are accounts of a flight to the countryside.

Iraq said it launched its missiles in retaliation for two Iranian rockets which struck Baghdad yesterday and killed or wounded "many civilians". This deadly game of tit for tat continued tonight when the Iranians fired a single rocket into the Iraqi capital.

It seems that the Iraqis have the edge in the missile duel simply because they have more rockets than the arms-starved Iranians.

The Iraqis claim that their rockets, named Al Hussein after a Shia saint, are home-made, but there is little doubt that they are Russian-made and are part of the heavy shipments of arms made by the Soviet Union (→20).

Afghanistan to be Soviet-free zone

March 3. The last obstacles to a Soviet withdrawal from Afghanistan were removed today when the Afghan and Pakistani representatives at the Geneva talks agreed on a nine-month timetable for the Red Army to retire across the Russian border.

Abdul Wakil, the Kabul government's Foreign Minister, also told a press conference that Kabul had agreed to Pakistan's demand that half of the Soviet troops in Afghanistan pull out in the first three months of the withdrawal.

Mr Wakil said there was nothing more to discuss and he considered the agreement complete (→7/4).

Car thieves find the break-ins easy

March 3. If you think your car is safe from thieves you had better think again: it takes only seconds to break into most popular saloons, according to a new report by the Consumer Association's magazine *Which?* Shocked by figures of over a million thefts of and from cars in Britain every year, *Which?* set its own "car thief" loose on 57 models. Boots and steering wheels stood up well, but most doors were vulnerable. The moral? Park in a garage or well-lit street, leave nothing visible in the car, know your serial numbers and get an alarm.

Two Oxfam workers missing in Beirut

March 4. Two Oxfam officials have been seized by an unnamed Palestinian group, apparently while taking photographs in the turbulent Ein el-Hinweh refugee camp outside Sidon. The two men, Peter Coleridge, the British head of Oxfam's Middle East operations, and Omar Treboulsi, the organisation's representative in Lebanon, were inspecting aid work inside the refugee camp. Mr Coleridge's disappearance raises fears that he has been seized as a hostage like Mr Terry Waite, who was kidnapped in Beirut 14 months ago (→8).

Ultra-right whites hit Botha reforms

March 2. The white backlash against President P.W. Botha's cautious reforms gathered strength today when ultra-right candidates easily won two by-elections. Botha has a huge majority in parliament, 133 seats to the Conservatives' 22, but the by-election setbacks are a warning that his support among the all-white electorate is being eroded. As the elections approached, Botha sought to appeal to right-wing voters by cracking down on 20 anti-apartheid groups. But most voters rallied to hard-line candidates (→15).

The Last Emperor, Bernardo Bertolucci's epic tale of the downfall and Communist re-education of China's Pu Yi, is packing the cinemas.

March
1988

Su	Mo	Tu	We	Th	Fr	Sa
		1	2	3	4	5
6	7	8	9	10	11	12
13	14	15	16	17	18	19
20	21	22	23	24	25	26
27	28	29	30	31		

6. English Channel: Relatives of the victims of the Zeebrugge ferry disaster a year ago throw wreaths into the sea.

6. Antarctica: An expedition reaches the continent after rowing 600 miles from South America.

7. Israel: Palestinians hijack a bus, killing three (→15).

7. UK: The Bank of England abandons efforts to peg sterling to the Deutschmark (→8).

7. UK: Doctors claim cash shortages closed 3,100 hospital beds last year (→9).

8. Marbella: The IRA Gibraltar bomb squad's car is found, packed with 140 pounds of explosive (→16).

8. UK: Mrs Thatcher rejects calls for cuts in the interest rate as sterling soars on the foreign exchanges (→15).

9. UK: The Queen Mother has asked the government why a hospital ward she opened last year is now closed (→15/4).

9. London: Police and bailiffs evict 370 squatters from a housing estate.

10. London: The Guinness share scandal deepens with the arrest of City financier Lord Spens (→7/4).

10. Austria: President Waldheim promises the country a fresh start.

11. UK: English pound notes cease to be legal tender at midnight tonight.

11. London: New collections by Bruce Oldfield and Rifat Ozbek open Fashion Week.

12. Mallorca: Seve Ballesteros wins the inaugural Open golf tournament (→10/4).

DEATHS

7. American film actor Divine (Harris Glenn Milstead) (*1945).

8. British jazzman Ken Collyer (18/4/28).

9. German politician Kurt Georg Kiesinger (*6/4/04).

10. British pop singer Andy Gibb (*5/3/58).

SAS gun down IRA bomb trio on Rock

March 7. In brilliant sunshine, three IRA members were gunned down at point-blank range in a Gibraltar street yesterday. Police believe that the three had been preparing a bomb outrage at the local Changing of the Guard ceremony, but refused to confirm that the SAS were involved in the shooting. The three armed men in civilian clothes who fired the shots were rushed from the scene in a police vehicle. The three dead were identified as Sean Savage, Daniel McCann and Mairead Farrell. All were known as IRA activists — McCann had served a two-year sentence and Farrell 10 years for terrorist activities — and are believed to have been trailed across the border from Spain.

The IRA confirmed in Belfast tonight that the three were an "active service unit" with 140 pounds of plastic explosive. Gibraltar police and Ministry of Defence spokesmen in London initially indicated that a bomb had been found in a white Renault car parked by the three in a square, but this was later denied by the Foreign Secretary, Sir Geoffrey Howe.

In a Commons statement today, Sir Geoffrey said that the three

Shot dead (l. to r.): Sean Savage, Mairead Farrell and Daniel McCann.

IRA members had been challenged by security forces. "When challenged, they made movements which led the military personnel operating in support of the Gibraltar police to conclude that their own lives and the lives of others were under threat. In the light of this response, they were shot dead."

The shootings were given widespread backing by MPs, especially when the Foreign Secretary described the potential carnage of soldiers — at least 50 would have been on parade — and watching civilians at the guards' ceremony.

However, witnesses claimed today that no warning was given to the three. Mrs Pepi Celecia, whose flat overlooks a petrol station in Winston Churchill Avenue, where two of the terrorists were killed, said: "Suddenly, from nowhere, there comes running a well-built man with blond hair in a light blue jacket and blue jeans. He fired at the couple. The man in a white suit fell over a low wall and the woman tumbled, splayed out.

"Then the blond man fired again at the couple on the ground. Four times he fired," she added. The third IRA member, McCann, was shot seconds later. All three were unarmed.

A search is continuing on the Spanish side of the border for a car containing explosives (→8).

Chinese troops move in to stop Tibetan independence demands

March 10. The Chinese army clamped an iron hand over the Tibetan capital of Lhasa today, preventing any trouble on the anniversary of the bloody uprising against Chinese rule in 1959, during which thousands died and the Dalai Lama fled to sanctuary in India.

With tension in the city high following last weekend's rioting, the Chinese authorities were aware of the danger of emotions exploding today, and so imposed a virtual curfew on the city.

Known nationalists have been rounded up, including some who were taken in a dawn raid on the Jokhang Temple, the holiest shrine of Tibetan Buddhism. Some reports say that 500 people have been arrested since Saturday's violent demonstrations.

The Chinese have also made it plain to Buddhist priests that nationalist activities would receive "rigorous punishment" (→4/4).

Trouble flares in New Delhi, where Tibetan monks are restrained by police.

Hart failure puts Gary out of White House race for good

March 11. For the first time today 17 American states held their primary elections on the same day, including ten southern States. On the Republican side, Vice-President George Bush led Senator Robert Dole easily, with TV evangelist Pat Robertson well beaten in third place.

The Democratic race was less conclusive. Senator Albert Gore, of Tennessee, and Reverend Jesse Jackson, who won the lion's share of the large black vote, prevented Governor Dukakis winning a commanding lead. The most striking result was the eclipse of Senator Gary Hart. It seems voters have not forgiven him his adventure with a model, Donna Rice, widely reported in the press (→27).

Gary is denied his Hart's desire.

Royal ski party in avalanche tragedy

Mournful royals accompany Mrs Sarah Lindsay, widowed by the fall.

March 10. The Prince of Wales narrowly escaped death this afternoon when an avalanche caught his ski party above Klosters in Switzerland. One member of the party was killed and another seriously injured. The party was standing together near the Wang run when the avalanche began 100 metres above them. Prince Charles stood helplessly by as his friends were swept away. He talked later of how they disappeared in "a whirling maelstrom as the whole mountainside seemed to hurtle past us into the valley below". The party was skiing off-piste in one of the most dangerous areas.

The dead man is Major Hugh Lindsay, aged 34, a former equerry to the Queen. His wife, Sarah, who works in Buckingham Palace, is expecting a baby in three months. The injured woman is Mrs Palmer-Tomkinson, wife of one of the Prince's close friends (→13).

Government attacks professional cartels

March 8. The days of professional privileges and business cartels could be numbered, if plans announced today by Lord Young, the Trade and Industry Secretary, go ahead.

The government intends to make it harder for businesses or professional groups to limit competition by "restrictive practices". These include keeping prices high so that no one — except the consumer — suffers, sharing markets among themselves and freezing out suppliers.

Lord Young said that the Office of Fair Trading, which keeps an eye on such practices, will get "greater teeth" to allow it to enter company offices and search for proof of cartel agreements. Culprits could end up paying massive fines, he said. The professions are exempt from most restrictive practice laws at the moment, but will soon have to justify why, for example, barristers but not solicitors can be heard in Britain's higher courts.

The government also plans to enable private legal actions by people who feel they have suffered because of a cartel or monopoly.

Stoppard keeps his audiences guessing

March 10. Tom Stoppard's first stage play for five years was received with polite bafflement by critics today. *Hapgood* combines a Le Carre-type spy thriller with lessons in quantum physics. It demonstrates that the Uncertainty Principle applies to moles as well as to molecules. "If the science is difficult to understand, the plot is impossible to unravel," wrote one.

Thatcher plans to transform inner cities

March 7. A ten-year timetable for renewal of Britain's rundown inner cities was announced today by Mrs Thatcher, with an accompanying blast from the government's public relations trumpets.

The Prime Minister told a news conference that injection of cash from private enterprise and the expertise of leading businessmen will be combined with government effort in the regeneration programme. The government has earmarked £3 billion to attack a host of innercity problems. Development and more jobs will be encouraged by removal of bureaucratic obstacles. However, Mrs Thatcher added: "I don't think there is a single new policy here. It is using the money, intensifying, concentrating it in a much more coordinated way."

Labour MPs dismissed the Prime Minister's statement as "tawdry and bogus".→

Oxfam workers are freed by Abu Nidal

March 8. The notorious terrorist Abu Nidal today released Oxfam officials Peter Coleridge and Omar Treboulsi, seized by his men at the Ein el-Hilweh refugee camp outside Sidon three days ago. According to Mr Coleridge it was all his own fault: "I made a mistake by taking photographs, not realising the security measures in force at the camp."

Roger Rees and Felicity Kendal.

March

1988

Su	Mo	Tu	We	Th	Fr	Sa
		1	2	3	4	5
6	7	8	9	10	11	12
13	14	15	16	17	18	19
20	21	22	23	24	25	26
27	28	29	30	31		

13. Austria: An avalanche kills seven tourists at the ski resort of St Anton (→4/4).

13. Pretoria: The South African government launches a new peace initiative for Angola (→22).

14. UK: Runner Zola Budd is criticised for attending a race meeting in South Africa (→16).

14. UK: A survey shows that 9 out of 10 women find facilities for cervical cancer screening are inadequate.

14. US: Comic strip hero Superman is 50 years old today.

15. Washington: Israeli Premier Yitzhak Shamir rejects US plans to exchange land for peace in the West Bank (→16).

16. Israel: The authorities cut off international telephone lines from the occupied territories (→19).

16. UK: Zola Budd withdraws from the British international cross-country team (→16/4).

17. UK: The base interest rate drops from 9 to 8.5 per cent after a sharp rise in the value of sterling (→20).

17. Pretoria: The Supreme Court postpones the execution of the Sharpeville Six (→29).

17. West Germany: A secret funeral is held for Nazi Rudolf Hess, who died in Spandau jail last August.

18. USSR: The Communist Party in Nagorny Karabakh votes for a return to Armenia (→29).

18. UK: The government launches a campaign to raise awareness of the single European market, to open in 1992 (→5/4).

19. US: Scientists say the recent treaty on ozone protection comes too late to save the ozone layer (→22).

19. Israel: Authorities slap a new ban on foreign reporting from the West Bank and Gaza.

DEATH

18. British gardener and broadcaster Percy Thrower (*30/1/13).

Sharpeville Six will hang, insists Botha

March 15. The Sharpeville Six, five men and a woman, sentenced to death after a black councillor was stoned and burned to death during protests against rent rises, have had clemency appeals rejected by South Africa's President P.W. Botha. No evidence was offered at their trial that they took part in the actual killing, but, because they were in the crowd which attacked the councillor, successive judges have ruled that they shared a "common purpose" with the killers, who remain unidentified. There is still a slight hope for the Six; Mrs Thatcher, President Reagan and Chancellor Kohl of West Germany have appealed for clemency (→17).

President Botha takes a harsh stand.

Dundee loses 1,000 jobs in union row

March 17. Ford today abandoned a plan to build a new electronics plant in Dundee. The decision means the loss of a potential 1,000 jobs in an area of high unemployment. The factory is now likely to be built elsewhere in Europe.

Ford's plan depended on a secret single-union deal agreed with the engineering union last autumn. This deal, like the one between Rupert Murdoch and the electricians, which radically changed Fleet Street, was opposed by the other unions. Ford was not prepared to wait any longer for the unions to resolve their differences (→25).

State of emergency declared in Panama

March 18. Panama's government, controlled by General Manuel Noriega, has announced a national state of emergency. What amounts to martial law is in force.

General Noriega said the measures were being imposed because of the "undeclared war" being waged by the United States against Panama. The general has been charged with drug smuggling by one American court. Another has frozen all Panama's assets in US banks after Noriega overthrew the president of Panama. Since the local currency is the US dollar, this has brought the economy to a standstill.

Income tax slashed in Lawson's budget

March 15. Presenting his fifth Budget, the Chancellor of the Exchequer, Nigel Lawson, fulfilled last year's election pledge by cutting the standard rate of income tax by 2p, to 25p in the pound. The highest rate is to be cut from 60 to 40 per cent. His total tax cuts today are worth a massive £4 billion, going mostly to high income earners.

Some economists have questioned such a large boost to consumer spending. They thought that the Chancellor's forecasts of inflation staying below four per cent and the payments deficit below £4 billion might be optimistic (→18).

Ferry firm sacks striking seamen

March 15. P&O European Ferries tonight sent out letters of dismissal to the 2,300 Dover seamen who have been on strike for six weeks. The strike erupted because the company wants longer working hours with no extra pay to meet the competition from the Channel Tunnel, due to be completed in 1992.

The company's plans involve 400 redundancies on its 11 Dover ferries. The unions now have until next Wednesday to agree new terms. Mr Peter Ford, the company chairman, said: "The industry and all those employed in it must change to survive."

March 17. Richard Dunwoody rides Charter Party, trained by David Nicholson, to victory in the Cheltenham Gold Cup.

France and Wales share the rugby spoils

March 19. France today won a share in the Five Nations' rugby championship by beating Wales in Cardiff. After their most successful season since the glorious years of the 1970s, the Welsh team lost by a single point to the French and had to settle for a share of a championship they thought they had won outright.

There was no sense of anticlimax at Twickenham, however, where a rejuvenated English team trounced Ireland 35-3. Without a try all season, England managed six, with Chris Oti scoring three and Rory Underwood two, in Ireland's heaviest defeat since 1912.

France on their way to victory.

Belfast bloodshed plumbs new depths at funerals

The lone gunman stalks Milltown cemetery, bringing more death to Ulster.

Moments before he was murdered, Corporal Derek Wood pulls his gun.

Loyalist assassin fires on IRA mourners

March 16. A loyalist gunman opened fire indiscriminately at close range and hurled grenades into a huge crowd of mourners at an IRA funeral today, killing three people and injuring 50. As furious nationalists threatened to turn Ulster once again into a bloodbath, the British and Irish governments appealed for calm.

The gunman — said to be an east Belfast Protestant who was once rejected as a candidate for the Ulster Defence Association — infiltrated triple funerals of Mairead Farrell, aged 31, Daniel McCann, aged 30, and Sean Savage, aged 23, the IRA team shot by SAS men in Gibraltar. Police believe he took advantage of the absence of security forces, who had stayed away from the funeral at Milltown cemetery by prior arrangement.

The shooting began as the bodies were being lowered into their graves. Panic ensued as grenades exploded among the 5,000-strong crowd, with mourners leaping for cover behind gravestones. Many of the victims were seriously hurt with shrapnel wounds. After holding the crowd at bay for a few moments with a Browning automatic pistol, the gunman threw more grenades before fleeing across a nearby motorway, past a crowd shouting "Kill the bastard!". He was overpowered and severely beaten before police intervened. His condition in hospital tonight was said to be "not serious".

A loyalist source in Belfast tonight described the attacker as a "loner who was rejected because he was highly unreliable and unpredictable. He was also into drugs. He didn't want to work with anybody. The UDA just didn't want him".

Both the Ulster Defence Association and the outlawed Ulster Freedom Fighters denied any part in the attack tonight. Funerals have always been regarded as sacrosanct by both organisations. Meanwhile, Sinn Fein President Gerry Adams accused the security forces of "collusion" — alleging the presence of a white police-patrol van close to the funeral which could have spotted the killer.

Crazed mob lynches two British soldiers

March 19. In full view of the television cameras, two British soldiers blundered at high speed into an IRA cortege in West Belfast today — to meet their deaths after several horrific minutes at the hands of a lynch mob. The recently introduced policy of "no policing" of terrorist funerals was under urgent review by the authorities tonight.

No explanation was given for the presence of the men, members of the Signals Regiment, in this highly sensitive area of the city. Cpl Derek Wood, aged 24, and Cpl Robert Howes, aged 23, tried to reverse their silver Volkswagen, but were blocked by a black taxi. The windows of their car were smashed and they were dragged out. Although one of the soldiers fired a warning shot, the two corporals were overpowered and savagely beaten and stripped before being dragged to nearby waste ground, where they were shot.

Despite a claim by Gerry Adams, president of Sinn Fein, that the men were "SAS soldiers on a dirty-tricks operation", a spokesman for the army revealed that Cpl Howes had arrived in Northern Ireland only last week.

Observers believe that the mob feared a repeat of last week's attack by a loyalist fanatic at Milltown cemetery. The barbaric and public nature of the killings has caused widespread revulsion, summed up in the words of local priest Alec Reid. "Our parish is seen as dripping in the blood of the murders," he said (→22).

Father Alec Reid administers the last rites to one of the victims.

March

1988

Su	Mo	Tu	We	Th	Fr	Sa
		1	2	3	4	5
6	7	8	9	10	11	12
13	14	15	16	17	18	19
20	21	22	23	24	25	26
27	28	29	30	31		

20. UK: A survey shows 60 per cent of the population oppose cuts in the top rates of income tax (→24).

20. UK: The West African AIDS virus, HIV2, has now been detected in Britain.

21. Tokyo: Mike Tyson knocks out heavyweight challenger Tony Tubbs in under six minutes.

21. Nicaragua: Peace talks open between the Sandinista government and the Contra rebels (→24).

22. UK: Television companies refuse to hand over footage of Saturday's incident in which two British soldiers died (→23).

22. France: François Mitterrand announces his candidacy for the presidential elections.

23. Perth: Ian Botham is fined 9c 320 for assault and disorderly conduct (→28).

23. UK: The Royal Ulster Constabulary wins a court order to obtain film of the IRA funeral murders (→25).

24. US: Messrs Poindexter, North, Secord and Hakim plead not guilty of Iran-Contra criminal charges.

24. UK: British Telecom promises to pay 9c 5 a day for failure to instal or repair telephones as promised.

25. UK: The High Court warns the seamen that their union's assets could be seized if they hold a strike ballot (→1/4).

25. UK: The TUC urges the unions to drop their opposition to a single union deal at Ford's Dundee plant (→31/3).

25. Arctic: British explorer Sir Ranulph Fiennes calls off his walk to the North Pole.

DEATHS

20. American jazzman Gil Evans (Ian Ernest Gilmore Green) (*13/5/12).

21. British gynaecologist, test tube baby pioneer Patrick Christopher Steptoe (*9/6/13).

25. American ballet master Robert Joffrey (Abdulla Jaffa Anver Bey Khan) (*24/12/30).

Iraq attacks Kharg oil terminal, kills 54

March 20. Iraqi warplanes today pounded the Iranian oil terminal at Kharg island with missiles and bombs. Two supertankers, the 316,739-ton Avaj and the 253,387-ton Sanandaj, were hit by missiles as they prepared to take on cargoes of oil. Both exploded into flames and are still burning fiercely.

The entire crew of the Avaj is believed to have perished when the missiles turned the ship into a raging inferno. Fifty-four men are known to have died and it is feared the death toll will be much higher.

"There is a great deal of confusion at Kharg," said one source in Kuwait. "The fires are still burning intensely, both on the tankers and among the shore installations."

This attack could prove to be a devastating blow to the Iranians, for they rely on oil shipments from Kharg in the northern Gulf to provide them with the foreign currency to carry on the war against Iraq.

It may now prove impossible for Iran to maintain its operations from Kharg. It no longer has the fighters to match Iraq and it cannot afford to risk the loss of any more supertankers.

One method the Iranians might adopt is to ferry their oil in small tankers along the coast to supertankers waiting in the comparatively safe waters around the Straits of Hormuz.

Meanwhile, the Iraqis have fired another missile into the heart of Tehran, the 105th in the past three weeks (→1/4).

The location of Kharg Island has made it a prime target for Iraq.

China's Li Peng promises major reforms

March 25. Li Peng, China's new Prime Minister, dressed in a smart Western-style suit, today told the National People's Congress that "we must put reform at the centre of all our undertakings."

In a carefully scripted speech lasting two and a half hours, he ranged over most of China's problems, but always came back to the need to modernise the economy without allowing it to run away.

Mr Li, aged 59, who has just taken over from Deng Xiaoping, aged 83, insisted that excessive price rises were "the outstanding problem in our nations's economic and social life" (→12/4).

North Africa's food supplies are threatened by heavy locust swarms.

Sterling rate splits cabinet ministers

March 24. The cabinet row over exchange-rate policy intensified tonight, with Sir Geoffrey Howe, the Foreign Secretary, openly backing Chancellor Nigel Lawson against Mrs Thatcher.

Sir Geoffrey denounced as a "delusion" the belief that currencies should be allowed to float freely in world money markets. Mrs Thatcher is continuing to argue that the pound's value should be left to the markets. Mr Lawson, meanwhile, is adamant that sterling should be linked loosely to the German mark.

In answering parliamentary questions, Mrs Thatcher and Mr Lawson are not bothering to hide this clash. They have agreed in the odd situation to stress that they both want to check inflation (→8/4).

Anglo-Irish deal to be given fresh start

March 25. Yet another bid for closer cooperation against terrorism was announced by British and Irish government ministers after talks in London tonight.

They met in an atmosphere of mutual suspicion following tough Royal Ulster Constabulary action to check paramilitary displays at IRA funerals. Officials said: "We recognise the urgent need to give new impetus to improvement of relations between the security forces and the community." (→31)

Vanunu is found guilty of treason

March 24. Mordechai Vanunu, the Israeli nuclear technician who formerly worked at Dimona, Israel's top-secret facility in the heart of the Negev desert, was found guilty today of three charges of treason and espionage.

His crime was to reveal to the *Sunday Times* details of Israel's capacity to build nuclear weapons. He could be sentenced to death, but the three judges who have been hearing the case in secret for a year are expected to send him to prison for life (→27).

Soldier is first Israeli victim of "Intifada"

Israeli blood seeps into West Bank soil, where Moshe Katz lies dead.

March 20. Sergeant Moshe Katz, an Israeli army reservist, was shot twice in the head with a 9mm pistol while on guard duty in Bethlehem today. He died in the street outside the Ministry of the Interior building he was guarding, while his attacker vanished into Bethlehem's maze of alleys.

Sergeant Katz thus became the first Israeli to be killed in the "Intifada", the uprising which began in the occupied territories 102 days ago and has led to the deaths of 100 Palestinians.

His killing represents a change of tactics for the Palestinians. Until now they have been content to rely on stone-throwing and civil disobedience, knowing that they are winning the propaganda battle when the Israelis reply to their stones with bullets.

It may be that this will prove to be an isolated incident. Lt-Gen. Dan Shomron, Israel's Chief of Staff, was cautious in his assessment of Moshe Katz's killing: "It is too early to say we are entering a transitional phase. We know there are weapons on the West Bank and in Gaza. It's possible we'll get more of these incidents as we gain control of the demonstrations." (→28)

Ceasefire agreed in Central America

March 24. The Sandinista government and the Contra rebels in Nicaragua have signed a 60-day ceasefire and agreed to negotiate a final end to six years of civil war.

The accord, reached after midnight the day before yesterday at the little town of Sapoa, took both Central America and Washington by surprise. Some Contras said they were "dismayed" by the "timidity" of the agreement. The deal is also a blow to the Reagan Administration in Washington, which has fought in Congress for military aid to the Contras. Nicaraguan President Daniel Ortega said the pact was "only a beginning" (→27).

Charles urges swift action on pollution

March 22. The government is dragging its feet on pollution and the environment, said the Prince of Wales in a speech to mark the end of European Environment Year. He claimed that few politicians or industrialists took public worries about the environment seriously.

Some people, said the Prince, still thought of environmentalists as "bearded, be-sandalled, shaven-headed mystics who retreat every now and then to the Hebrides or the Kalahari desert". More specifically, he said the government was weak on vehicle pollution, and called for greater powers for the Forestry Commission (→28).

Kremlin stamps on fresh Armenian unrest

March 23. Armenian nationalists, whose grievances Mr Gorbachev last month promised to consider, today received a stinging rebuff. After hearing a speech by the Soviet leader, the presidium of the Supreme Soviet branded as "intolerable" demands for the return to Armenia of the Armenian enclave in neighbouring Azerbaijan. And in a reference to new unrest in the Armenian capital, Yerevan, the presidium ordered local Communist Party officials to "stamp out any nationalist or extremist manifestations... eroding the friendship of Soviet peoples".

Troops with helicopters and armoured cars have been deployed, and an unknown number of Armenian activists who refused to sign pledges not to join future demonstrations have been arrested.

The authorities have now revealed that 32 people died and 197 were injured in anti-Armenian riots in the Azerbaijani city of Sumgait last month (→30).

South Africa pushes deep into Angola

March 22. South African-led forces in Angola have opened an offensive to cut off the last major government position in the southeast, Cuito Cuanavale, which is being defended by Cuban forces. White South African officers are commanding a mixed force of Angolan defectors, Ovambo tribesmen from Namibia, and Jonas Savimbi's Unita guerrillas.

Travelling in lorries by night to avoid attacks by Cuban MiGs, they are thought to have penetrated some 400 miles into central Angola, just short of the Benguela railway. Though Soviet pilots have been in action, the South Africans doubt whether the Russians will risk getting too deeply involved.

Thatcher makes the most of the mess made for her in the park

March 22. Margaret Thatcher was out bright and early today picking up litter from St James's Park in an effort to set an example to untidy Britain. "You really are quite ashamed," the Prime Minister said later about her experiences of escorting visiting statesmen through the streets of London.

What she did not say was that the banana skins, bus tickets and sweet wrappers which she so diligently picked up for the benefit of the media's cameras had been put there specially; park-keepers had dumped piles of litter as ready-made targets for the prime ministerial litter-stick. Nicholas Ridley, the Environment Secretary, unfortunately spoiled the tidy image by dropping cigarette ash in his leader's wake.

The Prime Minister's eagle eye spots a morsel of carefully-arranged rubbish.

March

1988

Su	Mo	Tu	We	Th	Fr	Sa
		1	2	3	4	5
6	7	8	9	10	11	12
13	14	15	16	17	18	19
20	21	22	23	24	25	26
27	28	29	30	31		

27. Israel: Mordechai Vanunu is sentenced to 18 years prison for treason.

27. Nicaragua: A hundred political prisoners are freed to comply with the terms of the recent ceasefire.

28. UK: The Test and County Cricket board decide not to discipline Ian Botham for his misbehaviour in Australia (→6/4).

28. Bristol: Kevin Weaver, who killed four in a crazed shooting spree, is sent to Broadmoor for life.

28. UK: A report says that Britain's civil defence arrangements would fail under a nuclear attack.

29. US: Republican Bob Dole quits the presidential race as Michael Dukakis wins the Connecticut Democratic primary vote (→19/4).

29. Wembley: Lloyd Honeyghan knocks out Jorge Vaca to win the world welterweight boxing title.

29. Paris: African National Congress spokeswoman Dulcie September is assassinated by an unknown gunman (→21/4).

30. Israel: The Palestine Press Service is closed, leaving the army the only source of news from the West Bank (→31).

30. London: Greenpeace activists climb up Nelson's column to protest against acid rain pollution.

30. USSR: Nagorny Karabakh is brought to a standstill by a general strike (→3/4).

31. UK: Amnesty International is to investigate the killing of the IRA squad in Gibraltar (→12/4).

31. Israel: Premier Yitzhak Shamir tells Palestinian rioters they will have their heads smashed (→2/4).

31. UK: Cliff Thorburn is banned from competitive snooker after failing a drugs test.

DEATH

30. French statesman Edgar Faure (*18/8/08).

Israel seals off West Bank and gags press

March 28. The Israeli authorities are taking the most drastic measures to prevent disturbances in the occupied territories of the West Bank and Gaza tomorrow when the Arabs mark "Land Day", the day in 1976 when six Palestinians were shot dead during protests against the expropriation of their land by the Israelis.

These measures include unprecedented restrictions on the foreign press, especially TV camera teams, blamed by Israel for providing a focus for demonstrations. No correspondent or TV crew will be allowed into the West Bank or Gaza without an army escort. At the same time an official news blackout is preventing government spokesmen from giving details of arrests, economic sanctions against demonstrators and detentions without trial.

These regulations are aimed at preventing news getting out and removing the protesters' acknowledged ability to set up a riot for the cameras.

Other new rules are designed to seal off the troublesome areas for three days. West Bank residents are not being allowed to enter Israel or cross the bridges to Jordan, and a curfew has been imposed on the Gaza Strip (→30).

An Israeli soldier sprays mace gas into the eyes of an Arab protester.

Scientists confirm "greenhouse effect"

March 28. Scientists claim that predictions, first made 50 years ago, of an atmospheric "greenhouse" effect, produced by burning fossil fuels, are finally coming true. Estimates of the average global temperature increase over the next 40 to 50 years range from 1.5 to 4 degrees centigrade. One of the results could be a rise in sea level of as much as a metre as polar ice-caps melt, threatening low-lying coastal plains in all five continents.

The greenhouse effect is caused by carbon dioxide in the atmosphere, which traps heat in much the same way as the glass of a greenhouse. The concentration of carbon dioxide is increasing steadily, with the burning of fuels such as coal and oil, and the destruction of tropical forests the main sources.

Meteorologists have attempted to produce models of the resulting climatic changes, using some of the world's most powerful computers. Detailed forecasts are beyond the state of the art, but it is generally agreed that the major climatic belts would move towards the poles. One consequence could be global food shortages, resulting from the grain-growing areas becoming deserts, with the suitable climatic belts moving to regions with much poorer soils (→30).

Dundee deal hopes dashed by unions

March 31. Last-minute efforts by Norman Willis, general secretary of the Trades Union Congress, to save the proposed new Ford plant in Dundee were thwarted by senior shop stewards at the company today. They refused to give assurances that the plant would not be blacked unless pay was the same as in other Ford plants.

Ford's plans depended on a single-union deal with the engineering union which would have given them labour costs 50 per cent below other Ford UK plants. They will now build in Spain.

Kinnock challenged for Labour lead

March 30. Tony Benn, backed by left-wing MPs, will challenge Neil Kinnock for the Labour leadership in an election at the party's annual conference in October.

The move — announced tonight — will plunge Labour into six months of internal strife. Mr Kinnock dubbed it "a deliberate, futile, selfish and unnecessary distraction". Mr Benn retorted: "Elections have an important educational role." Tories rubbed their hands and said: "Situation normal. The Labour Party's in flames." (→1/4)

March 30. Ian Botham, a modern-day Hannibal, starts his elephantine trek across the Alps. He hopes to raise £10 million.

Jesse Jackson's win stuns Democrats

Brussels looks into Rover takeover bid

March 27. Jesse Jackson's dramatic victory in the Michigan Democratic caucuses, where he won 55 per cent of the votes and easily led the favourite, Michael Dukakis, has sharpened the Democratic party's agonizing dilemma.

If it chooses Jackson, a black man and a radical by any standards of American politics, the polls say that it will be decisively defeated by the Republicans this November. If it seems to close ranks against Jackson, it will lose the votes of the blacks and Hispanic voters, who are exhilarated by Jackson's campaign, and who make up more than 20 per cent of the potential voters.

With Jackson running only just behind Governor Michael Dukakis in the delegate count, the party must now confront this choice.

Jackson is a truly inspired campaigner. Crowds besiege him whenever he speaks. No Democratic politician has possessed his charisma since Robert Kennedy who was assassinated in 1968. The per-

Jackson is an inspired campaigner, but colour remains a barrier.

centage of the white vote he has won has crept up to around 20 per cent in recent primaries.

Yet Jackson, the illegitimate son of a teenage mother who has never held public office, makes no concessions to the need to appear

moderate. He has outraged Jewish voters by his support for the Palestinians and by calling New York "Hymietown".

The irony is that the decisive test will now come for him in the New York primary on April 19 (→29).

March 29. The European Commission is to examine the terms of the proposed sale of the Rover Group to British Aerospace (BAe). This effectively blocks on the merger for up to two months. Lord Young, the Trade and Industry Secretary, had been on the point of announcing details of the sale, which has been under negotiation since the beginning of the month. Indications are that the government was preparing to pay over £800 million to wipe out Rover's accumulated debts.

The Commission's concern is with the amount of money that BAe is asking the British government to inject into Rover. Such national subsidies are seen as creating unfair competition for other European motor manufacturers. Last year the Brussels Commission forced the government to cut £80 million off the £750 million it proposed to inject into Leyland Trucks as a condition of its sale to the Dutch company DAF.

Canary Wharf skyscraper plans unveiled

AIDS kills surgeon at Exeter hospital

March 29. The biggest skyscraper in Britain — and Europe — was announced today as plans were unveiled for a £3 billion Canary Wharf development in London's docklands. The 800-feet office block, due to open in 1992, is the centrepiece of the 71-acre office, shop and leisure complex which the Canadian developers claim meets "the best international standards

within a high-quality urban environment". Despite this confidence the project has its critics. It has been slammed for its "inhuman" scale and for the fact that the skyscraper, taller than both the Telecom and NatWest towers, spoils the symmetry of the view from Greenwich Park, across the Thames, of Sir Christopher Wren's Royal Naval College.

March 27. A "dedicated and conscientious" surgeon who worked in Africa for several years died today from AIDS. David Collings, aged 30, who was happily married with an 18-month-old son, is believed to have caught the disease while operating in Zimbabwe.

More than 300 patients whom he operated on in Exeter and Redditch since his return to Britain are being

contacted by the authorities. It is stressed that there is no known case of a patient catching the virus from a doctor, but all are being offered HIV tests and counselling if they want them.

Collings learned he had AIDS only six days before he died from a lung infection. Colleagues described him as a man driven by a sense of duty and compassion.

An artist's impression of London's controversial proposed landmark.

French presidential candidate François Mitterrand sits for a sculptor.

April

1988

Su	Mo	Tu	We	Th	Fr	Sa
					1	2
3	4	5	6	7	8	9
10	11	12	13	14	15	16
17	18	19	20	21	22	23
24	25	26	27	28	29	30

1. UK: Neil Kinnock asks the big unions to support him in the Labour leadership battle.

2. London: Oxford win the 134th Boat Race.

2. Bethlehem: Israeli troops kill six Palestinians, the highest total for a single day so far (→6).

3. Zimbabwe: Joshua Nkomo's Zapu party votes for a merger with Robert Mugabe's ruling Zanu PF party.

3. Brazil: Alain Prost wins the Grand Prix.

4. London: Tibetan leader the Dalai Lama arrives for a state visit, but is forbidden to speak to the press.

4. UK: The final episode of the long-running television soap opera *Crossroads* is broadcast.

4. Austria: Four British school children die in a mountain fall.

5. Blackpool: Three children and two adults die in a fire at a DHSS bed & breakfast hotel.

6. West Bank: The first Israeli civilian victim of the troubles, a 15-year-old girl, dies (→7).

6. London: The King's Cross fire inquiry is told that safety was a lower priority than profitability on the tube.

6. London: A John Lennon cheque fetches 9c 5,280, and Michael Jackson's shoes fetch 9c 4,400, at an auction.

7. West Bank: It is found that the teenager who died yesterday was killed by an Israeli army bullet.

7. Yorkshire: Broadcaster Russell Harty is admitted to hospital with hepatitis.

8. UK: Bank base rates are cut to eight per cent, the lowest for ten years (→17/5).

8. UK: Assaults on the police in 1987 were up 20 per cent on the previous year at 17,000.

9. Aintree: Rhyme 'n' Reason, trained by David Elsworth and ridden by Brendan Powell, wins the Grand National.→

9. UK: Liverpool and Wimbledon win their semi-finals to go through to the FA Cup Final (→17/4).

Gorbachev to sign Afghan pull-out deal

The leaders of Russia and Afghanistan meet to finalise the agreement.

April 7. Mikhail Gorbachev has today announced his intention of signing the Geneva peace accord, thus enabling the Soviet Army to start pulling out of Afghanistan on May 15. However, the agreement was reached only because the Americans and the Russians decided to ignore the apparently insoluble problem of the supply of arms to the Afghanistan government by the Russians and to the Mujahidin by the Americans. The essence of the agreement, therefore, is that the Russians will leave Afghanistan, but the war will go on, fought with weapons supplied by the agreeing superpowers (→14).

Seamen's strike strands holidaymakers

April 1. More than 6,000 holidaymakers were stuck in a queue at Dover today. Children started football games in the bright sunshine, but their parents grew increasingly frustrated as they heard that the peace talks between P&O European Ferries and the National Union of Seamen had broken down.

P&O is the main Dover operator, and the six-week strike really began to bite today as the holiday rush reached its peak. Travellers face a wait of 12 hours for the few other ferries. P&O has offered to cut proposed redundancies by 100 to 362, but the union still objects. Now P&O is expected to bypass the union and appeal to the workers to agree new manning levels to help them to beat off competition from the Channel Tunnel (→22).

April 9. Rhyme 'n' Reason, who fell in the Gold Cup last month, clears one of the Grand National's 30 fences on his way to victory.

Top broker accused in Guinness probe

April 7. The City of London was shocked today by a new arrest arising from the Fraud Squad investigation into Guinness. David Mayhew, aged 47, a senior partner of stockbrokers Cazenove, was taken to Holborn police station and charged on three criminal counts.

Mr Mayhew is the seventh man to be charged in connection with the scandal. He comes from the City's top drawer. Cazenove has the most impressive client list of any stockbroker. It includes the Royal Family and many leading companies. Mr Mayhew has been widely respected for his honesty and tonight Cazenove said he would remain a partner.

He was an adviser to Guinness during its £2.7 billion bid for Distillers, but Cazenove believes he is innocent, and he has masterminded many other bids since the Guinness scandal broke.

Bishop attacks Tory policies as wicked

The angry Bishop of Durham.

April 3. The Bishop of Durham, Rt Revd David Jenkins, chose Easter Day to deliver another attack on Conservative policies. Speaking on BBC radio, he said it was morally wrong to make life harder for the less well off: "If they refuse to face this fact, which has been put before them again and again, then they are so clearly wrong that the only word to use is "wicked"."

Hijacked airliner lands in Cyprus

April 9. The Kuwaiti airliner which was hijacked by Shia militants four days ago at Mashad in Iran was allowed to land at Cyprus's Larnaca airport tonight after the pilot, passengers and hijackers had pleaded in vain to be allowed to land at Beirut.

But Beirut has had enough of hijacks and, despite warnings from the pilot that he might have to land in the sea, and threats from the hijack leader that he would "punish" the control-tower officials, they were turned away.

Now Cyprus has the task of trying to bring the hijack to an end without bloodshed. On board are some 50 crew and passengers, including some members of the Kuwaiti royal family, one of them suffering from a heart condition.

The hijackers have repeated their demand for the release of 17 men jailed in Kuwait for terrorist offences and have threatened that the hostages will be "in extreme danger" unless their friends are set free. They have already shown a capacity for brutality by beating up one of the hostages. Tonight the plane sits at the end of the runway, lit up by spotlights and surrounded by police, as the Cypriots wait for the next move (→16/4).

The hijacked Jumbo Jet sits paralysed on the runway as negotiations continue.

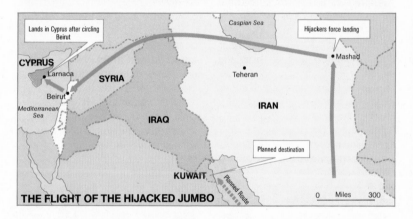
THE FLIGHT OF THE HIJACKED JUMBO

Pravda tells home truths about Brezhnev

April 3. Leonid Brezhnev, who ruled the Soviet Union for 14 years until 1982, was ridiculed by *Pravda* today for awarding himself medals for valour in the Second World War, when he hardly heard a shot fired in anger. He gave himself four gold stars as a Hero of the Soviet Union and added the highest mili-

tary honour, the Order of Victory. As a political commissar, he did no fighting, but was probably present at a minor incident in 1943, when German forces were stopped from landing at Malaya Zemlya, on the Black Sea. Brezhnev portrayed this as a second Stalingrad and a turning point in the war (→29/4).

West Indies collapse to defeat at home

April 6. Ten years of sporting invincibility came to an end today when the West Indies lost a test match at home. Their conquerors were the Pakistanis, who won the first test at Georgetown in Guyana by nine wickets with more than a day to spare.

Pakistan's star was their captain, Imran Khan, who was persuaded to come out of his short-lived retire-

ment by his country's president. Imran followed his seven wickets for 80 runs in the first West Indian innings with 4 for 41 in the second as the West Indies slumped to 172 all out. Top scorer was Gordon Greenidge with 43.

The West Indians hope that the return of their captain and top batsman, Viv Richards, will enable them to secure their revenge.

Sikh violence closes Punjab frontier

April 3. India's Prime Minister, Rajiv Gandhi, has today ordered the sealing of the border between the violence-torn state of Punjab and Pakistan. Mr Gandhi made no secret of his belief that Pakistan is training and arming the Sikh separatists who are pursuing a bloody campaign of murder in their attempt to carve out their own state of Khalistan from India.

Mr Gandhi also ordered a reorganisation of the Punjab intelligence services in an attempt to stop the violence which has already claimed 650 victims this year.

It is a matter of common knowledge in Amritsar, the Sikh holy city, that militants have infiltrated the Punjab police and paramilitary units and are warning the terrorists of police operations.

Iran accuses Iraq of using mustard gas

April 1. Iraq is again spreading silent, choking death among Kurdish villages, attacking the rebellious tribesmen with mustard and nerve gases, according to Iran's official Islamic Republic News Agency.

The agency claims that Iraqi warplanes dropped gas bombs on villages in Iraq's north-eastern Qara Dagh region between March 21 and 26, killing 75 people and making scores seriously ill.

These stories follow similar claims of gas attacks on villages later visited by Western journalists, who found hundreds of bodies in the streets and houses. Unmarked, they had died in agony, struck down by an unseen killer.

RIP: the traditional British passport

April 5. Britain's reluctant progress towards "Europeanisation" took a step forward today when the Home Office announced the phasing out of the traditional hardbacked blue passport. Its replacement will be a softer, burgundy-red passport, conforming to an agreed European Community format. The new passport, which will be standard issue by 1990, has a computer-readable strip on the cover to help tighten border controls.

Perestroika brings American pizza to Moscow, one of the more dubious aspects of reform.

April
1988

Su	Mo	Tu	We	Th	Fr	Sa
					1	2
3	4	5	6	7	8	9
10	11	12	13	14	15	16
17	18	19	20	21	22	23
24	25	26	27	28	29	30

10. Los Angeles: 24,000 square feet are needed to display Liberace's possessions, which are now up for auction.

11. Israel: The authorities expel eight Palestinian leaders to Lebanon (→16).

11. UK: A quarter of all deaths in Scotland last year were caused by cancer.

11. Los Angeles: Bertolucci's *The Last Emperor* wins nine Oscars at the Academy Awards. →

12. Dublin: Terrorist Dessie O'Hare, the "Border Fox", pleads guilty to kidnapping and maiming a dentist (→13).

12. Gatwick: Two hundred air passengers escape death when two aeroplanes nearly crash (→22).

13. Dublin: Dessie O'Hare is sentenced to 40 years jail for kidnap and mutilation (→28).

13. London: Mother Teresa of Calcutta visits Mrs Thatcher for a frank discussion.

13. London: An in-car, computerised route guidance system is unveiled.

14. Geneva: Afghanistan, Pakistan, USSR and US sign accords on Soviet withdrawal from Afghanistan (→25).

14. Hemel Hempstead: Armed bank robbers shoot dead a policeman.

15. UK: The Archbishop of York calls for strict rules on genetic engineering.

15. UK: The government proposes a 12 per cent pay rise for nurses, to placate angry backbenchers (→21).

16. Gaza Strip: Thirteen Palestinians are shot dead in riots over the assassination of Abu Jihad. →

DEATHS

12. South African writer, author of *Cry, The Beloved Country* Alan Stewart Paton (*11/1/03).

14. British politician and author John Stonehouse (*28/7/25). →

15. British actor and comedian Kenneth Williams (*22/2/26). →

Lyle is first Briton to win US Masters

Sandy Lyle drives his way to victory, via a bunker, at the 18th hole.

April 10. Sandy Lyle today became the first Briton to win the Masters golf tournament in Augusta, Georgia. The 30-year-old former Open champion had led from the second round, but it looked as though the title — one of golf's four major championships — might slip away at the final hole.

Wanting a par four on the 405-yard 18th hole to force a play-off with American Mark Calcavecchia, he drove into a bunker. But what could have been a disaster became a triumph, with a 150-yard shot out of the sand which came to a halt just eight feet from the hole. One putt gave him the title and the coveted green jacket of the US Masters champion. It was Lyle's third US win so far this year and makes him the tour's top money-winner — another first for a British golfer.

China opens the doors to free enterprise

April 12. China today tore down another of the cornerstones of Maoist Marxism when the National People's Congress voted overwhelmingly to pass laws allowing capitalist-style private enterprise and the transfer of the use of land between individuals.

The Chinese still baulk at outright private ownership of land; the campaign against "landlordism" is too recent and too painful for that. But the facade of "the use of land" covers the growth of what amounts to a land-owning class of prosperous yeomen who were "enemies of the people" under Mao.

It seems likely that the Congress will take another big step towards capitalism today with a new law designed to free state corporations from the dead hand of party bureaucracy and make them operate like capitalist businesses.

Thatcher gives in to backbench pressure

April 14. A threatened rebellion by Conservative backbench MPs against the general drift of government policies tonight forced Mrs Thatcher to start softening her reforms.

It was announced that poll-tax rebates will be extended to cover an extra million people. Word went round the parliamentary lobbies that social security changes will be less radical than at first stated. The Prime Minister also made a rare visit to the MPs' tearoom to chat up her backbenchers — a sure sign that government whips had reported trouble brewing.

A recent straw poll of Tory MPs showed nearly two-thirds seriously concerned that the government is getting a public reputation for hard-faced unfairness (→18).

Kenneth Williams dies, aged 62

April 15. The outrageously camp and much-loved Kenneth Williams was found dead in his flat near Regent's Park today. The comedian was 62 and not apparently ill, although he had been told he needed surgery for an ulcer.

He became immensely popular on radio, with Tony Hancock and Kenneth Horne, for his unmistakable whine and his catchphrase, "Stop messing about". He appeared in 22 "Carry-On" films — "I like smutty old jokes" — and became a panel-game celebrity. He had appeared on stage in revue and in his friend Joe Orton's play *Loot*. He lived in a bare flat next to his mother's. "He was a melancholy man," said his "Carry-On" colleague Barbara Windsor.

Those fabulously flared nostrils.

MPs want to see the back of Page 3 girls

April 13. A bill to ban sexually provocative press pictures of women was approved by 163 votes to 48 today after MPs heard how women found them degrading. Labour MP Clare Short told the Commons that among 500 letters of support she had received there were 12 from rape victims: "When they were raped the man said they reminded him of a woman on Page Three."

A similar debate two years ago was swamped by ribald remarks. This time the atmosphere was more serious, but there will be no time for the bill to progress further.

Top PLO man murdered

April 16. Abu Jihad, military commander of the Palestine Liberation Organisation and Yasser Arafat's closest friend, was murdered today at his seaside villa in Tunisia. It was an operation which bore all the hallmarks of Mossad, the Israeli secret service.

He was cut down in a hail of bullets by four men who had first killed his bodyguard and a gardener with silenced guns. Abdel Rahman, a senior PLO official, later told reporters: "I saw Abu Jihad's body later. His fingers had been shot off and his gun destroyed, as though they caught him trying to fire back around the corner of a doorway.

"Abu Jihad shot only once. I don't know if it injured one of them. There was so much blood everywhere, but I am afraid it was all Abu Jihad's blood."

Abu Jihad, whose real name was Khalil al-Wazir, was one of the founders of Fatah, and was remarkable for his loyalty to his teenage friend Arafat, when so many had turned against the PLO chairman.

What is surprising is that the

Deputy PLO leader Abu Jihad.

Israelis chose to kill him at this moment. He had never been a really successful guerrilla leader and the emphasis within the PLO has swung from acts of terrorism to the "Intifida" uprising in the occupied territories. Possibly Israel judged him responsible for this.

Zola storm could sink Olympic hopes

April 16. Zola Budd is again at the centre of an Olympics controversy. Four years ago it was her collision with the American runner Mary Slaney. Today it is her presence at an athletics meeting in her native South Africa which threatens this year's games in Seoul.

The International Amateur Athletic Federation said today that Zola Budd, who now runs for Britain, should be suspended for at least a year. "Moral blackmail," was the reaction of marathon runner Hugh Jones, but if British athletics chiefs fail to ban Zola the entire British team could be on the sidelines at Seoul this autumn (→18).

Will she stop our Olympic team?

Ammo explosion rocks Pakistan towns

April 10. "It's the end of the world," yelled a man as he ran through the streets of Rawalpindi, his house in ruins.

Entire districts of Rawalpindi and Islamabad were destroyed this morning when an ammunition dump halfway between the two cities exploded, raining down bombs, missiles and shrapnel. The area resembles a battlefield, with fragments of shells and unexploded missiles embedded in the ground.

Eyewitnesses described a huge mushroom-shaped fireball followed by a stream of rockets. Many spectators thought war had broken

out as bombs flattened houses and toppled electricity pylons. Panic spread as people rushed to the bus and railway stations for shelter.

Over 80 are believed killed and at least 850 injured by the barrage, which went on for two hours after the first blast. Extra staff are helping hospitals to treat a mass of burns and broken limbs.

An investigation into the cause is already under way. Many suspect sabotage by the Afghan secret service, which is blamed for several recent bomb attacks aimed at softening Pakistan's hard line on an Afghan peace settlement.

Kuwaiti hijack moves to bloody climax

April 16. The hijacking of the Kuwait Airlines jumbo, now in its eleventh day, seems to be moving steadily and cruelly towards its climax at Algiers airport.

After the killing of two hostages at Larnaca airport in Cyprus, the Shia terrorists, threatening "a slow, quiet massacre", exchanged 32 hostages for fuel and flew off to the more congenial atmosphere of Algiers, which has a long history of dealing with hijacks — usually to the hijackers' advantage.

Today, continuing their cat-and-mouse game with the hostages, the terrorists freed a middle-aged Kuwaiti man. The Algerian negotiators took this as a good sign and two police vans were driven up to the jumbo's stairs, apparently in expectation that more hostages would be freed.

At dusk, the lone, brave figure of Algeria's Interior Minister, El Hadri Khediri, disappeared into the aircraft. Just what sort of deal he is attempting to strike is not known. What is certain, however, is

that the Kuwaitis have been enraged by the murder of two of their citizens. They therefore seem unlikely to give in to the hijackers' demands for the freeing of the 17 Shias serving long sentences for terrorist attacks in Kuwait (→20).

The second victim is taken away.

This time it's true: Stonehouse is dead

April 14. John Stonehouse, politician, businessman and adventurer, died today, aged 63. He is remembered at Westminster as a reformed, repentant crook and the former Labour MP who once faked his own death in a bid to escape from a murky past.

Stonehouse, an efficient, smooth-tongued charmer, climbed the ministerial ladder right to the threshold of the Wilson cabinet in the late 1960s. Then, out of office, he encountered financial troubles. He disappeared, and his clothes were found on a Miami beach. It was reported that he had drowned. He turned up later in Australia and was later imprisoned for fraud.

Bertolucci clutches one of the nine Oscars won by "The Last Emperor," the most since "West Side Story" in 1962.

April

1988

Su	Mo	Tu	We	Th	Fr	Sa
					1	2
3	4	5	6	7	8	9
10	11	12	13	14	15	16
17	18	19	20	21	22	23
24	25	26	27	28	29	30

17. UK: The men's race in the London Marathon is won by Denmark's Henryk Jorgensen.

17. Wembley: The Football League celebrates its centenary.

18. UK: Thirty-eight Tory backbenchers vote against the government's plans for a flat rate poll tax (→27).

18. London: Labour MP Ron Brown throws the Commons mace after a debate on supplementary benefits (→20).

18. London: The International Amateur Athletic Association bans Zola Budd from taking part in competitions.

19. West Germany: Terrorist Abbas Ali Hamadei is sentenced to 13 years' jail for arms smuggling and kidnapping.

19. Turin: Ian Botham completes his trek across the Alps.

19. Kuala Lumpur: British drug trafficker Derrick Gregory loses his appeal against the death sentence.

20. UK: An opinion poll gives Labour one per cent more support than the Tories.

20. London: Ron Brown is suspended for 20 days for refusing to apologise for damaging the mace.

20. UK: A female condom is now available.

21. UK: The Home Office has a backlog of 270,000 unopened letters, mainly queries about nationality.

21. S Africa: President Botha promises reforms which will bring blacks into the cabinet.

22. UK: P&O announces plans to break the Seamen's strike by sailing non-unionised ships into Dover (→27).

22. UK: Air traffic controllers say their system is overloaded and undermanned.

23. US: Airlines ban smoking on all flights of less than two hours.

DEATH

23. British churchman Lord Ramsey, former Archbishop of Canterbury (*14/11/04).→

US bombs Iran oil base

A fire ship pumps water to extinguish a blazing Iranian oil platform.

April 18. The United States Navy today unleashed its power against the Iranians in retaliation for their mining of the Gulf. A series of actions left two Iranian oil platforms blazing, two frigates in a sinking condition and a patrol boat sent to the bottom.

The day's events started with US warships warning the oil platforms at Sirri and Sassan that they were about to be fired on: "Evacuate the platform. We will commence firing in less than thirty seconds." After the Iranians took to their boats, the Americans boarded the platforms, found anti-aircraft guns and SAM-7 missiles and blew up the platforms.

The Iranian boats then tried to interfere. It was a brave but fool-hardy gesture. They were blown out of the water. President Reagan, speaking in Washington, said: "If they threaten us, they'll pay a price."

Nurses get 15% pay rise — with strings

April 21. Nurses are to get an average 15 per cent pay rise — and the Treasury will foot the £794m bill. At the higher end of the scale the increases, approved by the cabinet today, will aim to reward specialist skills. The nurses will get an interim four per cent pending a major restructuring of grades. The move follows weeks of political agitation about the state of the NHS, not only from the opposition but also from the Tory back-benches, coupled with an unease that the Budget was weighted too favourably towards the well-off.

Now there is no excuse for not taking your work home with you. These battery-powered lap top computers are the ultimate executive toy.

Hostages released in Algiers as their captors go free

April 20. The hijack of the Kuwaiti jumbo is over. The hostages were released at dawn this morning and the men who had kept them so cruelly imprisoned on the plane for 16 days were allowed to slip away to an unknown destination, under the deal worked out by the Algerian government.

The hijack, which started in Iran, moved to Cyprus and ended in Algiers, was marked by the highly trained and brutal behaviour of the Shia terrorists, who murdered two of their hostages. Abdul Mahmood, the jumbo's purser, said after his release today that the hijackers, who wore pointed hoods, "looked like sharks in the water".

The brave pilot gets a warm welcome.

Brook's Indian epic staged in Glasgow

April 18. Britain's most admired director-in-exile, Peter Brook, is presenting his current theatre epic in Britain for the first time — not in a London theatre but in Glasgow's Old Museum of Transport. Asked why, he said: "We went to where we were invited."

The Mahabharata, which is based on the 2,000-year-old Indian religious poem, lasts nine hours. The trilogy, translated into English by Brook, grows to an heroic scale, involving gods and demons, kings, princesses and a great warrior, under the eye of Krishna.

Dukakis wins New York: now it's a two horse race with Bush for the Republicans

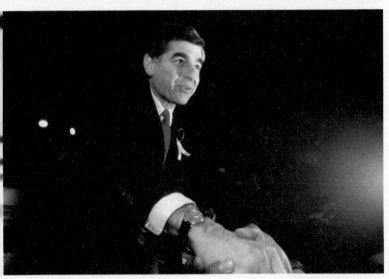

The first of thousands of handshakes for candidate Michael Dukakis.

April 19. Governor Michael Dukakis of Massachusetts was tonight heading for victory in the New York primary election and a commanding lead for the Democratic nomination.

Exit polls conducted by TV networks showed Mr Dukakis leading the Reverend Jesse Jackson, comfortably in New York State. In New York City, however, with its big black and Puerto Rican population, Mr Jackson was reported to be ahead. He delighted supporters by walking down Fifth Avenue, although he has recieved several death threats.

The third candidate, Senator Albert Gore of Tennessee, has already decided to pull out of the race for lack of money. He spent $600,000 on television advertising in New York to little avail, and his campaign is now $2.5 million in debt.

Before the New York vote Governor Dukakis already led Mr Jackson by 833 votes to 728, and now Mr Dukakis is more than halfway to victory at the Democratic convention. Mr Jackson's campaign has impressed observers with his ability to articulate issues on behalf of those white, as well as black, people who feel that they have been losers during the Reagan years.

In the Republican primary, also held today, Vice-President George Bush carried New York easily.

Pioneering archbishop Lord Ramsey dies

April 23. Lord Ramsey, the 100th Archbishop of Canterbury, died today at the age of 83. His 14-year primacy covered the permissive sixties, when the church faced challenges from within and without concerning its traditional beliefs. Lord Ramsey managed to retain the love of the traditionalists, while at the same time winning the respect of those who wanted change.

He was the son of a congregational minister who was converted to the high church. He became a pioneer of the ecumenical movement.

In 1966 he went to Rome to meet Pope Paul VI, the first meeting of the two church heads for four centuries. He worked equally hard, though less successfully, for more unity with the non-conformist churches.

He spoke out clearly on political issues — opposing the death penalty, fighting restrictions on immigration and attacking South Africa's

Lord Ramsey, Archbishop 1961-74.

apartheid policies. He also stressed the value of keeping quiet. "Do not speak unless you can improve on the silence," he told the younger clergy. And he set an example by introducing the practice of silent croquet at Cuddesdon College.

Demjanjuk convicted as Ivan the Terrible

April 18. "Without the slightest hesitation or doubt, we state that the accused, John Ivan Demjanjuk, is one and the same as Ivan Grozny (the Terrible), the SS camp guard who operated the gas chambers at Treblinka death camp and perpetrated the brutal crimes ascribed to him." So, after two months of deliberation, the judges in Jerusalem pronounced their verdict. Throughout the 14-month trial, Demjanjuk

claimed he was the innocent victim of mistaken identity.

Some found it hard to reconcile the image of this wheelchair-bound teddy bear of a man with Ivan "the Terrible", who took delight in mutilating his victims as he herded them into the gas chambers. But there was no doubt in the minds of the camp survivors whose eye-witness testimony helped to secure his conviction (→25).

Beirut car bomb kills 54 people

April 23. A vegetable truck packed with 330 pounds of explosives blew up in the middle of Tripoli marketplace in Lebanon today. The explosion killed 54 people, injured 125, demolished six shops, set surrounding vehicles on fire and blasted a crater in the road. Rescuers believe the rubble will give up more corpses as the search for survivors goes on.

Right-wing Christian extremists are thought to be behind the bombing. Tripoli is a Moslem city policed by Syria and her allies. The Christian militias oppose Syrian plans to give Moslems more power.

Were these verses by Shakespeare?

April 26. A set of 14 verses, signed with the initials "W S", was written by Shakespeare, says Oxford professor of poetry Peter Levi. The page of verses was discovered in the Huntington Library, California. The verses were written in 1607 to be spoken at the engagement of Anne, daughter of the Countess of Derby. The "W S" is followed by the letter "h", which has been altered to look like a "k". Today another Shakespearean scholar claims that it is identical with the signature of Sir William Skipwith, a family friend.

April 23. Kanellos Kanellopoulos pedals his Daedalus human-powered aircraft 74 miles, from Crete to Santorini, to set three world records.

April

1988

Su	Mo	Tu	We	Th	Fr	Sa
					1	2
3	4	5	6	7	8	9
10	11	12	13	14	15	16
17	18	19	20	21	22	23
24	25	26	27	28	29	30

25. UK: The government announces a £6,000 million investment in the RAF's "Eurofighter" programme.

25. Afghanistan: The army withdraws from the war zone near the Pakistani border.

25. UK: A survey finds that 22 per cent of teachers are not trained to teach or assess the new GCSE examinations.

26. The Hague: The World Court rules that the US must submit to arbitration on its closure of a PLO mission.

26. UK: Midwives complain that the medical establishment is cracking down on home births.

26. UK: Swiss food giant Nestle bids £2,100 million for York-based confectioners Rowntree.

27. UK: The government buys off a threatened backbench revolt with £100 million of benefit concessions.

27. Rotterdam: P&O fly in 247 crewmen to sail strike-breaking ships to Dover (→28).

28. Hawaii: One is killed and 61 injured when the fuselage of an Aloha Airlines Boeing 737 rips open.

28. UK: The waiting list for NHS hospital treatment is now 750,000 people long.

28. London: The High Court issues an order preventing the National Union of Seamen from moving its funds.

29. Moscow: Gorbachev promises greater religious freedom in a meeting with church leaders.

29. Moscow: McDonald's announces the opening of 20 hamburger restaurants to sell the "Bolshoi Mak".

30. Newmarket: The 2,000 Guineas is won by the Aga Khan's Doyoun, ridden by Walter Swinburn.

DEATHS

28. British politician and pacifist Fenner Brockway (*1/11/1888).

29. Scottish actor Andrew Cruikshank (*25/12/07).→

Mitterrand takes first step to second term

April 25. François Mitterrand, France's Socialist President, easily came first in the first round of the French presidential elections today, with just over one third of the vote. But he did so only because the Right, which won over half the votes, was split three ways.

By far the most striking result was the showing of Jean-Marie Le Pen, extreme right-wing leader of the National Front, who won over four million votes, or 14.38 per cent of the total. In Marseilles, Le Pen led with 28 per cent of the vote.

Former President Jacques Chirac of the neo-Gaullist RDP party came first of the three right-wing candidates, winning just under 20 per cent of the votes. Raymond Barre, of the UDF, won 16.5 per cent.

The other dramatic result was the near-extinction of the Communist vote. The Communist candidate, André Lajoinie, won 6.76 per cent of the vote, or about half the number won by Georges Marchais in 1981 and only two-thirds of the itself disappointing Communist vote in the last elections to the National Assembly.

Right-winger Jean-Marie Le Pen could give Mitterrand a bumpy ride.

Steel workers go on strike in Poland

April 29. In the worst industrial unrest since the 1981 martial law crackdown, 14,000 workers at the Lenin steel works at Cracow stopped work, another 6,000 came out at the Stalowa Wola defence plant, 120 miles south-east of Warsaw, and 600 bus and tram drivers in Bydgoszcz halted public transport for 12 hours until they were given a 63 per cent pay rise. The wave of strikes follows price increases of 40 per cent on food, 50 per cent on rents and 100 per cent on electricity. The government claims that a spell of austerity is necessary to restore economic stability, but Lech Walesa, the Solidarity leader, says Poles have no faith in Communist polices, which, he says, "have made us the beggars of Europe".

Jagger acquitted of plagiarism

April 26. A handful of fans waited outside the suburban courthouse in White Plains, New York, today as singer Mick Jagger was acquitted of plagiarism. Jagger, aged 44, is no stranger to controversy, but no one had ever questioned his originality until Patrick Alley, a little-known Jamaican reggae singer, claimed that Jagger's hit, *Just Another Night*, was a rip-off of one of his own songs, with the same title, written in 1979.

Jagger said he first heard Alley's song in 1986, when his lawyer played it to him, and that he had tapes to prove he had written his own song in France. After the verdict Jagger brushed off the case, telling the court: "When you're a celebrity people take pot-shots at you."

Ministers condemn TV Gibraltar probe

April 28. *Death on the Rock*, Thames Television's programme on the SAS operation in Gibraltar last October, was transmitted tonight, despite heavy pressure from the government on the Independent Broadcasting Authority (IBA) to stop what it claims is "trial by television" in advance of the official inquest.

The programme included a local witness claiming that the bombers had their hands up when shot. The Foreign Secretary, Sir Geoffrey Howe, spoke personally to Lord Thomson, the IBA chairman, two days ago, urging that the programme be postponed to avoid any risk of prejudicing the inquest.

Andrew Cruikshank dies at age of 80

April 29. Andrew Cruickshank, who died today aged 80, was so identified in the public mind with Dr Cameron, the crusty, old-fashioned GP of *Dr Finlay's Casebook* who distrusted all modern medicine, that it is hard to recall his career in the classics.

He once played in Olivier's *Macbeth*, Gielgud's *King Lear* and at the National Theatre. He might well have gone further in the classics had he not become typecast in television dramas, first as a judge and then as Dr Cameron.

Scotland's best-loved medic.

Sudan war adds to Ethiopia famine

Three years after "Live Aid", the song of hunger remains the same.

April 28. Only a few weeks after international relief officials were speaking of operations in Ethiopia as "the best-organised food programme ever", some three million people in the Horn of Africa are facing starvation because of guerrilla wars — two in Ethiopia itself — and one in neighbouring Sudan, which has sent tens of thousands of Dinka tribesmen fleeing into Ethiopia to escape Arab raiders. Relief workers say there are over a quarter of a million Dinka refugees in Ethiopia.

In Ethiopia, where government forces are fighting secessionist movements in Eritrea and Tigre provinces, guerrillas are ambushing food convoys and attacking food distribution centres.

Most of the 1.3 million tons of food estimated to be needed for the year is already on the way from EEC countries, the United States and the Soviet Union. But at the Red Sea port of Massawa it faces delays, because the badly paid and poorly fed Ethiopian soldiers are unable to keep the roads open.

Airlifting the food by C-130 transports is safer but expensive. A C-130 carries about 20 tons of grain, but costs about £100,000 a week to operate and can bring food only to the main centres and not to isolated villages, which are often the most in need of relief.

Fenner Brockway dies at age of 99

April 28. Fenner Brockway, the noblest old libertarian socialist of them all, died tonight seven months before his 100th birthday. Frail but still passionate, he was active in the House of Lords until quite recently.

There, and on public platforms, he continued to preach vehemently against war, racism and capitalism. He was first put in jail for his pacifism three-quarters of a century ago.

Lord Brockway, a parson's son who accepted a peerage "against my better judgement" in 1964, was the last direct personal link with the pioneers who formed the Labour Party.

April 25. The Jerusalem judges sentence former Nazi camp guard Ivan Demjanjuk to death.

Syria and Arafat patch up their quarrel

April 26. In yet one more twist to Middle Eastern politics, Yasser Arafat, chairman of the PLO, and President Hafez Assad of Syria today agreed to patch up their differences in order to support the Palestinian uprising in the Israeli-occupied territories of the West Bank and Gaza.

As part of the agreement, Syria has agreed to allow Mr Arafat to reopen his offices in Damascus, which were closed five years ago when Assad expelled him from Syria, backed a mutiny against him by some PLO officers, and almost succeeded in having him deposed as the PLO's leader. The agreement highlights the rethinking of tactics imposed on the established leaders by the success of the "Intifada".

Back in favour: Yasser Arafat.

NUS defies court ruling to oppose scabs

April 29. Two P&O ferries sailed from Rotterdam tonight as the company escalated its attempt to break the 13-week strike by 2,300 members of the National Union of Seamen. The *Pride of Bruges* and *Pride of Kent* are expected in Dover tomorrow morning. A large picket is gathering to demonstrate against the strikers, but P&O has arranged for a police escort to take in new crews for the ships.

The original dispute was over P&O's plans to reduce manning levels to meet competition from the Channel Tunnel. On Tuesday, however, some Sealink seamen refused to cross NUS picket lines. Sealink won a high court injunction against this secondary action. The company is said to be reluctant to press for the seizure of the NUS's £5 million funds. Today, however, the court froze the funds and frustrated attempts by the union to move more than a million pounds abroad.

James Sherwood, chairman of Sealink's owners, met Sir Jeffrey Sterling, the P&O chairman, today in an attempt to mediate. He failed, and P&O is now determined to break the strike.

Reporters quiz NUS general secretary Sam McCluskie about his next step.

May

1988

Su	Mo	Tu	We	Th	Fr	Sa
1	2	3	4	5	6	7
8	9	10	11	12	13	14
15	16	17	18	19	20	21
22	23	24	25	26	27	28
29	30	31				

1. Sri Lanka: Tamil guerrillas are blamed for a land mine which kills 26 bus passengers.

1. Poland: Widespread May Day demonstrations are broken up by riot police (→3).

2. India: A children's hospital at Jammu collapses, killing at least 21 patients.

2. Lebanon: Two thousand Israeli troops move in to search for terrorists.→

3. UK: Photographs of Zola Budd at a race meeting in South Africa bring her future into question (→10).

3. Poland: Lech Walesa, leader of the Solidarity trade union, calls for wide reforms or "bloody revolution".→

3. Leeds: Russell Harty goes into intensive care with liver failure (→6/6).

3. London: The BBC confirms an outbreak of legionnaire's disease in a cooling tower at Broadcasting House.

4. UK: Mrs Thatcher tries to stop a BBC Belfast *Spotlight* documentary on the Gibraltar shootings (→5).

4. UK: A Kuwaiti government stake of 22 per cent in British Petroleum is referred to the Monopolies Commission (→10).

4. Liverpool: Two policemen who kicked a suspect to death are imprisoned for life.

4. UK: Sequestrators seize the assets of the National Union of Seamen (→9).

5. Belfast: The BBC goes ahead with showing of *Spotlight* programme on the Gibraltar inquest (→15).

5. UK: The Football League is considering signing an exclusive deal with satellite TV companies (→8/6).

5. France: Three French hostages, freed yesterday, return from Beirut (→11).

6. London: A bogus doctor who "treated" hospital patients is jailed for 18 months.

7. Washington: US officials claim George Bush lied when he denied knowledge of drug charges against Noriega in 1985.

IRA death squad kills British servicemen

The body of the airman killed at Roermond returns to England.

May 2. A police hunt began across northern Europe tonight after an IRA "hit squad" killed three off-duty British servicemen in Holland. A senior aircraftsman died and two of his colleagues were hurt when their car was sprayed by machine-gun fire at Roermond. At Nieuw-Bergen, 30 minutes later, a car bomb killed two more servicemen and severely wounded a third as they left a disco.

In a "simple message" to Mrs Thatcher after the killings, the IRA said: "Disengage from Ireland and there will be peace. If not, there will be no haven for your military personnel and you will regularly be at airports awaiting your dead."

Scotland Yard anti-terrorist detectives were flying to Holland tonight to assist the Dutch and West German police in the search for an IRA "active service" squad who are believed have been based in West Germany for several years.

With 76,000 British servicemen stationed in West Germany, politicians were urgently reassessing security arrangements on the continent. The IRA has been active both covertly and openly in Holland, and tonight notices were placed on the Dutch-West German border stating: "BFG [British Forces in Germany] Persons advised not to enter Holland."

Condemning the outrages, a Labour Party spokesman questioned whether they were a response to the shooting in March of three IRA members in Gibraltar (→4).

House prices up 20 per cent in a year

May 5. Last month's budget has helped boost house price inflation to a record average of 20.3 per cent a year, according to figures released today by the Halifax Building Society. Prices have been fuelled by an influx of first-time buyers trying to beat the August deadline for multiple tax relief for shared borrowers.

London's inflation has stabilised at about 25 per cent a year, but housing in East Anglia is rising by over 40 per cent a year and still going up. The West Midlands and the North are starting to experience the same upward trend that southeast England started to feel a few years ago (→13).

Steve Davis wins fifth world title

May 2. Steve Davis has won his fifth Embassy World Snooker Championship. Yesterday, Welshman Terry Griffiths clawed back Davis's 5-1 lead to 8-8, but today Britain's most clinical snooker player faltered only a few times on his way to win by 18 frames to 11.

Griffiths said the collapse of the long potting skills, which had clinched his semi-final win over Jimmy White, was the worst aspect of his play today. Davis, £95,000 richer tonight, grandly declared: "There's no disgrace in getting beat by someone great."

Hick blasts his way into the records with score of the century

May 6. Graeme Hick, the 20-year-old Zimbabwe-born batsman, today struck the second highest first-class individual score ever achieved in England — and the eighth highest of all time. What's more he was undefeated on 405 runs when his Worcestershire captain declared the team's innings closed against Somerset.

Hick was then only 19 runs short of the highest score in England, also at Taunton, by Archie MacLaren in 1895. He struck 35 fours and 11 sixes during his record-breaking 469-ball innings. To round off his day, Hick took two wickets with his off-spin bowling (→19).

Worcestershire star Graeme Hick, getting into his high-scoring stride.

NUS faces fine and seizure of funds

May 3. Four accountants from the City firm of Spicer & Oppenheimer tonight moved in to the headquarters of the National Union of Seamen to take over the union's £2.8 million assets. The union will also have to pay a fine of £150,000 and substantial costs following the High Court ruling earlier today on the sequestration application brought by Sealink, whose ferries have been stopped by secondary action.

Mr Justice Michael Davies said: "The leaders have only themselves to blame. This is the clearest possible case of deliberate attempted suicide." The dispute began three months ago when P&O proposed redundancies and longer working hours to prepare for competition with the Channel Tunnel. After attempts at conciliation failed, P&O engaged crews to run strikebreaking ships. The union then called on all its 25,000 members to support the strike.

Reagan ruled by stargazers, says Regan

Regan: spilling the beans.

May 3. President Reagan allowed his wife's astrologer to dictate favourable or unfavourable times for meetings, including last December's summit meeting with Mikhail Gorbachev, according to his former chief of staff, Donald Regan. In his book, just published, Mr Regan says: "Virtually every major move and decision the Reagans made during my time as White House chief of staff was cleared in advance with a woman in San Francisco who drew up horoscopes to make certain that the planets were in a favourable alignment."

Mr Reagan says he has not been influenced by astrologers in making any decisions: "I'm making it a policy not to comment on these books that seem to keep flooding out."

He may have been thinking of the recent book by his former acting press secretary, Larry Speakes, who said he invented remarks ostensibly made by the President and gave them to the press.

The Reagans are known to have consulted astrologers in the past about the timing of events. For example, Mr Reagan was inaugurated Governor of California just after midnight because his wife was told that the stars would be more favourable than on the previous day (→31).

Cook's win stokes women's pay hopes

May 5. Cook Julie Hayward served up a victory for the "equal pay for work of equal value" campaign when the Law Lords ruled in her favour today, ending a four-year legal battle. Her wages must now be raised to match those of joiners, painters and insulation engineers in the same company. The ruling will have widespread implications for women's pay, now averaging £137 a week, compared to men's £207.

Alton's Bill aborted by talkative MPs

May 6. Time ran out today for David Alton's controversial bill to cut the legal time limit on abortions from 28 weeks to 18. The Liberal MP claimed after the five-hour debate that his opponents had "used shabby devices" to talk the bill out; they say that Alton is out of touch with majority opinion.

Police smash Polish steelworkers' strike

May 5. Riot police went into action with tear-gas and stun grenades in Poland today in a determined bid to smash the wave of strikes that has paralysed the Lenin shipyard in Gdansk and the giant Nowa Huta steelworks near Cracow. Several thousand police in trucks surrounded the steelworks while snatch squads went inside to seize the strike leaders. The steelmen had been seeking 50 per cent pay increases to compensate for raging price inflation. At Gdansk, Lech Walesa, the Solidarity trade union leader, barricaded himself in the shipyard with 3,000 workers. At midday riot police moved in, but Walesa and some strikers are still holding out tonight (→8).

Israelis launch border raid on Lebanon

May 3. An Israeli armoured force made a dawn foray into southern Lebanon today, with some 2,000 troops occupying four villages on the slopes of Mount Hermon, just short of Syrian army positions.

Advancing six miles beyond their "security zone", they rounded up villagers in an operation designed to warn the Lebanese not to help the Palestinians, who are becoming increasingly bold in their cross-border raids.

Major General Yossi Peled, Israel's commander in the north, said: " In our experience, it is an efficient way to give a message to the villagers... that they cannot co-operate with terrorists against Israel".

Poles march to support Solidarity, their banned trade union.

William Hurt stars in "Broadcast News", an indictment of the US media.

May

1988

Su	Mo	Tu	We	Th	Fr	Sa
1	2	3	4	5	6	7
8	9	10	11	12	13	14
15	16	17	18	19	20	21
22	23	24	25	26	27	28
29	30	31				

8. Poland: Strikers ignore an ultimatum to leave the Gdansk shipyard (→10).

9. UK: Neil Kinnock has told colleagues he is prepared to accept the protection of a US nuclear "umbrella" (→11/6).

10. UK: The Electricians' Union votes to continue with single union and no strike deals, to TUC anger.

10. London: A poll shows that 61 per cent of Londoners and 71 per cent of parents want ILEA abolished.

10. Gdansk: The Lenin shipyard strike ends (→19/6).

10. London: A judge orders charges against soccer hooligans to be dropped because the police fabricated evidence (→23).

11. Paris: Freed hostage Jean-Paul Kauffmann attacks British lack of concern over hostages Waite and McCarthy.

11. Dover: The truckers' blockade crumbles as the NUS is fined £150,000 (→12).

12. UK: David Steel confirms that he will not stand for leadership of the merged SLD.

12. UK: The NUS calls off its Sealink ferry strike (→16).

13. UK: Sir Geoffrey Howe says Britain should join the European Monetary System (→16).

13. India: Five Sikhs are killed in the continuing siege of the Golden Temple at Amritsar (→18).

13. Moscow: Kim Philby is buried, with full military honours.

14. US: Michael Dukakis pledges to scrap the Strategic Defence Initiative ("Star Wars") if elected President.

14. Wembley: Wimbledon win the FA Cup, beating Liverpool 1-0.→

14. Glasgow: Celtic win the Scottish Cup, beating Dundee United 2-1.→

DEATHS

11. British spy Harold Kim (H.A.R.) Philby (*1/1/12).→

13. American jazzman Chet (Chesney) Baker (*23/12/19).

Mitterrand beats Chirac

May 10. François Mitterrand was today re-elected President of France at the age of 71, after winning 54 per cent of the vote. He defeated the candidate of the disunited right, the prime minister Jacques Chirac, although the latter had negotiated the return of hostages from Beirut.

In a victory speech he indicated that, as the socialist president of a country where a majority voted for one of three candidates of the right in the first round of voting, he would not stress socialist policies. "Our first duty," he said, "is to national solidarity and social cohesion."

The election has been a personal disaster for Mr Chirac, who lost his seat in parliament and now ceases to be premier. Chirac took it with dignity, saying: "In a democracy it is the people who choose."

The candidate of the National Front, Jean-Marie Le Pen, was more scathing. "The stupidest right in the world," he said, "has for the

Veteran socialist François Mitterrand (r.) steps back into power.

second time in seven years assured the victory of the socialists." Earlier in the day President Mitterrand and Mr Chirac shook hands silently at a parade to mark VE day (→12/6).

Syria steps in to stop fighting in Beirut

May 9. The Syrian army today threatened to intervene in Beirut to put an end to the fierce fighting between rival Amal and Hizbollah militias which has killed 74 people in the past three days. As gunfire shook the city, Brigadier Ghazi Kenaan, the Syrian commander, warned: "You will force us to solve the problem if you do not agree on an end. I will not allow the situation to continue as it is." (→15)

Exhausted Zola Budd quits the racetrack

May 10. Zola Budd returned to her South African homeland tonight, suffering from what her doctor calls an "acutely depressed" condition caused by the political maelstrom which has swirled around the tiny, 21-year-old athlete ever since she was given a British passport.

Forced out of this year's world cross-country championships — an event she had won in the past — she was then criticised for attending an athletics meeting in South Africa. International bodies called for a ban and the pressure finally broke her. Her doctor said she had been unable to sleep and was suffering from headaches and high blood pressure. She has gone home to relax, but many doubt that she will compete again internationally.

Back home in Bloemfontein.

Kim Philby, perfect spy, dies at 76

May 11. Britain's intelligence agencies heard with relief today of the death in Moscow of Harold "Kim" Philby, the Cambridge-educated spy who seriously endangered Anglo-American relations. He died without writing a sequel to his book, *My Silent War*, in which he might have named more names.

Philby, a senior MI6 officer before his resignation, and eventual "clearance", fled to Russia in 1963. As liaison officer in Washington, he had been privy to FBI and CIA intelligence material invaluable to his KGB masters. He was the "third man" who tipped off runaway diplomats Burgess and Maclean. Many of Philby's colleagues in the secret service saw him as a future head of MI6 (→13).

"Gentleman" and master spy.

Thatcherite youth is "more sensible"

May 10. "Thatcher's generation" of teenagers and young adults are more mature and less confused than their alienated, rebellious predecessors, says a survey by market researchers Mintel, out today. Today's youngsters say they want to be seen as "sensible and responsible", but give most of their time and attention to television, fashion and style. Although they say they value their families above all, fewer of them choose to marry.

Starving refugees flee Sudanese war

Refugees from war-torn Sudan set up camp in Ethiopia.

May 8. Africa's longest-running racial war is sending tens of thousands — some reports put the figure at two million — of starving refugees fleeing from southern Sudan. Some are arriving on the outskirts of the capital, Khartoum, after having been on the move for four months. Others are fleeing into neighbouring Ethiopia. All have horrifying stories to tell of murder, pillage and rape.

The victims are Dinkas, a Nilotic people, animists and Christians. They claim that Moslem Arabs from the north are pursuing a deliberate policy of genocide. Arab bands, often accompanied by regular Sudanese soldiers, are system-atically destroying Dinka villages and carrying off the women.

The war began in 1955, when Britain was about to grant independence to Sudan. The southerners, fearing domination by the Arabs, launched a civil war to win separate independence. That round lasted for 17 years, until Khartoum promised the south some autonomy.

That did not work out, and the war was resumed, with the southern rebels organising the Sudan People's Liberation Army, and mounting "scorched earth" raids on villages in an attempt to prevent supplies getting to the Arab bands. Foreign aid workers have been unable to enter the region.

Iraq bombs Gulf tankers

May 14. The world's largest ship is burning uncontrollably tonight after being attacked by long-range aircraft of the Iraqi air force at Iran's supposedly safe Larak oil terminal in the southern Gulf. The devastating raid by ten Mirages caught the defences off-guard, and the 564,000-tonne Liberian-registered supertanker *Seawise Giant* was hit while pumping oil.

The effect was awesome, as flames and smoke from the tanker's cargo boiled into the sky. Three other tankers were also hit and one of them, the 235,000-ton Spanish-registered *Barcelona*, is reported to have broken up and sunk.

On previous long-distance raids it has been supposed that the Iraqi planes have been refuelled in mid-air, but Iraq does not have the capacity to keep ten aircraft in the air for the 1,500-mile round trip which they made today.

The belief is current, therefore, that the Mirages were allowed to refuel in either Saudi Arabia or Kuwait. If this is so, it will be a serious escalation of the war, and one which will enrage the Iranians.

However, from the Kuwaiti point of view, it would be a matter of simple justice to strike at the Iranians, for the Kuwaitis have no doubt that Tehran was responsible for last month's hijacking of a Kuwait Airways jumbo (→25).

Kremlin crisis puts perestroika in peril

May 10. Mr Gorbachev admitted publicly tonight that his *perestroika* programme for restructuring Soviet society was meeting opposition from Communist Party officials and bureaucrats, not only at local level "but also at the top". He said they were scared and confused by the prospect of change. "We must defeat the conservatism blocking our path," he added. His speech is seen as a scarcely veiled attack on Yegor Ligachev, believed to be the chief opponent of reform (→31).

Lorry drivers block Channel ports

May 9. Mounting anger by lorry drivers, added to the fury of the seamen, to bring chaos tonight to Dover and Calais. Lorry drivers blocked the ferry berths of P&O's strike-breaking ships, claiming that preference had been given to French lorries carrying perishable goods. Meanwhile, leaders of the National Union of Seamen were meeting at TUC headquarters to try and hammer out a peace formula to end the three-month long dispute (→11).

Swiss roll up with a bid for Rowntree

May 10. Opposition grew today to Nestle's £2.1 billion bid for the York-based Rowntree group, makers of such household names as Kit Kat, Quality Street and Smarties. The local Conservative MP, Conal Gregory, told Parliament that both shareholders and employees overwhelmingly wanted Rowntree to stay independent.

The bid poses critical questions for the government's monopoly and merger policy. Nestle already owns 12 per cent of Rowntree and fellow Swiss chocolate giant Suchard 29.9 per cent. Both Swiss groups want Rowntree as a bridgehead within the European Community (→25).

Celtic's late winner clinches the double, but Liverpool tumble

May 14. The domestic football seasons reached their traditional climax today with the two Cup Finals, but the two teams of the season — north and south of the border — experienced contrasting fortunes.

In Scotland, Celtic duly completed a League and Cup double by beating Dundee United 2-1 at Hampden Park, thanks to two goals by Frank McAvennie after United had taken the lead. The winning goal came one minute from time. There was no such reprieve for Liverpool at Wembley where their dream of the double became a nightmare, as their expensive stars tumbled to a drab 1-0 defeat against humble Wimbledon (→21).

Dundee's McInally (in orange) holds off a challenge from Celtic's McStay.

May

1988

Su	Mo	Tu	We	Th	Fr	Sa
1	2	3	4	5	6	7
8	9	10	11	12	13	14
15	16	17	18	19	20	21
22	23	24	25	26	27	28
29	30	31				

15. Beirut: Syrian troops mass to support the Amal militia, as the weekly death toll from gun battles reaches 200 (→21/6).

15. Belfast: Three are killed and nine injured when gunmen fire into a bar (→13/6).

15. Khartoum: Four Britons die in a hotel bomb attack.

16. Israel: Two Palestinians are killed in fighting at the end of Ramadan (→21).

16. UK: P&O ferries resume passenger sailings to try to break the seamen's strike.

17. UK: Bank base rates drop to 7.5 per cent, the lowest for ten years (→18).

17. UK: Sainsbury's announces sales of over £5,000 million last year, selling 10.7 per cent of British groceries.

18. UK: The foreign exchange value of sterling is still rising, despite low interest rates (→20).

18. UN: A report warns that the world's population is growing by 220,000 a day.

18. London: Maoris protest against the planned auction of a preserved chief's head (→19).

19. Edgbaston: England beat the West Indies by six wickets in a one-day international (→28).

19. London: The High Court orders that a Maori chief's head is withdrawn from sale.

19. Birmingham: A study concludes that 30,000 men regularly use the city's prostitutes.

19. UK: Wilberforce, the resident cat at 10 Downing Street since 1974, dies.

20. UK: Privatisation of British Rail is reported to be high on the agenda for a fourth Tory government.

20. UK: Inflation reaches 3.9 per cent a year, fuelled by rising house prices (→27).

21. Wembley: England beat Scotland 1-0, with one fan dead and 165 arrests (→18/6).

21. West Bank: Three Palestinians are killed, bringing the total of Arab deaths in the uprising to 186 (→8/6).

42

Preacher Thatcher gives Kirk Tory creed

May 21. Greatly daring, Mrs Thatcher today told the General Assembly of the Church of Scotland, in effect, that God is on her side. This was probably not what a majority of the Prestbyterian elders and ministers thought.

The Prime Minister asserted that wealth creation was encouraged by Christianity's manifesto. She quoted St Paul as saying: "If a man will not work, he shall not eat". Mrs Thatcher argued that tax-cutting is an incentive needed to help people to be responsible citizens: "It is not the creation of wealth that is wrong, but the love of money for its own sake."

She also worked into her speech the Biblical story of the sinner criticised for wasting ointment on anointing the feet of Christ. According to the Bible, Jesus praised that sinner saying: "Ye have the poor always with you. But me, ye have not always."

The Prestbyterian hierarchy listened restlessly, but politely to this

Preaching the Tory gospel.

sermon from its eminent visitor. Many of its members nursed their wrath to keep it warm. They prepared retaliation on the theme of political morality. There were also signs that some Anglicans will also take issue with the Prime Minister's venture into religion (→31).

Pomp marks Russia's Afghan withdrawal

May 16. Several thousand khaki-clad Soviet troops gathered on a dusty parade ground in Kabul this morning to be praised by President Najibullah, the Afghan Communist installed by Moscow. "Thank you for your heroism, your courage and your valour," he said as he handed out medals. "May your journey home be safe and your food be tasty." As he spoke, the gunfire of

the *mujahedin* reverberated in the hills outside the city.

A brass band played as the troops boarded trucks for the 80-mile journey to Friendship Bridge into the Soviet Union. In the next nine months Moscow has promised to pull out all the 115,000 troops it sent into Afghanistan in 1979. Official spokesmen have said 15,000 Soviet soldiers died in the war.

The first Russian convoy begins the long process of military withdrawal.

Longer time should please gentlemen

May 20. Brewers, publicans and drinkers throughout England and Wales gave a subdued greeting to impending changes in opening hours today, as the Licensing Act received the Royal Assent. Starting this summer, 65,000 pubs will be able to stay open from 11am until 11pm on weekdays, with restricted hours on Sundays — but how many will take advantage of the new freedom remains in doubt.

The Brewers' Society believes that most rural pubs will stay shut; and many urban pubs are concerned that the new hours will prove to be uneconomical.

"Carrie" flop is a horror tale for RSC

May 21. The horror-musical *Carrie* came off tonight after a Broadway run of less than a week, and the Royal Shakespeare Company's $7 million gamble to find a money-spinning successor to *Les Miserables* went down the pan.

Terry Hands, the RSC's director, yearned to repeat the commercial success of his predecessor, Trevor Nunn. This adaptation of Stephen King's novel, about a teenage girl who unleashes her supernatural powers on her high school, was dismissed by the critics at Stratford, and again in New York — where it had been dogged by trouble — as "a mismatched morass".

Rees-Mogg to head new TV watchdog

May 16. Sir William Rees-Mogg is to head the long-awaited Broadcasting Standards Council. Douglas Hurd, the Home Secretary, announced today that the BSC's powers would cover research into and the drawing up of voluntary codes on sex, violence and decency for television, video, cable and satellite.

Sir William, the chairman of the Arts Council, an ex-editor of *The Times* and deputy chairman of the BBC, would also like powers to comment on programmes before they are broadcast (→22/6).

Sikhs give up siege at Golden Temple

May 18. Sikh militants who have been holding out against Indian government forces in the Golden Temple complex at Amritsar for ten days suddenly surrendered this afternoon. But not all of them chose to live. Five committed suicide rather than surrender, and two who made a run for it were cut down by police marksmen.

The 46 who came out with their hands up looked gaunt and tired. Most of them had not eaten for four days, but they still carried out a last act of reverence at their most holy shrine, touching the marble of the temple courtyard before being marched into captivity.

No policemen entered the complex and the operation was marked by a sensitivity lacking when Mrs Gandhi sent the army into the Temple — an act which led to her murder by vengeful Sikhs (→21/6).

Sikh militants, their hands above their heads, emerge from the Temple.

Armenian turmoil topples party chiefs

May 21. Three months of turmoil in Soviet Transcaucasia this weekend led to the sacking of the Communist Party bosses in Armenia and Azerbaijan. Kyamran Bagirov, party first secretary in Azerbaijan for eight years, and Karen Demirchyan, in Armenia for 14 years, were dropped "on health grounds". But they went without a word of thanks and on the insistence of Gorbachev, who sent the hard-line ideology chief, Yegor Ligachev, and the Politburo member for propaganda, Alexander Yakovlev, to oversee the sackings.

The two men paid the price of failing to curb mass demonstrations by Armenians protesting at persecution by Azerbaijanis, and counter demonstrations by Azerbaijanis, which led to race riots and at least 32 deaths. The resulting trials have led to fresh unrest (→11/6).

May 19. New illuminations at London's Tower Bridge are switched on.

Boom and poverty cohabit in Britain

May 20. Two Britains have been revealed by government statistics this week. There is the Britain whose problems are those of coping with success, as indicated by Bank of England figures today showing a sharp rise in bank and building society lending. And then there are the 9.4 million people, said yesterday by a Department of Health and Social Services report to be living at or below the poverty line.

The rise in lending, along with the continuing fall in unemployment and soaring house prices, suggests that a consumer boom is gathering momentum. Some economists fear that what they call the "overheating" of the economy will lead to a balance of payments crisis as imports increase. Incomes and inflation are also exceeding Treasury forecasts.

Such worries may be remote for those below the poverty line or the supplementary benefit level. The DHSS indicated that the numbers living at this level increased by more than a quarter between 1981 and 1985. The government disputes this and has ordered a fresh statistical analysis, prompting Labour charges of ordering "a fix".

Interest rates drop as pound rises

May 16. An extraordinary public rift between Mrs Thatcher and Nigel Lawson, the Chancellor, over exchange rates was apparently healed this afternoon.

The Prime Minister claimed agreement between them after conceding a half percentage point cut in interest rates in a bid to check a further rise in sterling. Against her wishes, Mr Lawson has been arguing that too a strong pound is damaging export prospects.

Insiders whispered that Mrs Thatcher still wants sterling to float freely and has made only a tactical retreat to save face for the Chancellor whom she recently contradicted in Parliament (→17).

Peter Hall stages a tempestuous exit

Final curtain-call for Sir Peter.

May 22. After 15 years as director of the National Theatre, Sir Peter Hall is presenting as his farewell productions there, the three plays that Shakespeare wrote in 1610-11: *Cymbeline*, *The Winter's Tale* and *The Tempest*.

Rehearsals have not been calm. Two actors departed: the veteran Robert Eddison after disagreement with Hall about the way to speak Shakespeare's verse, and Sarah Miles — surprisingly, in view of her lack of recent stage experience-cast as the heroine of *Cymbeline*.

May
1988

Su	Mo	Tu	We	Th	Fr	Sa
1	2	3	4	5	6	7
8	9	10	11	12	13	14
15	16	17	18	19	20	21
22	23	24	25	26	27	28
29	30	31				

22. Hungary: Karoly Grosz succeeds Janos Kadar as Secretary-General.

23. London: A covert police investigation into soccer hooligans collapses (→28).

24. UK: One in six pregnant women will be asked to volunteer for a blood test to assess the spread of AIDS (→2/6).

24. UK: The Director of Public Prosecutions bans a lottery to help fund the NHS (→2/6).

25. UK: The government gives the go-ahead to Nestle's bid for Rowntree (→23/6).

25. US: The White House abandons efforts to remove Panama's leader General Noriega from office.

27. UK: The budget deficit for April is £525 million, £240 million worse than in March (→2/6).

27. US: The Senate approves the nuclear missile deal for signature in Moscow (→31).

27. London: Tube boss Tony Ridley tells the King's Cross fire inquiry that safety is still not his top priority (→24/6).

28. Worcester: Graeme Hick becomes the eighth batsman ever to score 1,000 runs before the end of May (→2/6).

28. London: 102 are arrested in violence at Chelsea's football ground (→16/6).

29. Pakistan: President General Zia ul-Haq sacks his allegedly corrupt civilian prime minister and cabinet (→3/6).

30. Seoul: Students battle police at the opening of the National Assembly (→9/6).

30. UK: ITV's *Telethon* closes after 27 hours, having raised a record £21,015,604.

31. UK: A DHSS crackdown caught 80,000 fraudulent claims last year.

DEATHS

28. American jazzman Sy (Melvin James) Oliver (*17/12/10).

29. Sierra Leonean statesman Siaka Probin Stevens (*24/10/05).

BBC Falklands play upsets the army

May 31. Despite strong Ministry of Defence concern, BBC1 tonight transmitted *Tumbledown*, a controversial play based on the experiences of Robert Lawrence, a Scots Guards officer badly wounded during the Falklands War.

The play, which cost the BBC £1 million, was branded "subversive" by the *Daily Mail* even before it was filmed. Critics of the BBC have seized on the play as evidence that the Corporation lacks patriotism. Richard Eyre, the play's director and the next head of the National Theatre, insists that the play should be judged as drama and not "drama-documentary".

Russia rewrites the history books

May 31. As they used to say in Stalin's time, when history was being re-written to suit the Kremlin: never mind about the future, it's the past that's so uncertain. Soviet children learned today that there would be no history books on their desks when they went back to school in the autumn. Mr Gorbachev has decided the time has come to tell it like it was and fill in the blank spaces in the Soviet past, especially those chapters of history that did not tell the truth about Stalin's purges in the 1930s (→3/6).

Basra battle turns tables in Iran-Iraq war

May 25. The Iranians, growing increasingly war-weary, have suffered a smashing defeat at Basra, where they have been driven out of their bridgehead east of the port. This defeat, following the loss of the Fao peninsula last month, marks a complete reversal of fortunes in the Gulf War. Iran, which has had the upper hand for so long, is now facing a grim future.

The mass-suicide tactics by fanatical recruits, which had rocked the Iraqi army, no longer work. There are no longer thousands of young men willing to march to their deaths chanting the praises of Ayatollah Khomeini. The economy is shattered and there is dissension in the government.

THE GULF WAR BATTLEGROUND

Church of England synod attacks PM

May 31. Members of the Church of England Synod today denounced Mrs Thatcher's recent speech at the Church of Scotland General Assembly — the Parliament of the Kirk. Then they fell out with some of its members over a letter sent by the Bishop of Gloucester, the Rt Revd John Yates, to the Prime Minister.

As chairman of the Synod's Board for Social Responsibility, the Bishop challenged Mrs Thatcher's enthusiasm for individual wealth-creation along with greater individual support for charity.

His letter suggested that Thatcherism is causing deep divisions and injustices and he argued that all governments must be generous to the poor.

The Board often reflects the views of the Anglicans' leftist tendency, and a conservative, Bill Westwood, Bishop of Peterborough, quickly criticised the letter. He said: "Christians — whether bishops or not — are welcome to share in the moral-political-social debate. However they do not speak for the Church of England which is a more complex body than the Board sometimes imagines."

Mystery MP caught in shower romp

May 19. One MP saw another naked and looking for a towel in the House of Commons shower room tonight. The second MP returned to a cubicle and the first one heard a female voice and "frolicking noises".

Ron Brown, a Scottish Labour back-bencher who was recently embroiled in a disorderly scene in the Commons' chamber when he picked up and damaged the mace, denied rumoured involvement in the incident. He said: "It is totally untrue. Some people say because I dropped the mace I must also have dropped my trousers."

Soviet experts, visiting the hitherto top secret chemical defence establishment at Porton Down, question a member of the Royal Green Jackets.

The Reagans woo the "evil empire"

May 31. On his first visit to the capital of what he once called "an evil empire", President Reagan has praised Mr Gorbachev for his *glasnost* and *perestroika* reforms, but then irritated the Soviet leader by calling for more progress in human rights. In an unprecedented two-hour news conference for foreign journalists — the first given by a Soviet leader at home — Mr Gorbachev spent at least 20 minutes criticising Mr Reagan for "propaganda gambits, all sorts of spectacles ... let us get back to real politics". Earlier, though, he had said his meetings with the President had "made huge breaches in the walls of the Cold War fortress".

After Geneva, Reykjavik and Washington, this meeting in Moscow is the fourth between the two leaders. It is a summit of gestures rather than substance. The formalities of signing the Intermediate Nuclear Forces treaty have been completed, and there is optimistic talk of a possible agreement on strategic arms. Mr Gorbachev again complained about American Star Wars research, but offered to share data on Soviet research into space weapons.

Whatever the political gains, Ronald Reagan, the Hollywood veteran, showed he still knows how to woo an audience. At Moscow University, in the shadow of a giant

Reagan and Gorbachev, on walkabout in Moscow's Red Square.

bust of Lenin, he told 1,000 students they were living in one of the most hopeful times in the country's history. "What he said about democracy was right," one student said afterwards. "Though whether it can happen here is another matter."

While Ronald talked, Nancy went sightseeing to the Czar's Summer Palace with Mrs Gromyko. "Overwhelming," she said. "Ceilings, paintings, the furniture, everything." As for Mrs Gromyko: "I'm 77. I'm tired." (→1/6)

Tate gives modern art a new home in Victorian Liverpool

May 26. The Tate Gallery has opened a new wing at Liverpool's Albert Dock and thereby rescued some of the finest Victorian dock buildings in the country from dereliction. Architect James Stirling has turned the interior into wide-open, well-lit galleries with spectacular views across the docks and the Mersey. Although the gallery is in an already existing structure, it has cost over £9 million. The government is contributing £5 million.

The Tate has moved much of its modern art collection which it has no room to display in London to Liverpool. The opening exhibitions are of the Surrealists, abstract paintings by Mark Rothko and modern British sculptors.

Rothko painted these abstracts for a New York executive restaurant. "I hope to paint something that will ruin the appetite of every son of a bitch who eats in that room," he said. Soon afterwards he committed suicide.

The sculpture includes pieces from the sixties, such as a glass of water on a shelf, entitled *An Oak Tree* — with the artist's explanation: "because I say it is". There is a good deal of junk sculpture, too; some prefer the gallery to what is on show in it.

Gay demonstrators invade BBC news

June 23. Viewers of tonight's *Six O' Clock News* were astonished to hear squeaks and slogans over the air, as the newsroom was invaded by three gay rights activists protesting against government moves to stop local councils "promoting" homosexuality. As the protesters chained themselves to a camera and desk, the presenter, Sue Lawley, calmly said: "We have been invaded and hope to return to normal shortly."

It took a dozen men to restrain the angry lesbians; newsreader Nicholas Witchell sat on one of the protesters while a hacksaw was found to release them. Afterwards the unflappable Miss Lawley was applauded by her colleagues.

Branagh takes Shakespeare on the road

Branagh with Sophie Thompson.

May 30. Kenneth Branagh, who founded his own company as actor-manager when he was 27, is touring the country with it in three Shakespeare plays after opening to packed houses in Birmingham.

His Renaissance company dispenses with directors and employs fellow-actors instead. Branagh's furiously energetic Hamlet is directed by Derek Jacobi (himself a notable Hamlet) in an Elsinore like a police state. In her Edwardian *As You Like It*, Geraldine McEwan turns Branagh into a music-hall comedian as the ingratiating clown, Touchstone. Finally, Branagh plays an amusingly lovesick Benedick in Judi Dench's summery Italian production of *Much Ado About Nothing*.

The baggy jacket's reign, which has lasted most of the 80's, is over. They are now cut short and shaped, to be worn with a mini.

June
1988

Su	Mo	Tu	We	Th	Fr	Sa
			1	2	3	4
5	6	7	8	9	10	11
12	13	14	15	16	17	18
19	20	21	22	23	24	25
26	27	28	29	30		

1. Moscow: The Reagan-Gorbachev summit closes with a sense of anticlimax. →

1. Epsom: Ray Cochrane rides Kahyasi, owned by the Aga Khan, to a Derby win. →

1. UK: The Countryside Commission proposes a new, extended network of trails and bridleways.

2. UK: An NHS manager says that health care can no longer be equal for everyone.

2. UK: The government says it will continue to fight *Spycatcher,* saying it lost the case on a technicality.

2. US: A Presidential commission urges legislation to protect AIDS sufferers from discrimination.

2. Scandinavia: Toxic, fast-spreading algae threatens marine life off the coasts of Norway and Sweden.

2. Trent Bridge: England's Gooch and Broad score 100 on the opening day of the Test against the West Indies (→7).

3. Pakistan: Opposition leader Benazir Bhutto announces her candidacy in the forthcoming elections (→26).

3. Johannesburg: A bomb, allegedly planted by the African National Congress, kills four people.

3. Somalia: Foreigners are evacuated as rebel fighting flares.

3. Telford: A private warrant orders the arrest of MP Ron Brown, who has failed to answer a summons for damaging the Commons mace.

4. Paris: Steffi Graf wins the women's tournament of the French Open. →

4. East Sussex: A hundred youths run amok, attacking police, in the town of Crowborough.

4. Cuba: Leader Fidel Castro promises to free most political prisoners.

DEATH

2. Indian film producer and actor Raj (Ranbirraj) Kapoor (*14/10/24).

"Spycatcher" battle won by Peter Wright

June 1. After a three-year legal battle, the *Spycatcher* saga in an Australian courtroom ended today with the failure of the British government's attempt to prevent publication of Peter Wright's book. The high court ordered the government to pay Wright's costs of £326,000. Their own costs will come to over £1 million.

The British government has claimed throughout that Wright's book was a breach of confidentiality, and that publication could endanger relations between Britain and Australia. In *Spycatcher,* Wright, a former MI5 agent, names his former boss, Sir Roger Hollis, as a possible Soviet spy and alleges that some MI5 agents had attempted to undermine Harold Wilson's 1974-76 Labour government.

The Thatcher government has fought hard in the courts to ban the publication of Wright's book in Australia and elsewhere. Wright, now retired in Tasmania, stands to make at least £4 million from the publication in countries other than Britain, where it remains banned pending further hearings later this year (→2).

Moscow sanctions Sakharov's rights plea

Human rights campaigner Sakharov talks to the world's press.

June 3. In an extraordinary display of *glasnost,* Soviet officials put on a press conference in the Foreign Ministry for the country's most famous dissident and human rights campaigner, Andrei Sakharov, who was released from internal exile by Gorbachev 18 months ago. Today Sakharov described the Soviet leader as an "oustanding statesman", but said he feared resistance by conservatives was threatening reforms. Sakharov went beyond the routine Gorbachev line when he called for the repeal of articles of the penal code which are used to imprison religious and political dissenters (→5).

Interest rates hiked as pound plummets

June 2. Interest rates were put back up again today as alarm grew over inflation. Nigel Lawson, the Chancellor, raised the base rate from seven-and-a-half to eight per cent. This was the fifth change this year and it reversed a reduction made just three weeks ago.

The announcement came as the pound fell sharply on world money markets for the third day running. Whitehall and City experts now think that a cheaper money policy has encouraged a credit and spending spree, inflated property prices and a weakened trading position. Mr Lawson is now ready to hoist interest rates a lot higher yet in order to combat inflation, despite misgivings from industry (→6).

Britain wants Jeux avec Frontieres

June 3. Common Market plans for abolition of all cross-border checks in 1992 were firmly rejected by Britain today. Douglas Hurd, the Home Secretary, told Lord Cockfield, British vice-president of the European Commission, to cool his enthusiasm. Free movement of goods, yes. But of people, no.

Mr Hurd hopes that his opposite numbers in other countries will agree that such uncontrolled movement cannot be allowed because it would prejudice the fight against terrorism and other crimes.

Lord Cockfield still insisted that Britain cannot opt out of the spirit of the Single European Act, which Mrs Thatcher has signed along with other national leaders. In Whitehall it is whispered that he has "gone native" and is probably talking himself out of another term in his job (→13).

Steffi slaughters tearful Natalia

June 4. Steffi Graf powered her way to the French tennis title today by demolishing the challenge of her 17-year-old Russian opponent, Natalia Zvereva, in just 32 minutes. The German teenager won without losing a set, the first time that anyone had done so in a grand slam final since 1911. "I just wasn't in the game," said an embarrassed and tearful Russian afterwards (→5).

Steffi brandishes her French trophy.

Edwina was right; North eats tripe

June 1. Fears that Britain's northerners are eating and drinking themselves into early graves are backed by a new survey out today. Leon Kreitzman, director of health studies at the Henley Centre for Forecasting, told a meeting of personnel managers in Leeds that by the first part of the next century life expectancy in the south could be four or five years more than in the north.

"Northerners tend to exercise less, drink and smoke more, and eat less healthily," he said. "Those in the south are more likely to belong to a sports club and go to the dentist regularly, and there are more vegetarians."

Junior Health Minister Edwina Currie caused an uproar recently when she suggested that the traditional chips-with-everything diet of the north was responsible for lower than average standards.

Health hazards of Suzuki jeeps

June 1. You could get a bumpier ride than you bargained for in a Suzuki "Samurai". If you take the nippy mini-jeeps round a sharp corner, even at 20 miles an hour, they are likely to topple over. Suzuki's handbook advises drivers to avoid abrupt manoeuvres. Consumer associations in Britain and the US say this is not good enough; even the most careful driver has to make the odd sharp turn.

Four wheels turn into two.

Pit explosion traps 57 men underground

The strain shows on the faces of the rescuers and those waiting for news.

June 2. Hoping against hope, rescuers are today striving to reach 21 miners who may have survived a series of explosions which blasted through the Stolzenbach coal mine near Borken in West Germany yesterday. The blasts destroyed several buildings on the surface, injuring eight workers, and collapsed parts of the network of tunnels below.

Fifty-seven men — the entire morning shift at Stolzenbach — were trapped underground last night, one of them a schoolboy who had gone down the mine for the first time to earn some pocket money. So far the bodies of 36 men, most of whom died of suffocation, have been recovered. The whole of Germany is in mourning for the dead.

Privatised Telecom fails to please

June 2. One in ten telephone calls are too faint or crackly to be useful, and one in 36 calls fail to connect at all, says a critical Consumers' Association report published today. "So far British Telecom has failed to achieve an overall improvement in its service since privatisation," it concluded, citing delays in repairs and installation and BT's poor handling of complaints and bill queries. "We are well on the way to providing the best service ever," retorted a BT spokesman.

Kahyasi's late run clinches the Derby

June 1. The Aga Khan won the Derby today for the third time in five years, but his horse in the winner's enclosure was 11-1 shot Kahyasi, not the more fancied Doyoun which finished third. Ray Cochrane on Kahyasi was in the middle of the pack as they rounded Tattenham Corner. It was only inside the final furlong that he headed Glacial Storm, going on to win by one and a half lengths. It was the 30-year-old Ulster jockey's first Derby win (→15).

President Reagan comes to London, preaching human rights

June 2. President and Mrs Reagan had tea with the Queen at Buckingham Palace today. After that he walked across a red carpet into 10 Downing Street. Then, at a Guildhall banquet, the President invited America's allies to join him and Soviet leader Mikhail Gorbachev in seeking "a newer world of freedom and individual rights for all".

He also said: "The entire world salutes the Prime Minister for being first to suggest we can do business with Mr Gorbachev."

The US leader is on his way home from summit talks in Moscow. Labour's leader, Neil Kinnock said caustically that the President is not really intending to hand over leadership of the West to Mrs Thatcher. Behind the huge cordiality there is sober diplomatic recognition that East-West disarmament will be a slow process.

Reagan inspects a guard of honour provided by the Welsh Guards.

June

1988

Su	Mo	Tu	We	Th	Fr	Sa
			1	2	3	4
5	6	7	8	9	10	11
12	13	14	15	16	17	18
19	20	21	22	23	24	25
26	27	28	29	30		

5. Woburn: Sandy Lyle wins the British Masters golf title (→20).

5. Cumbria: Twenty-five inmates break out during rioting at Haverigg prison.

5. Paris: Mats Wilander wins the French Mens' Open tennis championship.

6. UK: Interest rates go up to 8.5 per cent (→22).

6. Leeds: Russell Harty slips into a coma (→8).

6. UK: The Queen strips imprisoned jockey Lester Piggott of his OBE.

7. UK: The Commons rejects a motion to bring back capital punishment by 123 votes.

7. Trent Bridge: England draw with the West Indies in the first Test.→

8. S. Africa: Army reservists are called up to fight a build-up of Cuban forces on the Namibia/Angola border (→24).

8. Paris: President Mitterrand promises to forgive one-third of African countries' debt to France (→21).

8. Liverpool: Comedian Ken Dodd is charged with tax evasion.

9. Seoul: Riot police battle 10,000 students marching to North Korea, demanding the unification of Korea.→

9. Belfast: A doctor claims that babies can become addicted to soap operas while still in the womb.

10. UK: John Emburey is appointed the new captain of England cricket team (→21).

10. London: Labour MP Michael Meacher loses a libel case he brought against the *Observer* newspaper.

11. Chesterfield: The battle for the Labour leadership starts in earnest with the opening of the "Socialist Conference" (→14).

DEATHS

8. British writer and broadcaster Russell Harty (*5/9/34).→

11. Italian statesman Giuseppe Saragat (*19/9/1898).

Russell Harty loses struggle to live

Cheeky, homely Russell Harty.

June 8. Russell Harty died today after a long struggle against hepatitis. Despite the light, frothy personality he presented as a chatshow host, he was widely read.

He was from Blackburn, where his father had a market stall, and spent six years as a schoolmaster before he got into Radio 3, then into TV arts programmes. He found his metier hosting a chatshow to rival Michael Parkinson's.

Although he called himself "one", he pronounced it, in Blackburn fashion, "wonn". "Wonn does feel, does wonn not?" was a typical Harty opening. People did not mind this affectation because he was unpretentious, loved an audience and did not mind being boxed on the ears by Grace Jones. People liked him for his cheek.

Two million strike against apartheid

June 8. About two million black workers stayed at home today in response to a strike call from the Congress of South African Trade Unions. The Congress leadership is campaigning against the government's new curbs on anti-apartheid protests and against proposed legislation which, it is claimed, will reinforce racial divisions in the trade union movement. Least affected by the strike were gold, diamond and coal mines, where only a few thousand of the half-million workers stayed away.

Gatting sent packing by England selectors

June 9. Mike Gatting was today sacked as England cricket captain after two days of tabloid publicity about late-night romps with girls during the first test match in Nottingham.

Peter May, the chairman of the selectors, said that they had accepted Gatting's denial of the reports, but considered the England captain had behaved "irresponsibly" in inviting a hotel barmaid to his room for a drink. Mickey Stewart, the England manager, added: "No player must put himself in the position whereby the image of England cricket is damaged in any way."

Four other England players have been called to Lord's today in order to answer the more garish newspaper accounts in which maidens took on interpretations which do not appear in the MCC rule book. Gatting himself has denied the allegations and is threatening to take legal action. Meanwhile, he has asked not to be considered as a player for the next test.

Gatting led a successful tour of

Sacked for "irresponsibility".

Australia in 1987, but last winter was embroiled in controversy over umpiring decisions in Pakistan. John Emburey, his Middlesex teammate, seems the most likely successor, although for how long, few would like to predict (→10).

Russian church celebrates first millenium

June 5. It was almost as though Lenin had never lived, and his atheistic revolution had never happened. For four hours today in the ornate splendour of Moscow's Cathedral of the Epiphany, the bearded Patriarch Pimen, in jewel-encrusted vestments decorated with images of the saints, celebrated one thousand years of Christianity in Russia. After the main service, a requiem was said for past primates who led the Church in its years of travail. "Remarkable," said Dr Runcie, the Archbishop of Canterbury, one of the foreign visitors. "The Church has kept the candle of faith burning." The Soviet authorities admit that seven out of ten people are still believers (→13).

Members of the Russian Orthodox church at Zagorsk celebrate Easter.

Armenians and police reported killed as riots flare over Nagorny Karabakh

June 11. An Armenian militant told a rally in Moscow today that a policeman and several Armenians had been killed last Saturday in Baku, when knife-wielding Moslem Azerbaijanis stormed through the city hunting down Christian Armenians. The speaker, Levun Gambayan, said he had been given the news when he phoned a relative in Baku, the Azerbaijani capital.

In Moscow, an official spokesman denied that Armenians had been killed, but confirmed that a policeman had died when he was struck by a ricochetting bullet, apparently fired by an Armenian.

Mr Gambayan is campaigning for the return to Armenia of Nagorny Karabakh, an Armenian enclave inside Azerbaijan. The enclave was arbitrarily handed to Azerbaijan by Stalin in 1923, but Moscow refuses to consider handing it back.

In Armenia, though, the local Communist boss, Suren Arutunyan, faced with mass strikes and demonstrations by several hundred thousand people in the capital, Yerevan, today promised to back the popular demands for the return of the disputed territory. His promise is seen as a message for Armenia's Supreme Soviet, which is due to meet in the next few days (13/5).

Stars provide the music at Nelson's party

Wembley Stadium is the focus for a worldwide celebration for Mandela.

Democrats want Duke at the helm

June 7. Governor Michael Dukakis will be the Democratic candidate in the forthcoming presidential election. He won the last four primaries and has a 15-point advantage in the polls against the Republican candidate, George Bush. Dukakis now faces the delicate task of dealing with his still-buoyant black challenger, Jesse Jackson, who says he "deserves consideration" for the vice-presidential nomination.

Tycoons fight for TV satellite boom

June 8. Amstrad, the electronics company, has announced plans to put one million satellite receivers into Britain's homes next year. Backed by international media tycoon Rupert Murdoch, whose Sky Channel switches on in 1989, Alan Sugar, pioneer of the low-cost Amstrad computers, is launching a cut-rate "dish" at just £199 to try and capture the satellite TV boom predicted for the 1990s.

June 11. Eighty thousand fans packed London's Wembley Stadium today as musicians and singers staged a day-long tribute to mark the 70th birthday of jailed black South African leader Nelson Mandela. Mandela has been in prison since 1964, convicted of attempting to overthrow the state.

Stars from the whole world made their contribution to the occasion. Among many others were the Fat Boys, Stevie Wonder and Whitney Houston from the United States; George Michael, UB40 and the Eurythmics from Britain; Youssou N'dour from Senegal; and the Mahotella Queens from South Africa itself.

Despite attempts by the BBC and the Coca-Cola company, which had sponsored transmissions to American TV, to keep politics out of the concert, many performers resisted such censorship. For fans and stars alike Mandela is the ultimate symbol of the fight against apartheid and there was no intention of forgetting it.

Reference to "the terrorist state" and to Margaret Thatcher's stance on apartheid were frequent, and went out live to a billion-strong audience in 60 countries.

Seoul student demo quashed by police

June 9. Thousands of South Korean students waving black flags, calling for unity with the North and demanding "Yankee Go Home", battled with riot police at Seoul's Yonsei University today. Petrol bombs and stones rained down on the police, who replied with barrages of tear-gas grenades.

The students plan to march to the truce village at Panmunjon tomorrow to meet officially sponsored delegates from the North. But the Seoul authorities say the march will be stopped "at any cost" and have massed 60,000 policemen to prevent the marchers reaching Panmunjon. Some students have threatened to burn themselves to death if the march is blocked (→12).

West Bank revolt praised by Arab leaders at Algiers summit

June 8. The "Intifada" uprising in the Israeli-occupied territories of the West Bank and Gaza has produced a rare unanimity among Arab leaders at their emergency summit in Algiers.

King Hussein was applauded when he described the stone-throwing as a "revolution against a colonialist occupying power" and demanded: "we should support the uprising in an organised and effective manner."

Yasser Arafat demanded equality at the conference table for the Palestinians, and the summit ended with the adoption of a resolution calling for an independent Palestinian state, whose representatives would take part in an international conference to settle the Middle East conflict.

Yasser Arafat is dwarfed by the summit security guards.

June

1988

Su	Mo	Tu	We	Th	Fr	Sa
			1	2	3	4
5	6	7	8	9	10	11
12	13	14	15	16	17	18
19	20	21	22	23	24	25
26	27	28	29	30		

12. Paris: General elections leave President Mitterrand without a majority in Parliament.

13. Luxembourg: EC nations agree on a plan to end all curbs on movement of capital around the community.

13. UK: A study shows that young black offenders are more likely to face prosecution than white ones.

13. USSR: The first Miss Moscow, Mariya Kalinina, is crowned (→30).

13. USSR: A rally of 500,000 people in Yerevan calls for a one-day general strike for tomorrow (→15).

14. UK: Top executives' pay is rising at 22 per cent a year, compared with a national average of 8.5 per cent a year.

15. Ascot: Magic of Life, ridden by Pat Eddery and owned by Stavros Niarchos, wins the Gold Cup.

15. USSR: Armenia's Supreme Soviet votes for the return of Nagorny Karabakh from Azerbaijan (→17).

16. UK: Mrs Thatcher rejects EC demands that cash injections for Rover must stop before British Aerospace buy it.

16. Luxembourg: European ministers agree to halve production of ozone-destroying CFCs by 1998 (→23).

17. UK: Neil Kinnock warns the Labour Party that unless they accept his reforms, they will never gain power (→20).

17. USSR: The Azerbaijani parliament votes to block any moves to return Nagorny Karabakh to Armenia (→25).

17. London: Two animal rights activists are jailed for firebomb attacks which caused £9 million damage to shops.

18. London: An exhibition of French masterpieces from the USSR opens at the National Gallery.

DEATH

17. British lawyer Elizabeth Kathleen Coulburn (Lane), the first woman High Court judge in Britain (*9/10/07).

English soccer faces European shame

On the pitch: Irish joy, English despair

June 18. England and Ireland were knocked out of football's European Championships in West Germany today, but their teams will return home to contrasting receptions. Ireland (and their English manager Jack Charlton) will be welcomed as heroes: the underdogs who drew with Russia, lost by only a single goal to Holland and, best of all, beat England in the opening match.

England leave pointless, losing 3-1 to Russia today to finish bottom of their four-nation group. In truth, England never recovered from the shock of losing 1-0 to the Irish in Stuttgart last Sunday (→26).

Dusseldorf police arrest a drunken hooligan for street fighting.

In the cities: fans battle with police

June 16. The Prime Minister summoned ministers to Downing Street today to plan measures to combat the hooliganism displayed by English football fans in Germany.

Gangs of English fans have roamed the German cities where the national team has been playing, often fighting local youths. Police in riot gear battled with the fans and there have been demands to recall the English team. In fact, although the English have attracted most of the blame, of 500 fans detained by Dusseldorf police on Tuesday and Wednesday only 113 were English (→26).

Top financier Peter Clowes is arrested

June 15. On his way to pick up the morning papers today near his home in Prestbury, Cheshire, businessman Peter Clowes was arrested by City of London fraud squad officers. He is said to have diverted up to £100 million of investors' money from a Gibraltar-based fund managed by his company, Barlow Clowes International, to finance his own personal business empire. He will face charges before London magistrates tomorrow.

Women priests are coming in 1993

June 16. Women priests will be celebrating communion in the Church of England in five years time, if legislation published today goes through. It will have to be passed by the Synod and by Parliament. However, the measures have been drawn up carefully to pacify opponents.

Individual bishops and individual parishes will be able to refuse women priests. Clergy who are totally opposed to the ordination of women will be able to resign the priesthood and claim an average of £30,000 in compensation.

IRA bomb kills five soldiers in "fun run"

June 15. With cruel irony, it began as a "fun run". British servicemen joined 4,000 civilians in a half-marathon for charity through the streets of Lisburn today. Five of them died when a bomb exploded under them as they stopped at traffic lights on their way back to barracks. Their van was unmarked. Police believe that the IRA planted the bomb in a car park while the soldiers competed in the race.

The IRA has admitted fixing the bomb under the soldiers' vehicle. Last month, the military banned its men from competing in the Belfast marathon. Lisburn, a mainly Protestant town, was considered a "safe venue".

An eye-witness described the scene at Lisburn as "horrific". "There was smoke and then a loud explosion and I saw two bodies lying in the middle of the road," he said. "One was badly mutilated. It seems they were blown from the van. There was panic and people were running everywhere." Ten civilians were injured by the bomb, none of them seriously (→28).

The twisted and charred remains of the army runners' van.

Seoul is rocked by student protests

June 12. Park Ae Jun, the student who burned himself to death in protest against the Seoul government's ban on a "unity" march to meet North Korean students, was buried today in a theatrical ceremony perfumed with tear-gas.

There were two trucks in the funeral procession, one carrying the coffin and the other carrying a full load of petrol bombs. The bombs were thrown at police as the cortege drove away from the city hall. The police replied with tear-gas, then the students hurled stones, and a pitched battle ensued.

Fellow-students made emotional speeches over the coffin and a girl performed a "dance of death" inside a symbolic circle of flames as drums rolled, cymbals clashed and tear-gas grenades exploded.

All this took place beneath a huge clock which reminded Seoul's inhabitants that there were only 97 days to go before the opening ceremony of the Olympics. The students needed no reminding. They tore Olympic flags from their poles and burned them.

The Games have given them a cause — they believe the North should co-host them — and a showcase for their protest. TV cameras transmit their violent demonstrations to living rooms all over the world. It remains to be seen if they will keep up their protests once the Games start. To many Koreans, the loss of face would be shameful.

Seoul riot police surround students, who want unity with North Korea.

IRA suspect eludes extradition through legal confusion

June 13. To the dismay of the Irish and British governments, a Dublin judge today refused to extradite a known IRA suspect to Northern Ireland. Patrick McVeigh was immediately spirited from the courtroom as lawyers puzzled over where they had gone wrong.

The court ruled, against all precedent, that it had not been proved that the man named in the extradition warrant was the man in court, despite Irish assurances that no witness would be required. The warrant concerns bombings in London between 1981 and 1983 (→15).

Turkish PM injured by escaped convict

June 18. The Turkish Prime Minister, Turgut Ozal, was delivering the opening speech at the Ankara congress of his Motherland Party today when a man in jeans stepped forward and raised a gun. One shot narrowly missed Ozal's head; a second clipped his right thumb before guards brought down the gunman with a bullet in the leg. The man, a 32-year-old former schoolteacher named Kartal Demirag, escaped from jail this year. He was given a ten-year sentence in 1986 for murder.

Denzil Davies quits, castigating Kinnock

June 14. Neil Kinnock's efforts to revive Labour's fortunes by gradually shuffling away from its unilateral nuclear disarmament stance were dented when the party's chief defence spokesman resigned in bizarre style during the night.

At 1 am Denzil Davies, a volatile Welshman, telephoned the Press Association with his decision to quit.

"I am fed up being humiliated," he said before using colourful language in attacking Mr Kinnock's leadership style. He complained about not being consulted before Mr Kinnock put a new gloss on their non-nuclear policy. Mr Kinnock said he was amazed (→17).

Davies: not happy with Kinnock.

US faces its worst drought for 50 years

June 16. Catastrophic crop failures are looming in the American mid-West as the worst drought since 1934 enters its fourth month. The Mississippi River has fallen to its lowest level since records began, and farmers are selling their cattle simply because they cannot feed them. Forecasters say the weather, with temperatures in the 90s and no rain, is expected to hold for the next ten days at least.

The government has set up an action committee to deal with the drought. Richard Lyng, the Agriculture Secretary, warned today that unless the weather breaks before the end of the month, a national disaster could be declared.

A fish is stranded by the drought.

June

1988

Su	Mo	Tu	We	Th	Fr	Sa
			1	2	3	4
5	6	7	8	9	10	11
12	13	14	15	16	17	18
19	20	21	22	23	24	25
26	27	28	29	30		

19. Poland: Moves towards democracy are mocked by a low turnout in the local elections.

19. East Berlin: Scuffles and arrests take place as youths gather to hear Michael Jackson give a concert in West Berlin.

20. Haiti: A military coup led by Lieut-Gen Henri Namphy ends four months of civilian rule.

20. Wimbledon: Seventeen ticket touts are arrested on the opening day of the tennis championships.

20. Cheshire: Jodrell Bank radio telescope is listed as a Grade One building of architectural interest.

21. India: A bomb planted in the Hindu market at Amritsar kills 15 people.

21. London: West Indies beat England in the second Test.

21. Wiltshire: A thousand police hold rioting hippies back from Stonehenge.

21. New York: A pair of crimson shoes worn by Judy Garland in *The Wizard of Oz* fetches $165,000 at auction.

22. UK: The base interest rate rises to nine per cent as fears grow of higher inflation (→ 27).

22. UK: The government wants to replace the TV licence fee with a subscription scheme.

23. UK: Rowntree accepts Nestlé's £2,550 million bid to buy out the company.

23. UK: Post Office managers threaten to close 1,000 rural post offices.

24. Cairo: South Africa, Angola, Cuba and the US attend talks to bring peace to Angola (→ 27).

24. London: Counsel for victims of the King's Cross tube fire lists 40 known safety hazards on the Underground.

25. USSR: Armenians in Nagorny Karabakh vote to end their five-week-old strike.

DEATH

21. British journalist Thomas Edwin Utley (*1/2/21).

Curfew imposed to quell Burmese riots

Anti-government rioters stage another protest against General Ne Win.

June 21. Riots swept through Rangoon today as students protested against the "Burmese Nazi government". The rioters burned down a police station, set fire to policemen's homes and wrecked cinemas. Armed with swords, cudgels and powerful catapults, they killed five policemen and injured 26. One rioter also died.

The government retaliated by imposing a dusk-to-dawn curfew on Rangoon for two months, closing the universities and ordering students from the provinces to leave Rangoon. It seems doubtful if this will curb the rioters. One Western diplomat said that the violence was the worst in the 26 years of General Ne Win's socialist government.

The authorities' situation has been made more tricky by the clandestine circulation of letters written to Ne Win by his former deputy, Brigadier Aung Gyi, who resigned from the government in 1963.

In these letters Aung Gyi called on Ne Win to act against food shortages, corruption and the violation of human rights. Aung Gyi, who leaked his own letters, is now believed to be in prison.

Much of the discontent has been caused by Burma's economic problems, which have caused the food shortages in some areas of this lush country.

Thatcher says No to central Eurobank

June 23. Britain will not join a proposed European central bank. Mrs Thatcher emphatically rejected the idea when she told MPs today that such a super-bank could only be created if the House of Commons is abolished and the 12 Common Market countries become a United States of Europe. "That," she said, "is not on the cards."

The Prime Minister agreed, however, that central bankers need to co-operate closely in keeping currencies steady. She added that interest rates will be used as one of the best ways of checking inflation which she says remains a constant threat.

Strange pips Faldo to win US Open

June 20. So close, but so far. Nick Faldo today failed to match Tony Jacklin's achievement in winning both the US and British Open championships in the same year. He lost the 18-hole play-off to American Curtis Strange after they had tied, two shots ahead of the field on Sunday. In the end, Strange won by four shots, but there was only a shot or two between them until the 17th when, attacking to recoup ground, Faldo overhit the green to take a bogey five.

Summit lauds prosperity, but spurns help for smaller nations

June 21. After a brief security scare caused by rumours that IRA and Japanese Red Army terrorists had arrived in Toronto, the summit of Western powers, plus Japan and Jacques Delors of the EEC, passed off in a mood of self-congratulation, with both Mrs Thatcher and President Reagan enthusing over "the longest period of continuous economic growth since the war".

But Mr Reagan failed to get agreement on a plan to phase out farm subsidies within 12 years. Japan's Noboru Takeshita led a move to ease black Africa's multibillion dollar debt burden by cutting interest rates, but his bid to help middle-rank states, including Argentina and Brazil, was rejected.

Western leaders line up for some tough talking at the Toronto summit.

Dutch skill lands European soccer trophy

Netherlands goal scorer Ruud Gullit (l.) celebrates the 2-0 win over Russia.

June 25. The Netherlands finally won a national football title today when they beat the Soviet Union by two goals to nil in the final at Munich of the European nations' championship. Even the Russian manager, Valery Lobanovsky, later paid tribute to the skill of the Dutchmen after an engrossing and competitive final.

Holland took the lead after 32 minutes when Ruud Gullit headed home. Then, after 54 minutes, Marco van Basten fired home an unstoppable volley from an oblique angle; it was his fifth goal and made him the tournament's top scorer. Six minutes later Russia had a chance to get back into the game,

but Belanov missed a penalty. The 1988 Dutchmen had reached the final by succeeding where their illustrious predecessors of the 1970s had failed.

Twice, then, the country, whose fluid style of play had prompted the description "total football", had lost to host nations in World Cup finals. This time they had to overcome another host nation, West Germany, in the semi-finals. They did so 2-1 while the Soviet Union conquered Italy 2-0. Holland lost once in the qualifying matches that saw England slump so miserably from the competition; they lost to Russia, but today there was no doubt about the victors.

Estonians press for greater autonomy

June 20. In an extraordinary gesture of solidarity with Estonian nationalism, Vaino Vaelaes, the new Communist party boss of the Baltic republic has publicly endorsed demands for a wide-ranging devolution of economic power from Moscow.

Vaelaes has approved a programme by Estonian economists for the republic to be allowed to manage its own budget and control prices and wages, with a simple commitment to making a yearly contribution to the central Soviet budget. Last month Moscow slapped down these demands, but the Estonians responded by saying over-centralisation was blocking economic growth.

New hope is kindled for Beirut hostages

June 21. New hope for the 15 Western kidnap victims still missing in Beirut came today with news from Syrian intelligence that all of them could be held hostage in the same place — the Hay Madi barracks, a stronghold of the Iran-backed Hizbollah organisation. Although Syrian troops control most of the surrounding area, they say there is no way to storm the heavily fortified building, which is guarded by over 200 armed members of the Iranian Revolutionary Guard and Hizbollah. However, they claim that there is no chance of the kid-

nappers moving the hostages around Beirut undetected.

This week, Hussain Fadlallah, the leader of the Hizbollah in Lebanon, confirmed that all the hostages, including Britons Terry Waite and John McCarthy, were alive and well. It is hoped that the net around the hostage prison, and Syria's desire to bring peace to Beirut, will bring freedom nearer for the 15. A British delegation is currently in Tehran trying to negotiate with Iran's influential speaker of parliament, Hojatoleslam Ali Akbar Rafsanjani.

I will axe Polaris and Trident — Kinnock

The disarming Neil Kinnock.

June 20. Neil Kinnock today reaffirmed Labour's non-nuclear defence policy. He also repeated his party's pledge to scrap Polaris and Trident weapons systems if it wins the next election. This appeared to contradict his own recent rejection of "something for nothing unilateralism".

The Opposition leader has been warned by Ron Todd, the Transport and General Workers Union leader, not to forsake Labour's "bedrock" policies. There is now confusion about where the party stands and this may continue until things are sorted out at its annual autumn conference. Mr Kinnock said: "We are in a rapidly changing set of circumstances." (→29)

Pregnant Marie is slain on motorway

June 20. West Mercia police have found the body of heavily pregnant 22-year-old mother, Marie Wilks, who disappeared on Saturday when her car broke down on the M50 near Ledbury. She had left her sister and 13-month-old son Mark in her broken-down Marina car in order to walk half a mile to an emergency telephone. Her attacker, who broke her jaw and stabbed her in the neck, struck as she spoke to the police operator.

A hundred police are working on the enquiry. Marie's husband, Adrian, said: "The person responsible is not a him or her, it's an it. It's not a human being." (→26)

Celebrations this week mark 40 years since Britain's first mass of West Indian immigrants arrived on the SS Empire Windrush.

June

1988

Su	Mo	Tu	We	Th	Fr	Sa
			1	2	3	4
5	6	7	8	9	10	11
12	13	14	15	16	17	18
19	20	21	22	23	24	25
26	27	28	29	30		

26. Pakistan: Mass demonstrations protest against General Zia's policy of Islamisation.

26. UK: Seventy people are under arrest after a night of drunken rioting nationwide (→28).

26. Worcester: A night club bouncer is held for questioning about the murder of Marie Wilks.

27. Paris: Seventeen die in a rush-hour collision between two trains.→

27. Angola: Twelve South African soldiers are killed in a border clash with Cuban troops.

27. London: A Van Gogh still life, dismissed as "second rate", fetches £7 million at auction.

28. Paris: The death toll from yesterday's train crash has risen to 59.

28. UK: The government says it is ready to resume diplomatic links with Iran, broken off in 1980.

28. Birmingham: Labour deputy leader Roy Hattersley links drunken louts to the attitudes espoused by Mrs Thatcher.

29. Great Yarmouth: Neil Kinnock rebukes Arthur Scargill's reactionary brand of socialism.

29. Belfast: The RUC decides not to discipline chief Sir John Hermon over "shoot-to-kill" allegations.

29. UK: Rumours that metal-eating ink will destroy their compact discs alarm owners of CD players.

29. UK: A barrister alleges professional jurors, standing in for those summonsed, make a nonsense of the jury system.

30. UK: The Cannon Group announces the closure and sale of Elstree film studios.

30. Switzerland: Archbishop Marcel Lefebvre severs all links with Rome, installing four bishops by the Latin ritual.

30. UK: Author Harold Pinter warns of a new spirit of barbarism sweeping Britain.

Airbus crashes during French air display

The lopped trees bear witness to the last moments of the Airbus.

June 26. Europe's aircraft hopes received a setback today when the much-admired A320 Airbus crashed in front of a crowd of thousands at an air display on the French-Swiss border. At least four people were killed, 98 injured and 30 are still unaccounted for. Some may be trapped in the charred wreckage; others may have escaped into the woods.

The aircraft was diving over the airfield with flaps and under-carriage down when it hit turbulence and crashed into the Hardt forest. The French pilot, Michel Asseline, who suffered only a gash on his forehead, said: "I tried to open the gas, but it just didn't respond." The aircraft has a sophisticated computer system which the makers claim increases safety by preventing the pilot from making dangerous moves. Critics, however, say the computer has too much control.

Tonight Air France and British Airways grounded their A320s as a precautionary measure. Until today there have been no passenger deaths, but last September an A320 crashed on a training flight near Luxor, killing all five crew. The makers, which include British Aerospace, are hoping that the inquiry will show that the accident was not caused by any technical problems with plane (→14/9).

Stephen Hawking is unlikely bestseller

June 16. A book about some of the most abstruse aspects of modern physics has become a runaway bestseller. *A Brief History of Time*, by Stephen Hawking, a Cambridge professor, has topped the charts in the United States for many weeks, and seems likely to do as well in Britain. Professor Hawking, aged 46, is acknowledged to be one of the most brilliant minds of today and his book covers the latest ideas about the origin of the universe. The fact that the author is severely paralysed by a nervous disease has helped capture public imagination.

Crippled genius Stephen Hawking.

£5 billion wiped off shares in new slide

June 27. A massive £1.2 billion UK trade deficit in May, announced today, knocked more than two cents off the pound, pushing it down to $1.7015. It also wiped some £5.5 billion off the total value of shares traded in London. Markets expected that the Chancellor, Nigel Lawson, would now be forced into his fourth rise in base interest rates this year to damp consumer demand and to protect the pound.

The May current account deficit was far worse than anything that the Chancellor had predicted in his March Budget and compares with a deficit of only £1.5 billion for all 12 months of 1987 put together. Some Conservative politicians, notably John Biffen, a former Chief Secretary to the Treasury, joined Opposition spokesmen in arguing that Mr Lawson's substantial income tax cuts in this year's Budget were to blame for fuelling the current consumer spending boom which is sucking in such a high volume of imports.

Bank base lending rates, which were at 7.5 per cent in the Spring, have already been raised three times since then in an effort to control inflation. Mr Lawson's problem is that higher UK interest rates aimed at reining back the consumer spending released by his March tax cuts also prop up the exchange rate, which makes exporting harder and importing easier.

Teen dreams Bros top the charts with "I Owe You Nothing". Will they now get some new jeans?

Glasnost on trial at Moscow congress

June 30. In Moscow's great Palace of Congresses things have been said this week which, as one delegate put it, one would not have dared to whisper over the telephone even a few weeks back. Mr Gorbachev opened the special Soviet Communist Party congress with a call to the 5,000 delegates, and the Soviet people generally "to express their opinion on any matter. For much too long, uniformity, conformity and mediocrity were made out to be the hallmarks of progress".

He admitted that food shortages were widespread, that poor quality goods were still being sold and that in his three years of power "far more could have been accomplished".

After listening to a three-and-a-half hour speech from the Soviet leader, delegates responded with a will, some criticising the policies of *glasnost* (openness) and *perestroika* (restructuring), but most earnestly endorsing Mr Gorbachev's drive to galvanise the arthritic Soviet econ-

Mikhail Gorbachev is open to questions at the Party congress.

omy. A delegate from a remote village in European Russia said people who flourished in the Brezhnev era should be removed from high office. Mr Gorbachev asked whom he had in mind. The speaker named the dour 78-year-old former For-

eign Secretary and now state president, Andrei Gromyko.

The conference, called by Mr Gorbachev to give momentum to his reforms, endorsed his plan for giving US-style executive powers to the Soviet President.

Royals blamed for deadly avalanche

June 27. A Swiss examining magistrate today blamed Prince Charles's skiing party for the avalanche which killed his friend, Major Hugh Lindsay, last March. The accident happened near Klosters on slopes known to be dangerous even for good skiers and after warnings to avoid the area.

According to his report: "Prince Charles's group itself set off the fatal avalanche. By deliberately leaving the marked slopes and skiing off-piste, the six-member group placed itself in great danger." No charges are to be pressed and tonight Buckingham Palace said the Prince had nothing to add to his full press account.

New official secrets law is proposed

June 29. The government published long-awaited proposals today to reform the Official Secrets Act. It favours convictions in future only when a jury considers that unauthorised disclosure of information has prejudiced the national interest.

So it need no longer be a crime for the general public to know how many cups of tea are drunk daily in Whitehall — and that sort of thing. However, many MPs think a new law will still be repressive.

Girl hurt as school bus bombed by IRA

June 28. The IRA claimed its latest victim today: a 14-year-old girl severely injured when a terrorist bomb exploded in a school bus. Gillian Latimer, a third-former at Enniskillen Collegiate Girls' School, was in intensive care tonight with chest and arm injuries.

The bombing — at Lisnaskea, Co. Fermanagh — was condemned as a "callous outrage" by community leaders. The IRA admitted its responsibility in a statement which said that it would hold an inquiry into the "regrettable injury" of a civilian.

The bomb exploded shortly after the driver — believed to be a part-time member of the Ulster Defence Regiment — began his journey, picking up children on the way to Enniskillen.

At the European Community summit in Hanover, Mrs Thatcher and the Irish premier, Charles Haughey, pledged their "full determination to defeat those who seek to advance political aims by violent means".

Tyson launches 91-second demolition job

June 28. It took Mike Tyson just 91 seconds tonight to despatch the challenge of Michael Spinks and to retain the world heavyweight title. Tyson hardly broke sweat, as he demolished Spinks, first with a right and then a left hook which put Spinks down onto the canvas. The

challenger was swiftly up, but almost as swiftly down again — this time as the result of a short right — and this time he stayed down. Yet Spinks had never been knocked down even once in his career. Next in the firing line for the mighty Tyson is Britain's Frank Bruno.

Paris train collision traps commuters

27 June. As many as 22 people are feared dead tonight after a collision between commuter trains at Paris's Gare de Lyon underground station. Police and firemen are expected to continue their search for people trapped in the wreckage late into the night.

A brake failure is thought to be the cause of the accident, in which a train travelling at speed apparently ignored signals and rammed into another train which was stationary. Passengers on board the rammed train said the massive bang, followed by smoke and flames, was like a bomb blast (→28).

June 26. Grace Bumbry takes the title role in Britain's biggest ever opera, Verdi's "Aida" at Earl's Court. She is promptly sidelined by tonsillitis.

July

1988

Su	Mo	Tu	We	Th	Fr	Sa
					1	2
3	4	5	6	7	8	9
10	11	12	13	14	15	16
17	18	19	20	21	22	23
24	25	26	27	28	29	30
31						

1. Moscow: Communist Party delegates endorse Gorbachev's reforms in the final session of conference (→10).

1. London: Savoy Hotel share-holders see off a takeover bid from Trusthouse Forte (→20).

2. Wimbledon: Steffi Graf wins the women's tennis trophy, beating Martina Navratilova 5-7, 6-2, 6-1 (→4).

3. UK: The government endorses the US shooting of the Iranian airbus.→

3. France: Alain Prost wins the Grand Prix (→10).

4. Wimbledon: Stefan Edberg beats Boris Becker 4-6, 7-6, 6-4, 6-2.→

4. UK: The bank base rate rises half a percentage point to ten per cent (→15).

4. UK: *Burke's Peerage* reveals that US presidential candidate George Bush is the Queen's 13th cousin (→12).

5. Brussels: Ex-priest Patrick Ryan is arrested under suspicion of being involved with IRA terrorists (→23).

5. London: Karl Bowers is the first person to drive a battery vehicle non-stop round the M25 motorway.

6. UK: British Steel and British Rail announce their highest profits ever (→2/8).

7. Moscow: The Soviet Union launches Phobos, an unmanned spacecraft heading for Mars.

7. Tehran: Mourners at a mass funeral for the victims of the Airbus disaster shout anti-American slogans (→14).

8. UK: Red Adair inspects the Piper Alpha platform, as Occidental Oil boss Armand Hammer meets Mrs Thatcher (→12).

9. UK: It is reported that Douglas Hurd, the Home Secretary, is expecting urban race riots this summer.

DEATHS

7. British comedian and actor Jimmy Edwards (*1905).

9. British animal trainer and broadcaster Barbara Woodhouse (*9/5/10).→

US warship shoots down Iran airliner

Mourners are more angry than sad.

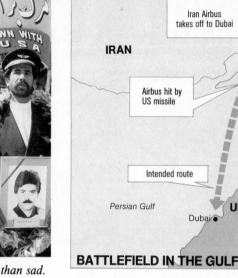

BATTLEFIELD IN THE GULF

0   Miles   50

July 3. The US guided missile cruiser *Vincennes* today shot down an Iranian airliner on a regular flight over the Gulf. All 286 people on board the Airbus A300 died when it was blown apart by a direct hit from a Standard missile.

The *Vincennes*, which had been engaged in a skirmish between one of its helicopters and Iranian armed speedboats, at first claimed that it had shot down an attacking F-14 Tomcat fighter. Only gradually did it emerge that the *Vincennes*, commanded by Captain Will Rogers III, had made a terrible error.

The tragedy has provoked outrage in Tehran where Prime Minister Mousavi threatened that the United States will "not be exempt from the consequences". He accused the Americans of "entering a direct war with our nation".

Washington was stunned by the news, not only by the tragedy itself and the fear of retaliation, but also by the fact that the cruiser's Aegis missile system could not tell the difference between a Tomcat with its 64-feet wingspan and an airliner almost three times as big.

Admiral William Crowe, chairman of the US Joint Chiefs of Staff, told a hurriedly summoned press conference that the *Vincennes* possessed one of the most sophisticated weapons systems on any US ship "but one of the most difficult problems is from a radar blip, particularly from a head-on target, to identify the type of aircraft".

President Reagan said that he was "saddened by this terrible tragedy", and announced that he had ordered the Pentagon to conduct a full inquiry.

However, both the President and Admiral Crowe insisted that the *Vincennes* had taken "proper defensive action" and the ship's crew was not to blame (→7).

Church says Yes to women priests

July 5. The Church of England General Synod voted today to push on with the laws for the ordination of women priests, but with a majority of only just under 60 per cent. The process is due for completion by 1992 and will require a two-thirds majority in the Synod.

Dr Robert Runcie, the Archbishop of Canterbury, voted against, although he is in favour of the principle of women's ordination. He dislikes the present proposals which allow bishops, priests and parishes to refuse women priests. Like many others who voted against, he fears this will lead to a divided church (→30).

July 4. Stefan Edberg defeats former Wimbledon champion Boris Becker at the end of a final delayed by bad weather. After losing the first set, Edberg outplayed Becker with a dynamite serve and a wicked return.

Over 150 feared dead in oil rig fire

July 6. An explosion which one eye-witness described as "like an atom bomb going off" shattered an oil rig tonight in the Scottish part of the North Sea, 120 miles east of Wick. Only about 70 of the rig's 227 workers are believed to have survived the raging inferno which brought the sea to near boiling-point.

One survivor, James McDonald, a rigger from Sterling, said: "There was this big bang, it shook the whole rig." Ten minutes later there was a second explosion and a ball of flame burst across the oil platform. Another survivor, Derek Ellington, described the scream of escaping gas before the blast: "About 30 seconds later there was the first explosion. It wiped out the control room and that was it, our nerve centre was gone." Flames more than 500 feet high helped reduce the platform to two molten stumps of metal and two twisted derricks.

Mr McDonald described how "some of the boys just sat in the room and gave up the ghost". He just said to himself: "Either I stay here and get roasted alive or I get out." He jumped 40 feet into the scalding sea.

Some men jumped 200 feet into a sea which seemed to be on fire. One diver said: "If it hadn't been for the waves washing over our heads I think we would have been fried in the water like pieces of bacon." High-speed rescue dinghies got in as close as possible, but some men could not swim. "I saw two men disappear and just drift away, they had never been in water deeper than a bath. It was a crying shame," wept the diver.

Tonight seven Nato warships, 21 smaller boats and six helicopters were still searching for survivors.

Rescue efforts are hampered by the fierce fire on board the platform.

But with fire still raging and cranes from the rig crashing into the sea there is little hope for them.

The rig, Piper Alpha, is operated by Occidental Petroleum, one of the biggest international oil companies. It passed a Department of Energy safety check just eight days ago. However, four years ago there was an explosion on it. Then 175 men had to be taken off by helicopter. The inquiry report into that accident was never published.

Until tonight the worst North Sea rig disaster was in 1980 when the Alexander Kielland rig capsized in high winds in the Ekofisk field killing 123 men (→8).

Cleveland report slams local health staff

July 6. Families caught up in the Cleveland child sex abuse scandal were victims of a battle between personalities and social agencies, according to the long-awaited report on the affair. In the clash between the ignorant and the over-zealous, it says parental rights were ignored and children damaged.

In her 320-page report, Lord Justice Butler-Sloss criticises all the leading figures in the scandal, including paediatricians Marietta Higgs and Geoffrey Wyatt for "over-confidence".

The report came on the same day as Tony Newton, the Social Services Minister, announced new measures to ensure cooperation between doctors, police and social workers. At least 12 families plan to take legal action.

European unity is on the way, says Commission chief

July 6. The prospect of a united Europe becoming an economic superpower equal to the United States, and bigger than Japan and the new industrial states of the Pacific combined, was opened up today by Jacques Delors, president of the European Commission (EC). He told the European Parliament in Strasbourg that, within ten years, 80 per cent of economic and social decision-making would pass from national parliaments to the EC.

He added: "Some wish to go very far and some less far." This is seen as a rebuke for Mrs Thatcher, who has dismissed the idea of a central European bank and a common currency because that implied the extinction of national sovereignty (→22).

End of "Walkies" Woodhouse-style

July 9. Barbara Woodhouse, whose stern but loving cry of "Walkies!" and headmistressy style endeared her to generations of British dog lovers, died today in her Buckinghamshire home. A long career of caring for animals went unsung until 1980 and her first series of *Training Dogs the Woodhouse Way* for BBC television. The result was instant celebrity for her, and better behaviour from the nation's dogs.

Ulster officers face disciplinary action

July 4. Senior Royal Ulster Constabulary officers face disciplinary proceedings following a lengthy series of inquiries into an alleged "shoot-to-kill" policy in Northern Ireland. The investigation, initially led by John Stalker, began in 1982. At least 20 men, including two superintendents, are involved (→5).

Barbara Woodhouse and friend.

Su	Mo	Tu	We	Th	Fr	Sa
					1	2
3	4	5	6	7	8	9
10	11	12	13	14	15	16
17	18	19	20	21	22	23
24	25	26	27	28	29	30
31						

11. Warsaw: Mr Gorbachev proposes a European conference to speed up the process of disarmament (→19).

11. Lusaka: Neil Kinnock has talks with African National Congress acting leader Oliver Tambo (→18).

11. UK: 8,500 people are known to carry the AIDS virus.

12. USSR: The parliament of Nagorny Karabakh votes to secede from Azerbaijan (→16).

13. UK: British Aerospace threatens to withdraw from the Rover sale (→14).

14. UK: The government steps in to salvage the sale of the Rover Group to British Aerospace (→18).

14. Mexico: Carlos Salinas de Gortari is chosen as president-elect after a controversial general election (→16).

14. UK: Chris Cowdrey is appointed captain of the England cricket team (→26).

14. London: A dilapidated Mercedes-Benz roadster, made in 1936, fetches 9c 1.6 million at auction.

15. UK: Inflation last month reached a two-year peak of 4.6 per cent (→18).

15. Kabul: Guerrillas kill 20 in a city centre bomb attack.

15. UK: Riots at Lindholme Prison cause 9c 70,000 worth of damage (→1/8).

16. USSR: Troop reinforcements are sent to Yerevan in order to crush Armenian activists (→19).

16. Mexico City: Over 200,000 people march to protest against the way votes in the general election were counted.

16. Indianapolis: Florence Joyner runs the fastest women's 100 metres ever, in 10.49 seconds.

DEATHS

10. British actor and playwright Errol John (*20/12/24).

11. British social scientist Barbara Frances Adam, Baroness Wootton of Abinger (*1897).

Texas conservative to run with Dukakis

Dukakis and Bentsen look forward to five months of campaigning together.

July 12. Michael Dukakis, the Democratic presidential candidate, surprised the pundits today by choosing Senator Lloyd Bentsen as his running-mate. They were expecting him to opt for the space hero, John Glenn. Mr Bentsen, aged 67, is far less well-known outside his home state of Texas.

Washington observers, however, thought it was a shrewd choice. Like John F. Kennedy, also from Massachusetts, Mr Dukakis has chosen a conservative senator from Texas who has the respect of professional politicians in Washington. The Democrats probably need to take Texas if they are to win the campaign. They also need to convince the floating voters that Mr Dukakis is not "too liberal".

The choice has upset Jesse Jackson, the black clergyman whom Mr Dukakis beat in the primaries. His support is necessary to bring out the votes of the blacks and other minorities. Today Mr Jackson said he would keep his name on the ballot for the final vote on the nomination next week (→18).

Iran airbus radio counters US claims

July 14. Iranian representatives at the UN today scorned Mr George Bush's argument that the destruction of the Airbus shot down by the US cruiser *Vincennes* was the Iranians' fault because they allowed it to fly "over a warship engaged in active battle".

"What was the *Vincennes* defending itself against," asked the Foreign Minister, Ali Velayati, "the scheduled flight of an airliner, flying within a recognised civilian airway?" He read the transcript of radio messages from the air traffic controller to the airplane before it was destroyed. "Have a nice day," said the controller (→14/8).

Super-league plan by top soccer clubs

July 13. English soccer is today at the crossroads. Ten Division One clubs are threatening to break away and form their own "super league" Television is the temptor, offering multi-million pound deals which would shatter the Football League.

Arsenal, Tottenham and Manchester United have spearheaded the breakaway movement, with other clubs invited either because of their size (such as Liverpool) or their importance to regional ITV companies (such as Sheffield Wednesday). Talks are continuing both with ITV and within the football establishment to try to avoid an outright rift (→21).

Tories retain seat with cut majority

July 14. The Tories staggered to an embarrassingly narrow victory in today's Kensington by-election — the first polling test since Mrs Thatcher won her third term 13 months ago. A strong Labour challenge cut the government's majority from 4,447 to only 815.

Despite the anti-Tory swing, the divorced ex-partners in the now-defunct Liberal-SDP Alliance fared disastrously with the David Owen's SDP barely saving its deposit (→25).

Thousands turn out for Jacko's UK tour

The superstar struts his stuff.

July 16. The American rock star, Michael Jackson, played to a packed Wembley Stadium tonight and proved that, for all the hype and hostile press coverage, "Wacko Jacko" is a supreme entertainer.

Jackson hit the top 18 years ago as the 11-year-old singer for his family group, the Jackson Five, and has stayed there, first as black America's original teen idol and now as a solo artiste rumoured to be worth 600 times his weight (8.5 stone) in gold.

Jackson earns £700,000 an hour on stage, but the 75,000 fans were sure he deserved it as the man, who apparently thinks he came from Mars, danced his way through hits like *Billie Jean* and *Thriller* (→25).

Terrorists kill nine on Greek liner

July 11. Terrorists turned a Greek ferry, the *City of Poros*, into a bloody shambles today when they opened fire with automatic rifles and threw grenades at the tourists packed on the boat as it neared the end of its day trip round the Aegean islands.

At least nine people died and 78 were wounded. There was panic as fire broke out and passengers jumped into the sea to escape the hail of bullets. Some were pulled from the sea by rescue boats, while others, too badly injured to jump to safety, were rescued from the burning ferry.

French holidaymakers Jean and Natalie Wogewda were both wounded. He was shot in both legs, but managed to crawl to safety. "I was on deck when I heard automatic fire. I turned round and was thrown into the air by the bullets hitting my legs," he said.

"I saw the man who was shooting and I couldn't believe it," he said. "I thought it was a joke. When I saw others falling to the deck, it turned out to be real. I only saw one gunman as he reloaded his weapon.

Passengers flee the "City of Poros" after the shooting started.

Then he hurled a grenade at the ship's smoke-stack, setting off a fire. Then he approached my group and started firing at us again."

There is much mystery surrounding the terrorists. Some reports say they were driven away from the ferry by a speedboat. They made no demands and did not identify themselves. A connection is being made, however, with the death of three people yesterday, when a car carrying explosives blew up close to the ferry's home-port near Athens.

One theory is that the attack was mounted by the Abu Nidal group, the most ruthless of all Palestinian terror groups, one of whose members comes up for trial in Greece later this month.

British Grand Prix victory for Senna

July 10. Brazilian Ayrton Senna drove through an English summer blend of rain and sunshine to win his first British Grand Prix at Silverstone today. The rain made driving difficult and Senna only narrowly missed his team-mate, Alain Prost, when taking the lead on the 14th lap.

Prost later retired, leaving England's Nigel Mansell to offer the only real challenge to Senna. As the track dried out, Mansell drove with great flair, advancing from seventh position to second and setting the fastest lap time at an average speed of just over 129 miles per hour. But Senna was never really threatened and finished 23.3 seconds ahead of Mansell.

Ayrton Senna sweeps through the rain to a Silverstone victory.

Police raids mark Mandela's birthday

July 15. In a nationwide swoop, South African police have detained at least 25 black activists who were planning to stage concerts and sporting events to mark the 70th birthday of Nelson Mandela, who has spent 25 years serving a life sentence for sabotage and treason.

The authorities followed up their crackdown with an unprecedented offer to allow Mandela's wife, Winnie, and other members of his family to make a six-hour visit to him in his Cape Town prison. Mandela was also allowed to receive a gift from film director Bernardo Bertolucci — a copy of his Oscarwinning *The Last Emperor*.

Mandela accepted the film, but rejected the offer of a family visit, saying he did not want to be given privileges not granted to other black nationalist prisoners. Mrs Mandela will spend the birthday quietly at home — as she has done for the past 25 years (→17).

Settlement closer for war in Angola

July 13. After three days of talks in New York diplomats from South Africa, Angola and Cuba today agreed in principle to a plan which could end two of the continent's long-running bush wars.

South Africa has agreed to stop helping anti-government guerrillas in Angola and to grant independence to neighbouring Namibia, where Swapo guerrillas have been fighting for 25 years. In return, Cuba will withdraw its 50,000 troops that have been propping up Angola's Marxist regime. But no timetable has been agreed, and the American mediators said the plan was only "the basis for final steps to a settlement" (→5/8).

Red Adair's men board Piper Alpha

July 12. Two of Red Adair's team of troubleshooters tonight managed to get on to the Piper Alpha oil rig, still blazing a week after the blast which killed 166 men. The veteran Texan oilman has been trying to get his men aboard for three days but high winds stopped him.

The wells have to be capped in order to put the fire out. It is likely to be many weeks, however, before the accomodation module, where most of bodies are thought to be, can be raised from 400 feet down on the sea bed (→29).

Red Adair approaches the rig.

17. London: A rally is held in Hyde Park to demand Nelson Mandela's release (→18).

17. UK: The government proposes a code of practice to curb unscrupulous and incompetent estate agents.

18. S. Africa: Mrs Thatcher is the only western leader not to send Nelson Mandela a birthday card (→20).

18. UK: Bank base rates rise 0.5 per cent to 10.5 per cent (→21).

18. US: Jesse Jackson and Michael Dukakis agree a role for Jackson's supporters in the presidential election. →

18. UK: Rover Group announces that 4,900 redundancies will follow the sell-off to British Aerospace.

19. UK: Beacons are lit to commemorate the sighting of the Armada 400 years ago today.

19. USSR: Mr Gorbachev rejects Armenian demands for Nagorny Karabakh in a national TV broadcast (→20).

20. Yerevan: Armenians call a 48-hour general strike (→25).

20. UK: The government reveals its 9c 7,000 million share plan for the English and Welsh water authorities (→27).

21. UK: Building societies raise their mortgage lending rates to around 11.5 per cent.→

21. UK: West Ham put a 9c 2 million transfer fee on their striker Tony Cottee, wanted by Everton and Arsenal (→3/8).

22. UK: Leon Brittan is appointed Britain's senior European commissioner, succeeding Lord Cockfield (→3/8).

23. Yugoslavia: Four thousand Serbs join a march demanding regional autonomy.

23. Rangoon: Bloody anti-government riots force Ne Win, Burma's leader for 26 years, out of office (→26).

DEATHS

18. German rock singer Nico (Christa Paffgen) (*1945).

20. British cartoonist and journalist Charles Mark Edward Boxer (*19/5/31).→

Tour de France leader fails drug test

July 21. Pedro Delgado, race leader in the Tour de France, has failed a drug test. Delgado has protested his innocence and a further test will be carried out today. If it proves positive, the Spaniard will be out of the Tour which is due to end in Paris next Sunday. Meanwhile, Delgado continues to ride in the race.

News of the positive dope test was only released yesterday, although it was derived from a urine sample given last week. Five riders are tested each day, including the race leader which for the last week has been Delgado.

Gerard Porte, the race doctor, said: "The drug detected is benemide, a masking agent, which has only just been added to the list of proscribed substances." (→24)

Under suspicion: leader Delgado.

Midsummer madness at Britain's airports

July 17. The foreign air traffic controllers' strike has kept package tourists stranded in British airports for up to 48 hours. The outlook, as the holiday season reaches its peak, remains poor, despite the French controllers' last-minute decision today to call off their planned total strike. Industrial action by Greek and Spanish controllers continues, and heavy disruption is expected over France for some weeks.

MPs today noted that delays in other European countries were measured in hours rather than days. The Civil Aviation Authority, whose response to the airports crisis is simply to state that nothing can be done to alleviate it, is being criticised for its inertia and apparently chronic lack of foresight.

The tour operators agreed. One said that the CAA didn't even have enough telephone lines to take bookings for charter flight slots. The CAA blames the operators for creating an unforeseeable rise in the number of flights. Whoever is at fault, the tourist suffers: Luton lacks the attractions of Marbella.

Seve pulls off third British open victory

July 18. Seve Ballesteros today won his third British Open championship with one of the great final rounds in golfing history. It was the Spaniard's first success in one of golf's four major championships for four years and he said later that he had never played better.

What began as a three-way tussle involving Nick Faldo became a head-to-head confrontation between Ballesteros and Nick Price of Zimbabwe. Ballesteros produced some blistering golf, with a succession of birdies, but Price did not wilt until Ballesteros put his second at the 16th just three inches from the hole. A chip at the last skimmed the hole and Ballesteros was round in 65 shots to win by two strokes.

An elegant swing from Seve.

Greenham opens gates for Russians

July 19. British and American commanders today welcomed 20 Soviet military personnel to the top secret Greenham Common air base. Their arrival marks the implementation of the arms control treaty signed by Mr Gorbachev and President Reagan last December, which was ratified last month.

The Soviets, led by Vysacheslav Lebev, are here to check that the 96 missiles declared at Greenham by the Americans are actually in place. As they got out their geiger counters to start their work, women from the "peace camp" at the gates tried unsuccessfully to break through the perimeter fence. Eight were arrested.

Russian boss Vysacheslav Lebev (l).

House-buyers face mortgage rate leap

July 21. Led by the Halifax, all major building societies decided today that they could no longer hold out against the present trend of rising interest rates. They raised their base mortgage lending rates by almost two percentage points — from 9.8 to 11.5 per cent.

On Monday the clearing banks put their base lending rates up to 10.5 per cent, the sixth half-point rise in two months. The mortgage rise will add 0.7 per cent to the retail price index, pushing the inflation rate once again over the five per cent mark (→27).

Fragile peace moves in Iran-Iraq war

July 22. The fragility of the prospect of peace in the Gulf War was exposed today when Iraq launched an offensive aimed, according to a spokesman, at recovering land lost in the early days of the war. Nevertheless, the UN Secretary General, Perez de Cuellar, is going ahead with his plan to send a team to Iraq and Iran to work out details of a ceasefire under the terms of Resolution 598 which was accepted by Iran five days ago.

He would seem to be justified; for while Tehran says "we will reply to the enemies of Islam on the battlefield", it is becoming increasingly obvious that Iran can no longer continue the war. Ayatollah Khomeini confirmed this when he admitted he made the ceasefire decision: "Taking this decision was more deadly than taking poison. I submit myself to God's will." (→24)

Teenage members of the Iranian army, now Iraqi prisoners of war.

Family murdered in IRA bomb "mistake"

July 23. A family of three died by mistake today when a bomb exploded on a border road in Northern Ireland. Security forces believe the bomb was intended for a judge who was travelling on the same road after flying on the same flight as the family from New York.

Robert Hanna, aged 44, his wife Maureen, also 44, and their six-year-old son, were killed when a 1,000-pound bomb, planted near a derelict house, blasted their car off the road just north of the border.

An hour later, Mr Justice Ian Higgins, a Catholic, and his wife and daughter, arrived on the scene with the RUC escort which had accompanied them from the border. The judge's house has been a target for an IRA mortar attack.

The IRA later admitted to this latest blunder — one of several which have killed more than 17 civilians since the Enniskillen outrage — and tendered its "deepest sympathy" to the victims. The Hannas died less than 100 yards from where a bomb killed Lord Justice Gibson last year (→1/8).

The Hannas' car is wrecked, blasted by the IRA bomb meant for another.

Eleven killed in Hyderabad riots

July 17. Troops are patrolling the silent streets of Hyderabad today enforcing a curfew imposed after the killing of 11 people in renewed ethnic violence between Sindhi nationalist groups and Muhajir settlers from India.

The violence broke out when Sindhi gunmen tried to murder the Muhajir mayor of Hyderabad. He survived, but the enraged Muhajirs rampaged through the town, burning Sindhi shops (→5/8).

1988: the year of "bonking bimbos"

July 19. There is nothing particularly new in older men having affairs with glamorous, younger women. But, as politicians, businessmen and preachers have found to their cost, the pleasures can have a price: exposure in the public prints where the girls are "bimbos" and sex becomes "bonking". This week it was Burton boss, Sir Ralph Halpern, in the spotlight in a court case over the alleged theft of diaries in which Fiona Wright described her affair with Sir Ralph.

Dukakis patches up split with Jackson

July 21. At the Democratic convention in Atlanta tonight, Michael Dukakis accepted his nomination as the presidential candidate with a speech aimed at healing the splits in the party and setting the tone for his campaign.

"It's time to meet the challenge of the next American frontier — the challenge of building an economic future... for every citizen in the land," he said. Dukakis paid special tribute to his rival Jesse Jackson, who "lifted so many hearts with the dignity and the hope of his message throughout the campaign" (→3/8).

Zimbabwe soldiers hold up Kinnock

July 18. Zimbabwe's president, Robert Mugabe, apologised to Neil Kinnock today for the treatment which Labour's leader, his wife Glenys and a posse of London journalists got on arrival in the country.

Bad light forced the party, which was flying from Mozambique, to land without warning at a remote airstrip. A Zimbabwe army lance-corporal hustled the unexpected visitors at gunpoint into a hut.

During an hour's detention Mr Kinnock, although not amused, led his fellow prisoners in hymn singing. A Zimbabwe official said: "They had white faces and might have been South African raiders."

July 20. Mark Boxer, whose "Marc" cartoons pilloried the affluent for over 20 years, dies. He also edited the Sunday Times magazine, Tatler and Vogue.

July

1988

Su	Mo	Tu	We	Th	Fr	Sa
					1	2
3	4	5	6	7	8	9
10	11	12	13	14	15	16
17	18	19	20	21	22	23
24	25	26	27	28	29	30
31						

24. Iran: Iraqi troops start to withdraw after an offensive aimed at bolstering their position in peace talks (→8/8).

25. UK: Mrs Thatcher reshuffles her cabinet. →

25. USSR: Workers in Nagorny Karabakh call off their general strike.

25. Johannesburg: David Bruce, aged 25, is sentenced to six years jail for refusing to do national service (→3/8).

25. London: A Michael Jackson lookalike brings traffic to a halt in the West End.

26. Burma: Sein Lwin replaces Ne Win as the head of state (→2/8).

26. Oxford: Scientists start testing a piece of the Turin Shroud, trying to find its true date (→13/10).

26. Headingley: England lose the fourth Test against the West Indies (→2/8).

27. UK: The balance of payments deficit last month was 9c 1,020 million (→29).

27. London: Mercury Communications open the first non-British Telecom payphones, at Waterloo Station.

28. Vienna: A proposed monument to the victims of Nazism brings widespread objections.

28. Palma: Howard Marks denies being the "Mr Big" in a huge drug operation.

29. UK: The last fire on the Piper Alpha oil platform is extinguished.

29. UK: Roads seize up as the holiday weekend begins (→26/8).

30. Jordan: King Hussein says the PLO has sole claims on former Jordanian land in the West Bank (→4/8).

30. UK: Mrs Thatcher says she personally backs the ordination of women (→1/8).

31. Nigeria: The cargo ship *Karin B* sets sail for Italy, loaded with illegally dumped toxic waste (→28/8).

31. India: The discontinued Hindu soap opera *Ramayana* is reinstated after strong protests including strikes.

Thatcher cuts off funds for space plane, saying HOTOL money can be better spent

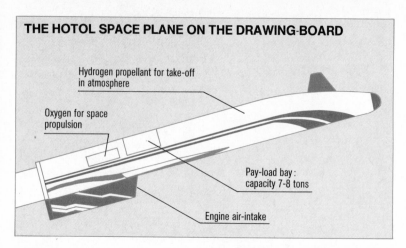

THE HOTOL SPACE PLANE ON THE DRAWING-BOARD

Hydrogen propellant for take-off in atmosphere

Oxygen for space propulsion

Pay-load bay: capacity 7-8 tons

Engine air-intake

July 26. The government has refused further funding for the Hotol plane project which, its supporters claim, could slash the cost of getting into orbit by a factor of ten.

Hotol exploits a novel weight-saving concept in which the engines for the space plane are air-breathing in the atmosphere and then switch to rocket propulsion when the air becomes too thin.

Hotol, backed by Rolls-Royce and British Aerospace with some government support, is still in the initial study phase. The next phase would have cost about £6 million, a minute fraction of what it almost certainly would cost to make Hotol a reality (→7/8).

Couples rush to beat mortgage deadline

July 29. Mortgage lending has jumped to a massive £3.6 billion in the last three months from £2.2 billion in the second quarter, according to the Bank of England figures today. Much of the rise comes from couples buying now to beat the August deadline, after which unmarried couples will no longer be able to claim two lots of tax relief of up to £30,000 each.

Even allowing for this, however, city analysts think the boom is out of control and inflation will top 6 per cent next year. Nigel Lawson, the Chancellor of the Exchequer, does not agree; he called them "teenage scribblers" (→8/8).

July 30. Stars of television's "Grange Hill" do their bit to help "Shop Assistance" in London's Covent Garden raise money for AIDS charities.

Briton arrested as police smash huge drugs conspiracy

July 25. Drug squads in Britain, Spain and the US have broken what is allegedly the world's largest and most successful cannabis smuggling ring. They have arrested 22 people across the three countries, including Oxford graduate Howard Marks, aged 42, who is described as the ringleader of the $100 million operation.

In 1982 an Old Bailey jury cleared Marks of drug smuggling charges when he satisfied them that he had been working undercover for MI5. Since then, he claims, he has had a legitimate career running a chain of travel agencies (→28).

Alleged ringleader Howard Marks.

Drugs storm sours Delgado's victory

July 24. Pedro Delgado duly won the Tour de France which ended in Paris today, but his triumph was soured by continuing controversy over his escape from a positive drug test. Two tests on the Spanish rider proved positive, but the international jury for the tour said they would take no action because the offending product has not yet been banned by the International Cycling Union. However, other bodies, including the Olympic and French cycling authorities, have proscribed the drug which helps combat dehydration and can allegedly mask the use of steroids.

Cabinet shake-up splits DHSS in two

July 25. The huge Department of Health and Social Security was split in two tonight as part of a government reorganisation involving a minor ministerial reshuffle.

In the hope of greater efficiency there will now be separate departments for Health and Social Security — each with its own cabinet minister. Kenneth Clarke is the new boss at Health, while John Moore keeps the other part of the divided empire.

The DHSS was formed by a Labour government in 1968. It has been by far the biggest Whitehall spender, accounting for more than 40 per cent of public expenditure.

Paddy Ashdown wins his leadership spurs

July 28. A hunky, 47-year-old ex-commando, Paddy Ashdown, was today elected as leader of the new Social and Liberal Democratic Party. In a ballot of party members he got 41,401 votes against 16,202 for his rival, fellow Liberal MP Alan Beith.

Mr Ashdown immediately declared that Labour can never again rule Britain and his target is to replace it as the alternative to the Tories. David Owen, the leader of the continuing SDP, sent him a congratulatory message. Mr Ashdown replied with a flea in the ear. The SDP, he said, is "an irrelevance". The SLD's position now is that it will have no pacts or coalition and will fight for power on its own.

Ashdown salutes his win over Beith.

South Africa halts Biko film showings

July 29. South African police today raided cinemas throughout the country, confiscating copies of Sir Richard Attenborough's film, *Cry Freedom*, even though it had been passed by the censors. A government spokesman said the police knew better than the censors what should be shown.

The film presents the life and death in police custody, of the black activist, Steve Biko, and is based on a book by the former newspaper editor, Donald Woods, who is a banned person and whose writings may not be quoted. Before copies of the film were seized, bombs exploded in cinemas where it was shown.

Schools shake-up wins Royal assent

July 29. The biggest shake-up in Britain's education system for over 40 years becomes law today when the Education Reform Bill receives the Royal Assent. The Act introduces a national curriculum for state schools, regular testing of pupils and a facility to opt out of local education authority control. Although the changes affect schools only in England and Wales, Scottish universities will be affected by new financial arrangements. Much criticism has focused on the greater powers accorded to the government under the Act.

Thatcher attacks idea of a united Europe

July 27. Mrs Thatcher today scornfully dismissed the concept of a United States of Europe. She said: "It will never come in my lifetime and I hope never will."

This was her retort to the vision of European Union recently conjured up by Jacques Delors, the president of the European Commission. He predicted that within ten years 80 per cent of social and economic law-making will be at the level of Europe rather than national parliaments.

The Prime Minister snapped: "He went over the top. He should never have said it." As for monetary union and a European central bank, such notions are just "airy-fairy", and too much time has been spent talking about them.

She also rejected as dangerous the idea of people travelling without passports or border checks and said that she will never surrender the British parliament's sovereignty in general.

Mrs Thatcher has shown many signs recently of wanting to slow the pace of West European integration. But she said that this does not mean she is against closer collaboration between the 12 Common Market nations "on the things we would do better together". It was just best not to rush (→21/9).

"Cry Freedom": banned.

Guinness face huge takeover payout

July 28. A ruling by the Takeover Panel, the City's own watchdog, that Guinness must pay up to £100 million more to former shareholders of Distillers was upheld today by the Court of Appeal. In a takeover, all shareholders should be offered the same price for their shares. The Panel found that a subsidiary of the Swiss Bank Leu was "acting in concert" with Guinness last September, when it paid well over the odds for 10.6 million shares in Distillers after a promise from Guinness to cover any losses it suffered as a result (→12/8).

Winnie Mandela's house burnt down

July 28. Winnie Mandela lost almost all her possessions this afternoon when fire gutted her four-room house in the black township of Soweto, outside Johannesburg. Eye-witnesses said black students from a nearby high school smashed windows and poured petrol inside.

The attack comes after clashes between the students and members of the self-styled Mandela United soccer team, who act as Mrs Mandela's bodyguard. Her husband, serving a life sentence for treason, was told of the fire. He said no comment should be made (→12/8).

America's Yellowstone Park is closed while firefighters try to save it.

August
1988

Su	Mo	Tu	We	Th	Fr	Sa
	1	2	3	4	5	6
7	8	9	10	11	12	13
14	15	16	17	18	19	20
21	22	23	24	25	26	27
28	29	30	31			

1. Australia: Mrs Thatcher arrives in Perth on a state visit.

1. London: Prison officers at Holloway strike in protest at staffing levels. →

1. Cleveland: Charlotte Hughes, believed to be the oldest person in the UK, is 111 years old today.

2. Burma: Sein Lwin arrests all war heroes, fearing they might be possible leaders for opposition (→3).

2. India: A virulent cholera epidemic in New Delhi has killed 220 and affects a further 20,000 people.

2. UK: Graham Gooch replaces Chris Cowdrey as captain of the England cricket team (→19).

3. US: Michael Dukakis releases medical records to quash rumours that he has had psychiatric treatment (→10).

3. Johannesburg: 143 young people refuse the military call-up.

3. Burma: Sein Lwin declares martial law. →

4. Ulster: IRA gunmen shoot dead two builders who had worked on a police station (→5).

4. West Bank: King Hussein of Jordan sacks his employees in a move towards recognising Palestinian self-rule (→10).

5. Dusseldorf: Four soldiers are injured in a suspected IRA bomb blast at a British army base at Ratingen (→8).

5. Amritsar: The bodies of 41 people tortured to death by Sikh extremists are found.

5. Worcestershire: Naturalists are trying to save Britain's last 16 marsh warblers, in danger of extinction.

6. Geneva: A United Nations report alleges that 200,000 youths under 15 are fighting in the world's armies.

6. Newmarket: A man dies after a brawl, bringing fears of racetrack hooliganism.

DEATH

2. American short story writer Raymond Clevie Carver (*25/5/38).

Angola peace talks end in optimism

Aug 5. Peace in Angola came a step nearer tonight when delegates from South Africa, Cuba and Angola, meeting in Geneva, agreed on what they described as "a sequence of steps" for disengagement of the five separate armed forces in the region: the armies of South Africa, Angola and Cuba, and the guerrilla bands of Unita, the anti-Marxist Angolan rebels, and Swapo, fighting for Namibian independence.

Before the Geneva meeting, the fifth in a series sponsored by the United States, the South Africans made a bid to seize the initiative by publishing their terms for a deal. They offered to withdraw their forces from southern Angola, to pull their troops out of Namibia within ten months, and to hold free elections there as a prelude to full independence.

In return, they said the 50,000 Cuban troops must leave Angola within the same ten months and the Angolan camps of the black nationalist organisation, the African National Congress, which is banned in South Africa, must be closed down. Swapo guerrillas in Angola must be confined to their camps.

The South African package was not taken up by the Angolan and Cuban delegates. They are reported to be sceptical about South Africa's willingness to grant independence to Namibia. As for South Africa, a Cuban withdrawal from Angola is an essential for any agreement.

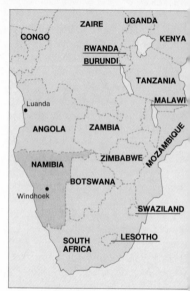

Soldier dies as IRA bombs London camp

Aug 1. At 6.53 this morning the IRA's first mainland bomb for four years blasted through the accommodation block of the Inglis Barracks in north London, killing one soldier and injuring nine others. The explosion has resurrected the spectre of another IRA bomb campaign on the mainland.

Experts, who say the death and injury toll was remarkably low, believe the bomb was planted inside the barracks. People who work and live there say they have long been worried by the lax security in the camp, which had facilities used by local residents and acted as a short cut for drivers. The police have started their inquiry. A review of security at military bases is sure to follow.

The barracks keep on blazing.

TV deal spells end of "Super League"

Aug 3. Football's flirtation with a "super league" and satellite broadcasting is expected to come to an end today with a £44 million deal giving ITV exclusive rights to televise English league soccer for the next four years. The BBC and their new-found partners, British Satellite Broadcasting, last night withdrew from what they called an "auction" for TV soccer rights.

It was ITV's original proposal to concentrate coverage on just ten clubs which first gave rise to the prospect of secession from the century-old Football League. But now, after a month of financial jockeying, a rift has been averted — for the time being, at least.

British Rail panned for poor services

Aug 2. British Rail came under fire from its watchdogs today with accusations of overcrowding — "it has reached epidemic proportions" — dirty coaches and inadequate catering. The Central Transport Consultative Committee also attacked BR's recently-introduced policy of pricing passengers off popular routes with inflated fares and blamed the overcrowding on shorter trains at busy times.

China is stricken by floods and drought

Aug 2. The worst flash floods for centuries in eastern China have killed at least 250 people, swamped 200 million acres of farmland and isolated at least 100,000 people. About 350 are missing, feared dead, as a huge clean up operation begins.

China has recently suffered a spate of weather-related disasters. Hailstorms, drought, typhoons and landslides have struck in swift succession, causing loss of life and physical and economic devastation.

This week's floods are the result of 20 inches of rain in 12 hours running straight off the hard, drought-baked earth.

Over a hundred ships were sunk and an unknown number of people killed when a flash flood hit a transport canal in Shandong province.

Over four million people face the threat of food shortages this winter. The floods have polluted supplies of drinking water and further damaged crops which were struggling to survive the drought.

Ceasefires herald end of two wars

Angola: Cuba and Pretoria call truce

Aug 8. After three months of negotiations in an atmosphere of mutual mistrust, South Africa, Angola and Cuba have agreed to a ceasefire in the bush war that has lasted for almost 20 years. Swapo, the black African guerrilla organisation fighting for Namibian independence from South Africa, has agreed to join the ceasefire so long as it does not come under attack from South African forces. But Unita, the anti-Marxist guerrilla force, says the fight will continue until the Angola regime agrees to negotiations.

A joint statement, issued simultaneously in Washington, Pretoria, Havana and Luanda, said that the next stage was agreement on a timetable for withdrawing the 50,000 Cuban troops from Angola. The Cubans have been in Angola since the territory gained independence from Portugal in 1975, and the survival of the Marxist regime in the capital, Luanda, was threatened by anti-Marxist guerrillas.

South Africa wants to see the Cubans leave within seven months; the Cuban-Angolan timetable speaks of four years. In that case, South Africa says it will not proceed with its promise to grant independence to Namibia. The South Africans fear that if the Cubans stay in Angola, they would be used to back a Marxist take-over in an independent Namibia (→30).

UN Secretary-General Perez de Cuellar announces the Gulf ceasefire.

Gulf: UN announces Iran-Iraq peace deal

Aug 8. The war in the Gulf is over. After eight years of bloody conflict with horrendous casualties of nearly a million dead, Iraq and Iran have today agreed to a ceasefire which will come into effect formally on August 20. The truce will be followed by direct talks between both countries under the auspices of the UN in Geneva five days later.

The agreement was announced at a special meeting of the Security Council by the UN Secretary General, Perez de Cuellar, who has worked so hard to bring peace to the Gulf. He said: "The restoration of peace will bring to the peoples of both countries victories far greater than those of war."

The war started when Iraq accused Iran of subversion and border violations and President Saddam Hussein sent his tanks into Iran, counting on an easy victory. But the Iranians, sustained by religious and nationalist fervour, fought back and the war turned into a long war of attrition which threatened to drag in the rest of the world.

Both sides are now claiming victory. President Hussein has announced a three-day national holiday in Iraq, while in Iran, Foreign Minister, Ali Akhbar Velayati, said the ceasefire was the first step "in the achievement of a just, comprehensive and honourable settlement returning peace to our region" (→25).

Coe is left out of the Olympic squad

Aug 8. Sebastian Coe, twice an Olympic champion, was today left out of Britain's athletics team for the Seoul Olympics which are to begin next month. The selectors were split over Coe, who failed to qualify even for the final of the 1,500 metres trials on Sunday, but ultimately gave the vacant final places to the men in form — Steve Cram and Peter Elliott. With old rival, Steve Ovett, also missing out, it's the end of an awesome era in British running (→23).

Interest rates rise again to 11 per cent

Aug 8. In the seventh rise in the cost of borrowing in less than three months the Chancellor, Nigel Lawson, today pushed up bank base rate by another half-point to 11 per cent. So there is now dearer money than for nearly 18 months.

The Treasury explained: "Some small tightening is needed to check over-rapid economic growth and signs of rising inflation." Opposition MPs complained that Mr Lawson's last tax-cutting budget was obviously a mistake (→19).

Nelson Mandela is taken to hospital with tuberculosis

Aug 12. Nelson Mandela, South Africa's 70-year-old black nationalist leader who has been in prison for 25 years, was taken to a Cape Town hospital last Friday after becoming short of breath and coughing up blood. Today the hospital said he was suffering from chronic inflammation of the lungs, but there were no signs of cancer. Mandela was responding to treatment and was "without pain or discomfort".

His wife, Winnie, visited him on Saturday afternoon and, because he was undergoing an examination, she had to wait almost four hours before she was able to see him. She is said to have been shocked by his condition. The family lawyer said Mandela was suffering from tuberculosis. The authorities were so anxious about his condition that they moved him to a civilian hospital in Cape Town.

New royal princess greets her public

The Duke of York: a proud father.

Aug 12. The Princess of York made her public debut today as she left the Portland Hospital in London with her proud parents. The newest — still unnamed — royal was born four days ago and is fifth in line to the throne. The Duke and Duchess and their baby later flew to Balmoral to join the Queen (→22).

Eddie Murphy plays a confused prince in "Coming to America".

Su	Mo	Tu	We	Th	Fr	Sa
	1	2	3	4	5	6
7	8	9	10	11	12	13
14	15	16	17	18	19	20
21	22	23	24	25	26	27
28	29	30	31			

14. US: The officer who ordered the shooting of the Iranian Airbus is to get a "mild reprimand".

14. Edinburgh: The Festival opens, with over 10,000 shows on offer.→

15. Belfast: Speakers at an anti-internment rally praise the IRA's campaign of murdering troops.→

15. UK: A man who unlawfully collected 7,960 wild bird eggs is told he could face a £7.3 million fine (→18).

16. UK: British Rail announces huge fare rises for long distance commuters.

16. UK: Education Secretary Kenneth Baker urges teachers to put more emphasis on basic mathematics and science.

17. Poland: Coal miners stage a national strike.

17. UK: The report on the Haverigg prison riots blames the trouble on illegal drugs.

18. Ulster: A Catholic is murdered and a Unionist MP is sent a parcel bomb.→

18. Burnley: Wild bird egg thief David Brierley is fined £880.

19. Burma: Dr Maung Maung is appointed as the country's first civilian president (→28).

19. UK: Inflation is now running at 4.8 per cent a year (→25).

19. UK: P&O resumes sailings from Dover to Boulogne.

19. London: Graeme Hick scores the fastest century so far this season, hitting 100 in 79 balls at the Oval (→28).

20. Donington: A violent dance craze, "slam dancing", is blamed for the death of two fans at a heavy rock festival.

DEATHS

14. Italian racing car magnate Enzo Ferrari (*18/02/1898).→

17. British politician Lord Silkin of Dulwich (*6/3/18).

17. Pakistani President Zia ul-Haq (*12/8/24).→

19. British ballet choreographer Sir Frederick Ashton (*17/9/1904).→

Zia killed in plane crash

The late president's coffin is borne by a solemn guard at Islamabad.

Aug 17. Pakistan's military ruler, President Zia ul-Haq, was killed today when his Hercules transport plane blew up in mid-air after taking off from Bahawalpur, where he had been inspecting armoured troops. Arnold Raphel, the US Ambassador, was also killed along with the senior US military attache to Pakistan, Brigadier-General Herbert Wassom, and several members of the Pakistan armed forces.

There is, as yet, no explanation for the crash of the Hercules, which is regarded as a safe and sturdy aircraft. Tonight, Ghulam Ishaq Khan who, as chairman of the Senate is now acting president, said: "Sabotage cannot be ruled out."

The list of people who wanted Zia dead is long. He seized power in a coup in 1977 and later hanged the democratically-elected Zulfikar Ali Bhutto on charges of murder. He instituted a strict code of Islamic morality and imposed an iron-fisted military dictatorship.

He also became the main ally of the US in the region and provided the infrastructure for the Afghan *mujahideen* to wage war against the Russians. Sabotage is therefore a distinct possibility.

Bank robbers held after death spree

Aug 18. A gun battle outside Bonn was the climax today of a hostage-taking and murder spree by two desperate, drug crazed armed criminals. The terror started on Tuesday in Gladbeck, when Dieter Degowski and Hans-Jurgen Rosner took two staff hostage during a bank robbery. The next evening, they hijacked a crowded bus and shot dead a 15-year-old Italian boy when police seized an accomplice. After driving into Holland, they abandoned the bus but took two women hostage. As they drove back into Germany, they were finally captured at a police roadblock. In a last exchange of gunfire, an 18-year-old hostage died.

Fires destroy huge areas of Amazon

Aug 15. Two of Brazil's most important wildlife reserves have been devastated by farmers using fire to clear tropical rain forest for pasture. Over 40,000 square miles of virgin tropical forest has disappeared in the last year alone.

Scientists, concerned by the destruction to wildlife as fires raged through areas made bone dry by three months of drought, also believe the fires are adding to the worldwide "greenhouse effect" by releasing massive quantities of gas and ash into the atmosphere. Ecologists argue that the belt of tropical rain forest has a crucial role to play in maintaining the equilibrium of the earth's climate.

Nurses plan more protest stoppages

Aug 17. Nurses are to stage a one-day stoppage in several London hospitals tomorrow in pursuit of their pay claim. Today's vote for action by two health service unions comes despite plans to resume pay talks. These were broken off last week after the unions accused the government of sabotaging the 15 per cent wage deal. They claim that regrading will make 30,000 nurses £1,500 a year worse off.

Ashton, choreographer supreme, dies

Aug 19. Sir Frederick Ashton, who died in his sleep last night aged 83, was the leading British choreographer who did most to establish the repertoire of the Royal Ballet, which he joined in 1935. "He was to our national ballet what Fokine was to the Russians," said Dame Ninette de Valois today.

Ashton became a dancer in the face of severe family disapproval and first won fame with the ballet he created for Walton's *Facade* music in 1931. One of its wittiest dances was the tango which he danced himself. He also created *La Fille Mal Gardee*, *Marguerite and Armand* for Fonteyn and Nureyev, and the film ballet *Tales of Beatrix Potter*, in which he danced as Mrs Tiggywinkle.

Ballet master Sir Frederick Ashton.

Bomb kills six soldiers

The dead and injured soldiers' personal belongings litter the road.

Aug 20. Six British soldiers died today when a land-mine exploded on an Ulster road, hurling their unmarked bus into a field. The men were returning from home leave to their Omagh barracks from Aldergrove Airport, near Belfast. Bodies were scattered over a wide area. A further 27 casualties were flown to hospital in Dungannon, County Tyrone. Six are dangerously ill.

The 200-pound bomb, hidden under a drainage culvert and detonated by remote control, was made of Semtex, an explosive widely used by the IRA in their latest campaign which has claimed more British service lives than at any time since they arrived in Northern Ireland for the latest round of troubles which began in 1969. Most of the men have been killed off-duty.

Service chiefs are concerned about the increasing level of sophisticated weaponry available to the IRA. Apart from Semtex — which has no smell and is easily smuggled through border checks — terrorists are believed to possess at least one "Stinger" ground-to-air missile which could pose a serious threat to patrolling British helicopters.

US media open Quayle-hunting season

Aug 19. George Bush said he had chosen "an inspiring young leader" as his vice-presidential running-mate, but so far his choice of Senator Dan Quayle has generated controversy and astonishment rather than the excitement sought by the Bush campaign team.

The man at the centre of the storm is a 41-year-old senator from Indiana, little known outside his state and considered a rank outsider amongst the list of candidates to join Vice-President Bush on the Republican ticket in this year's presidential election.

The initial surprise over Senator Quayle's selection has now been overtaken by controversy. A hesitant performance at a press conference alongside Mr Bush did not help remove doubts, but what is particularly embarrassing for the Bush campaign managers is the revelation that Quayle, a military hawk, avoided military service in Vietnam by joining the Indiana National Guard.

Service in the Guard enabled him to avoid active service and there have been suggestions that he used his newspaper-owning family's influential contacts to secure enlistment. Quayle admits that "a number of calls were made". George Bush now risks having his acceptance speech at the New Orleans convention overshadowed by the furore as 13,000 journalists go Quayle-hunting.

Mrs Bush and Mrs Quayle stand by their Republican nominee husbands.

Aug 18. Liverpool pay an undisclosed sum to re-sign striker Ian Rush from Juventus, who paid £3.2 million for him last year.

New riots in Seoul on eve of Olympics

Aug 15. The riot police were out in force in Seoul again today. Looking like ancient warriors with their shields and helmets, they clashed with thousands of students attempting to march to the border to meet North Korean students. Demanding the reunification of Korea, the students attempted to break out from the campus of Seoul's Yonsei University, but the police swiftly and none too gently arrested the ringleaders and dispersed the rest. The feeling here is that, although these protests have been deliberately mounted on the eve of the Olympics, the students have too much national pride to interfere with the Games.

Ferrari dies, but the name lives on

Aug 14. Enzo Ferrari, the man behind a racing car legend, died today aged 90. His sports cars, driven by Niki Lauda, Juan Manuel Fangio, Jody Scheckter and a host of others, have chalked up 93 Grand Prix victories and 13 world titles since they started racing after the Second World War.

He started as a driver for Alfa Romeo in 1920, founding his own company called Scuderia Ferrari in 1940. Ferraris have never been produced in great quantities: when Enzo retired in 1977, just 3,500 vehicles a year were being made. Their sleek looks, and superb engine design, make Ferrari ownership a dream for any sporty driver.

Russians put on a show at Edinburgh

Aug 14. The Edinburgh Festival, now 42 years old, opened yesterday with a giant parade of floats to herald 8,000 performers in companies from all over Europe, the Soviet Union, Canada and Japan.

Highlight of the drama programme is Yukio Ninagawa's renowned Japanese company in *The Tempest*. The Georgian Actors Film Studio from Tbilisi are presenting a spectacular *Don Juan*. Another attraction is a Russian hit play by a personal friend of Mr Gorbachev, Aleksandr Gelman. Called *A Man with Connections* it is described as "a thoroughly enjoyable example of *perestroika* in action".

August

1988

Su	Mo	Tu	We	Th	Fr	Sa
	1	2	3	4	5	6
7	8	9	10	11	12	13
14	15	16	17	18	19	20
21	22	23	24	25	26	27
28	29	30	31			

21. Burundi: 24,000 Tutsis have been massacred by Hutus in tribal feuding.

22. UK: Pubs are allowed to stay open all day from today onwards.

22. London: The Duchess of York names her child Beatrice Elizabeth Mary.

23. UK: Athletes protest against a plan to give Sebastian Coe a "wild card" to enter the Seoul Olympics team (→24).

24. UK: Liquidators at Barlow Clowes International say investors will get back up to 40 per cent of their money.

24. UK: Postal workers vote for a national 24-hour strike over bonus payments.

24. UK: The proposal to offer Coe a "wild card" invitation to run at the Olympics is withdrawn.

25. Geneva: Peace negotiations open between Iran and Iraq.

25. UK: The first GCSE exam candidates receive their results.

26. UK: The bank holiday weekend starts with an 11-mile snarl-up on the M1 and a 14-mile tailback on the M3.

28. UK: Worcestershire beat Warwickshire to retain the Sunday cricket league title (→16/9).

28. UK: The *Karin B*, with its cargo of poisonous waste, is sighted off Land's End.→

29. S. Africa: Thirteen die in violence in a Natal township.

29. UK: Graham Gooch's participation in South African cricket puts England's tour of India in doubt (→9/9).

30. Japan: It is announced that Emperor Hirohito is suffering from a fever.

30. Angola: South Africa completes her military withdrawal.

31. Bangladesh: An international appeal is launched after a devastating monsoon kills at least 700 people.→

DEATH

26. British politician Thomas Frederick Peart (Lord Peart) (*30/4/14).

Another IRA "mistake" kills two civilians

The wreckage of a booby-trapped car in which a Navy officer was killed.

Aug 31. The IRA bungled yet another "operation" today — killing two middle-aged Derry people who were concerned about a neighbour. This followed an upsurge in violence last weekend with almost 200 attacks on troops and police. Among the shootings and bombings was a booby-trap car bomb in which a Royal Navy officer killed.

Today's killing in Derry occurred when Sheila Lewis, aged 60, and Sean Dalton, aged 55, had gone to their neighbour's flat because they had not seen him for several days. Mr Dalton climbed through a window, triggering a booby-trap bomb.

The missing neighbour is believed to be held hostage by the IRA with the bomb planted to kill members of the security forces when came to look for him. The flat was demolished.

This latest act of violence represents a major downturn in the IRA's fortunes. With the SAS shooting three members of an IRA "active service unit" in County Tyrone this week and the arrests of two suspected Irish terrorist in Holland, security forces appear to be fighting back hard after weeks of renewed violence.

Over 500 dead in Himalayan quake

Aug 21. Houses and roads along the border of India and Nepal splintered, and over 500 people are believed dead after a serious earthquake in the Himalayan foothills this morning. The quake, the worst in the area for over 50 years, measured 6.7 on the Richter scale at its centre and affected a 1,000-mile long strip. India's poorest state of Bihar, and Biratnagar and Dharan in Nepal, were especially badly hit. The death and casualty toll is expected to rise once rescue efforts get under way. Doctors say they have already run out of blood to treat the many thousands of injured.

Indian Prime Minister Rajiv Gandhi will visit Bihar tomorrow to inspect the damage.

Nepal clears up after the quake.

Mortgage rates to jump as record trade gap puts up bank rate

Aug 25. The government today announced a record £2.2 million balance of payments deficit for the last month. The City panicked. The Bank of England again increased interest rates — from 11 to 12 per cent. Another big rise in mortgage rates is inevitable and the government's economic strategy has been seriously damaged.

With Britain in the middle of a spending spree financed by huge personal borrowing, Nigel Lawson, the Chancellor, said: "You can have too much of a good thing. I have now had to apply the brakes." Some Tory MPs asked: "Has our magician begun to lose his touch?"

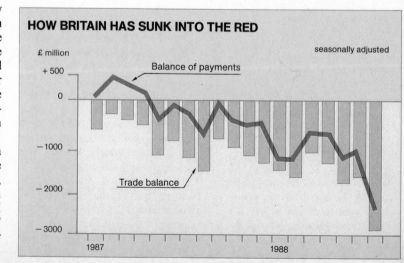

HOW BRITAIN HAS SUNK INTO THE RED

£ million

seasonally adjusted

Balance of payments

Trade balance

+ 500

0

− 1000

− 2000

− 3000

1987   1988

Jets crash into spectators at airshow

The split-second timing of the "Frecce Tricolori" fails when one of the pilots makes a fatal misjudgment.

Aug 28. Thirty-three people died today when three Italian air force jets collided during an aerobatics display at Ramstein in West Germany. One of the stricken jets tumbled into the crowd of spectators and then blew up, engulfing the area in a huge fireball. All three pilots died, and 60 people injured by flying, blazing wreckage are said to be in a "critical" condition tonight.

The manoeuvre which led to catastrophe, in which a single plane flies across the path of nine others, was criticised by British safety experts tonight. Germany has banned all aerobatic displays, but organisers of next week's Farnborough Air Show say it will go ahead as usual.

The tail of one of the stricken planes sticks up, a monument to disaster.

Polish government to talk to Solidarity

Aug 31. After talks with Polish ministers, Lech Walesa, the leader of the banned Solidarity trade union movement, has called on coal miners, shipyard and transport workers to end their strikes. Walesa's action followed reports that the authorities had agreed to discuss legalising Solidarity.

An official spokesman, referring to Walesa's meeting with ministers, significantly perhaps, did not mention Solidarity, but spoke only of Walesa as "representative of a mass movement". Only a week ago the government rejected Walesa's appeal for talks. The change of mind appears to have been brought about by the failure to end the wave of strikes by sending truncheon-wielding police into factories to beat up strikers as they prayed.

No sign of end to Burmese violence

Aug 28. Protest marches took place in most of Burma's cities today as hundreds of thousands of people took to the streets to challenge the rule of the new president, Maung Maung. The demonstrators took great care to keep their protests peaceful while the army took equal care not to provoke any violence.

These mass protests have already forced the resignation of Sein Lwin, who was president for only 17 days. There is no doubt they will continue and diplomats fear more violent confrontations.

Censors expose filmgoers to temptation

Aug 26. *The Last Temptation of Christ*, a film which has provoked a "holy war" in the US over its alleged blasphemy, was passed last night by the British film censors with an "18" Certificate. After consulting four Church of England bishops, they said no cuts were required for British cinemas.

The controversy about the film, directed by Martin Scorsese from a novel by Nikos Kazantzakis, centres on a vision which the fictional Jesus has on the cross. He imagines what it would be like to abandon his mission, make love to Mary Magdalene, bring up a family and live like an ordinary man.

Mr Scorsese, a Catholic who wanted to enter the priesthood, insists that "the film is my way of trying to get closer to God". But Bible belt preachers have called for it to be burned and crowds besieged Universal Studios in Hollywood with placards. Churches, including the Catholic bishops of England and Wales, have urged Christians not to see it. It opens in London on September 9.

Britain turns away poison cargo ship

Aug 30. Environmentalists were triumphant today when Virginia Bottomley, a junior environment minister, banned the *Karin B*, with its 2,000-ton cargo of toxic chemicals, from landing in Britain. Tonight, the ship was spending a second night at anchor off Plymouth harbour, while the captain searched for a country which would take his cargo.

The original destination was Ravenna in Italy, but the mayor organised a blockade. Since then the ship has been turned away from Spain and West Germany and Neath in Wales. There are now fears that the waste may be leaking from five damaged drums.

The move suggests that the government may be having second thoughts about its policy of encouraging British companies to cash in on the lucrative waste disposal. The Hazardous Waste Inspectorate last July made public the difficulties of monitoring such waste disposal. The *Karin B* affair has proved that toxic waste is a politically explosive issue.

Su	Mo	Tu	We	Th	Fr	Sa
				1	2	3
4	5	6	7	8	9	10
11	12	13	14	15	16	17
18	19	20	21	22	23	24
25	26	27	28	29	30	

1. S. Africa: Nelson Mandela is moved to a luxury clinic in Cape Town (→12).

1. UK: A report says that Europe's farm policy costs every consumer £13 per week in taxes and higher food prices (→21).

2. Yorkshire: A £400 million plant is commissioned to cut sulphur emissions from the Drax power station (→7/10).

2. North Sea: The seal virus has spread from common to grey seals.

3. London: Middlesex win the NatWest one-day cricket final.

3. Ulster: Five hundred police and 100 soldiers guard an IRA funeral (→6).

4. UK: Nutritionists blame young people's diet of junk food for increased youth violence (→14).

5. Bournemouth: The electricians' union, EETPU, is expelled from the TUC.

5. UK: There are now 1,730 reported cases, and 949 deaths, of AIDS (→7/10).

6. Ulster: Police uncover a loyalist gun factory (→8).

7. UK: Property developer Peter Palumbo is named Chairman of the Arts Council.

7. North Sea: Divers begin the search for the bodies of the 120 men still missing from the Piper Alpha disaster (→22).

7. Russia: The Soviet spacecraft lands back on Earth.

8. US: Polls show George Bush has an eight per cent lead over Michael Dukakis (→25).

8. Gibraltar: The inquest hears of a "frenzied attack" on the IRA bomb trio, with one member shot 16 times (→27).

9. London: The sale of Elton John's collection closes, having made £4,838,022.

10. Harare: The Pope arrives for a tour of "front-line" states in southern Africa (→14).

DEATH

1. American nuclear physicist Luis Walter Alvarez, Nobel laureate in 1968 (*13/6/11).

Mail delayed by postal workers' strike

Undelivered mail piles up in a Central London sorting office.

Sept 7. Angry postmen brought Britain's mail to a near standstill today. Five more of the 80 main sorting centres came out on strike leaving only Belfast working normally. Over 100 million items of mail are now caught in the logjam.

The dispute began with a one-day strike last week called by the Union of Communication Workers to protest against the management's plans for flexible pay rates for new recruits in the south-east. The management wants to pay them more to deal with labour shortages, but the UCW fears that the principle of regional pay will lead to postmen in the poorer parts of the country being underpaid.

Anger changed to fury in the sorting offices when casuals were brought in to help clear the backlog of mail held up by the one-day strike. Bill Cockburn, the managing director of the Royal Mail, denies that more than the usual number of casuals are being used. He said that the present strikes were "a smokescreen to get unjustifiably high levels of overtime to clear the backlog which they caused in the first place" (→12).

Steffi completes Grand Slam with US win

Sept 10. Steffi Graf today became only the fifth person to win the "Grand Slam" of the four top tennis tournaments in the same calendar year by beating Gabriela Sabatini 6-3, 3-6, 6-1 to clinch the US Open. It was only the second time in this year's four major tournaments — Australia, France, Wimbledon and the US — that she had dropped a set.

Miss Graf, who is still only 19, blamed the wind rather than nerves for a slightly below par performance, although her Argentinian opponent proved a worthy rival.

Previous winners of the Grand Slam are Donald Budge (1938), Maureen Connolly (1953), Rod Laver (1962 and 1969) and Margaret Court (1970).

Steffi Graf of West Germany looks very pleased by her win.

Isabel leads exiles back to Chile

Sept 2. Isabel Allende, daughter of the former president of Chile, flew back to Santiago today within hours of the lifting of the ban on political exiles' return. Jose Oyarce, a communist who was minister of labour in the Allende government, returned on the same flight.

It was an emotional return for Miss Allende who was put on a plane and flown to Mexico after the coup 15 years ago in which her father died, gun in hand, in the smoking ruins of the presidential palace.

The exiles were allowed to return by strongman General Pinochet as a conciliatory measure before next month's plebiscite in which he will seek re-election (→6/10).

Returning from a long exile.

Cosmonauts are stranded in space

Sept 6. A Soviet spacecraft, with a Russian and an Afghan cosmonaut on board, is orbiting the earth at a height of about 200 miles after the failure of two attempts at bringing it back to earth. Supplies vital for life support are running low.

Vladimir Lyakhov and Abdul Ahad Mohmand blasted off from Baikonur on August 31 and then docked with the Mir space station.

Later they re-entered a Soyuz spacecraft for their return journey to earth. One attempt at coming out of orbit was blocked by the spacecraft's computer when a sensor was fooled by rays from the sun, a second when the engines switched off early. The Soviets say that nothing is seriously wrong (→7).

Flood waters devastate Bangladesh

Sept 4. Bangladesh, once described by Dr Kissinger as "a basket case", has once again been struck by an appalling natural disaster, with more than 20 million people being made homeless in one of the most serious floods even by that disaster-prone country's standards.

Two-thirds of the land is under water, at least a quarter of this season's crops have been washed away, roads and dykes have been breached, the international airport cannot be used and even the British-built railways, constructed three feet above the estimated high water mark, are now under feet of water.

The damage to the infrastructure of the country will cost millions of pounds to repair, but before that can even be contemplated, emergency help is urgently needed. Some 300 people have already died and it is estimated that many more will be infected by diseases from contaminated wells.

As the extent of the disaster became apparent today, representa-

The streets of Dhaka, the capital city, are covered in flood waters.

tives of the nations already engaged in relief work in Bangladesh held meetings with government officials to draw up a list of priorities.

The main problem is going to be getting the aid to where it is most needed. Mahabur Rahmanthe, the

information minister, is appealing for helicopters to distribute emergency relief. He said: "We are hoping for an inspired response. No other country in the region has suffered so much damage from natural calamity." (→16)

Weak Brezhnev "all but dead" in final six years

Sept 7. A gruesome account of the last years of Leonid Brezhnev appears today in a Moscow newspaper just as the trial gets under way of the Soviet dictator's son-in-law, Yuri Churbanov, accused of corruption.

According to the Soviet historian Roy Medvedev, physicians diagnosed Brezhnev as clinically dead after a massive stroke in 1976. They managed to revive him, but it was three months before he was able to think or speak with any degree of normality. Even then he could not properly understand what was going on around him. For the next six years, until his death in 1982, doctors equipped with revival kits never left his side.

The Churbanov trial is intended not only to discredit Brezhnev by exposing corruption he allowed to flourish, but to warn corrupt officials to mend their ways (→16).

Burmese demos drive out diplomats

Sept 8. Diplomats' families were evacuated from Rangoon today as mobs rampaged through the Burmese capital, sacking government buildings and looting factories and warehouses.

Army trucks carrying soldiers with itchy trigger fingers patrolled the streets, carrying out the threat made on Rangoon radio that they

would open fire "to impose control" on looters. The stage seems set for more violence as the government prepares for a nationwide strike and what the protesters hope will be the largest demonstrations yet. In an ultimatum tonight they demanded the resignation of President Maung and the holding of democratic elections (→11).

Visa row could stump Indian cricket tour

Sept 9. Half the English cricket team chosen to tour India this winter will be denied visas because of their past sporting links with South Africa, it was announced in New Delhi tonight.

Although talks are promised between the cricket authorities, neither country expects the tour to take place, leaving cricket poised on

the brink of a split on racial lines. The tour has been in jeopardy ever since Graham Gooch was chosen as England captain. Not only did Gooch captain a "rebel" tour of South Africa in 1982, but he was due to play there again this winter. Seven other players in the tour party have played or coached in South Africa (→16).

Buddhist monks join the demonstrations against the government.

"Last Temptation of Christ" has a stormy start to its London run (→28).

September

1988

Su	Mo	Tu	We	Th	Fr	Sa
				1	2	3
4	5	6	7	8	9	10
11	12	13	14	15	16	17
18	19	20	21	22	23	24
25	26	27	28	29	30	

11. Walsall: Anthony Haskett goes on a gun rampage, shooting three people before killing himself.

11. Burma: The government votes to dismantle the one-party political system (→19).

12. Mozambique: South African premier P.W. Botha holds peace talks with President Joaquim Chissano (→17/10).

12. Geneva: The International Amateur Athletics Association says Ben Johnson jumped the gun at last year's World Championships in Rome (→24).

12. UK: The postal strike, estimated to have delayed 150 million letters, ends.

13. West Germany: Rudolf Cordes returns from being held hostage in Beirut (→20).

14. UK: Crime figures show an overall drop in crime but a sharp rise in sexual and violent offences (→4/10).

14. Oslo: Scotland beat Norway 2-1 in a World Cup qualifying match.

14. Paris: Air France fires the pilot of the Airbus A320 which crashed at an airshow in June.

15. UK: Inflation is now running at 5.7 per cent (→16).

15. Australia: The Supreme Court quashes the murder convictions of Lindy and Michael Chamberlain in the "dingo baby" case.

15. UK: Home Secretary Douglas Hurd says the Independent Broadcasting Authority is superfluous (→9/10).

16. Moscow: Gorbachev proposes the scrapping of US and Soviet bases in the Pacific (→22).

16. UK: The government warns workers not to use high inflation as a basis for high wage claims (→20).

17. Seoul: The Olympic flame is lit at the stadium (→24).

DEATHS

12. British illustrator Roger Hargreaves, creator of the *Mister Men* (*1935).

17. British politician John Alec Biggs-Davison (*7/6/18).

Bus hijack gun battle mars Papal tour

Sept 14. A furious gun battle between security forces and a gang holding 70 Roman Catholics hostage in a bus marred Pope John Paul II's visit to Lesotho today. The Pope had travelled there from Johannesburg where his plane had been diverted because of bad weather. Ironically, the Pope had pointedly omitted South Africa from his itinerary.

When the Pope reached Lesotho, he found South African commandos storming the hijacked bus, which had crashed into the British High Commission. The hostage gang, who claimed to be anti-government guerrillas, had demanded a meeting with the Pope. Four of the gang and a girl of 14 hit by crossfire were killed (→11/10).

The Pope visits Swaziland.

Charles slams purveyors of violent films

Sept 15. Prince Charles opened London's new Museum of the Moving Image today with a speech attacking the "incessant menu of utterly gratuitous violence" on cinema and television screens, comparing it with the standards which used to exist in film-making. "Those of us with children are very concerned by the appalling lack of restraint shown by those who make such films and videos," he declared. "I hope people won't think he means the films we are showing," said Sir Richard Attenborough.

MOMI, as the new museum is known, contains more than 100 screens showing clips of film, from magic lantern shows and the Lumiere cinematograph to *Star Wars*. On show are Charlie Chaplin's hat, cane and contract with Keystone, Fred Astaire's tails and Marilyn Monroe's shimmying dress worn in *Some Like It Hot*, for which the museum bid almost £20,000 at auction this year.

The Museum cost £12 million to put together. Its biggest benefactor is J. Paul Getty Jnr (→28/10).

His Royal Highness did not like what he saw — and said so.

Envoys expelled in London gun affray

Sept 13. The Cuban Ambassador and one of his envoys were expelled today after shots were fired in a London street. The shooting incident followed what seems to have been a bungled attempt by MI5 to woo the Cuban Third Secretary Carlos Manuel Medina Perez.

Cuba claims that a Cuban defector to the west, accompanied by three MI5 agents, approached Medina Perez outside his Bayswater flat and "in a menacing way instructed (him) to defect". Frightened for his life, the envoy pulled out his gun and fired, injuring an MI5 officer, before running off. The police have offered no alternative version of events.

Film veterans bring burlesque to stage

Miller + Rooney = a great team.

Sept 14. Two veterans of Hollywood, Mickey Rooney, aged 67, and Ann Miller, who is 65, began previews at the Savoy Theatre in London last night in "Sugar Babies", a Broadway hit that has run for nine years. It recreates an old-style American burlesque show in all its raunchy vulgarity.

Rooney, in a set of monstrous wigs, exhibits his vaudeville timing — he was a child performer in burlesque before he went into films as Andy Hardy. Miss Miller dances three exhausting numbers with machine-like precision.

"Gilbert" causes havoc in Caribbean

Sept 16. The nightmare of Hurricane Gilbert continues tonight, after the western world's worst storm this century swung away from Texas to lash the coast of Mexico for the second time. Hundreds of thousands of people have been made homeless and damage costs are estimated at several billion dollars since September 10, when the storm became a hurricane.

The serious devastation started in Dominica, where flood waters killed 11 people and wrecked roads and farmland. In Haiti, 29 people died including ten who drowned when their boat was swamped. The harbour at the port of Jacmel was simply washed away by tidal waves, wind and rain.

Gilbert then moved on to Venezuela, where torrential rain brought mudslides and floods. In Jamaica, police have reported 36 deaths and half a million homeless; damage is estimated at $8,000 million and a state of emergency has been declared. The hurricane, blowing at 140 miles per hour, then swept through the Caribbean on to Mexico.

When it hit Mexico's Yucatan peninsula on Wednesday, at a staggering 175 miles per hour, the effects were like a massive bomb. Cars and lorries were swept off roads, large ships pushed right inland, buildings flattened and trees ripped out of the ground like darts out of a board. At least 26 people died and 20,000 were made homeless. However, the storm is beginning to weaken (→22/10).

The terrifying strength of the hurricane pushed this ship inland.

Yucatan peninsula in the centre of the storm in this satellite photograph.

Worcestershire are cricket champions

Sept 16. Worcestershire today rounded off the 1988 English cricket season by winning the county championship by a single point from Kent. The race for the title was only decided on the final day of the season when Worcestershire beat Glamorgan by an innings and 76 runs. Appropriately, it was Graeme Hick who starred for the new county champions, hitting 197 to end the season much as he began it with his record-breaking 1,000 runs in May.

Serbs march for freedom in Yugoslavia

Sept 15. Mass Serbian demonstrations are threatening the stability of communist Yugoslavia's increasingly shaky federation of six ethnic republics and two provinces. Today they staged a rally of some 20,000 people outside Belgrade to protest against the persecution of Serbs by ethnic Albanians in the province of Kosovo. The rally took place as government ministers left for Kosovo in an attempt to defuse the ethnic tensions in the province.

Kosovo, once the home of Serbian culture, where a Serbian king ruled for two centuries, is today populated by 1.7 million ethnic Albanians and only 200,000 Serbs. But many Yugoslavs fear that the Serbian Communist Party leader, Slobodan Milosevic, is exploiting the tensions in Kosovo in a bid to win power at the national level. Serbs make up 40 per cent of Yugoslavia's 23 million population, and Milosevic is appealing not only to Serbian nationalism, but also to the general resentment at economic disorder, with annual inflation soaring to 200 per cent. It was the Serbs who organised strikes and mass rallies against a wage freeze (→22).

Bangladesh floods toll exceeds 1,300

Sept 16. The death toll in the Bangladesh flood disaster is now 1330, and disease is threatening to kill thousands more among the homeless millions who are living in the most squalid conditions with only contaminated water to drink.

Some 500,000 people are already reported to be suffering from intestinal diseases, and it is feared that many of the malnourished children could be blinded by vitamin deficiency unless help reaches them soon.

Many areas are still cut off, except by boat or helicopter, with lorries trapped on islands of dry roadway between the flooded areas. It will be some days yet before the aid gets through.

Bloated nudes win retrospective view

Sept 17. Henry Moore's sculpture, once denounced by a president of the Royal Academy, Sir Alfred Munnings, as "bloated, heavyweight nudes with knobs in place of heads", took over the Academy's galleries today in a retrospective exhibition of 120 of his works. It was planned as a 90th birthday tribute but Moore died in 1986.

"Being an institution almost beyond criticism for nearly half his long life did not do Moore any good," wrote one critic. His early work is admired the most.

Sept 13. Cyril Smith, the SLD MP for Rochdale, prepares to receive his knighthood on Nov 2.

Su	Mo	Tu	We	Th	Fr	Sa
				1	2	3
4	5	6	7	8	9	10
11	12	13	14	15	16	17
18	19	20	21	22	23	24
25	26	27	28	29	30	

18. Haiti: A military coup, led by Prosper Avril, ousts premier Henri Namphy.

19. Torquay: At the SDP conference, leader David Owen launches a crusade for proportional representation.

19. Japan: Emperor Hirohito has an emergency blood transfusion.

19. Poland: Prime minister Zbigniew Messner resigns, a scapegoat of the recent wave of strikes (→26).

20. Beirut: a car bomb kills five people on the eve of the presidential elections (→22).

20. UK: The mortgage rate rises to 12.75 per cent (→27).

21. Reading: Junior Health Minister Edwina Currie tells pensioners to wrap up warm this winter.

21. Pakistan: Opposition leader Benazir Bhutto gives birth to a seven-pound boy (→2/10).

21. UK: Minorco, a South African-controlled investment firm, makes a controversial bid for Consolidated Goldfields (→29).

22. North Sea: One person is feared dead after a blow out at the *Ocean Odyssey* oil rig (→23).

22. Lebanon: General Michel Aoud replaces Amin Gemayel as President.

23. UK: A newly-discovered planet is named "Len Carter" after the secretary of the British Interplanetary Society.

23. North Sea: The *Ocean Odyssey* is cut free of its moorings to enable firefighters to attack the blaze (→29).

24. Abingdon: Two RAF pilots die in a crash while practising for an air display.

24. London: Camden Council bans *Whizzer & Chips* comic and Enid Blyton books as ideologically unsound.

DEATHS

20. British actor Roy Kinnear (*8/1/34).→

21. British actress and post-war sex symbol Christine Norden (Mary Lydia Thornton) (*28/12/24).

Russian tanks smash Armenian rioters

Soviet tanks roll in to Yerevan as ethnic violence flares.

Sept 22. Moscow has sent in the tanks again in an attempt to quell unrest in Armenia, where strikes and demonstrations have paralysed the capital, Yerevan, for the past week. Trouble flared when reports reached Yerevan of anti-Armenian attacks in the neighbouring republic of Azerbaijan, where a gang stormed a busload of Armenian students.

In the battle that followed, 49 people — 33 Armenians and 16 Azerbaijanis — were injured and one man, still unidentified, was killed, according to a Soviet official spokesman. Houses and cars were set on fire, and the situation is becoming more threatening.

Only recently were Armenia and Azerbaijan reopened to foreign reporters — a sign that Moscow believed the situation was calm. Now visits have been banned again and a night-time curfew has been ordered. Moscow denies that a state of emergency has been imposed, but admits that "special measures" are in force. The strikes and protest marches have continued in Yerevan despite the authorities' show of force. The unrest is the most widespread since last February, when 32 people were killed in clashes (→30).

Belgrade talks of Politburo sackings

Sept 22. The Serbian leadership is stepping up the pressure on Yugoslavia's Communist Party Politburo by staging mass demonstrations in protest at what is claimed to be the persecution of Serbs in the province of Kosovo, where ethnic Albanians are in a majority. Thousands of Serbs flee from Kosovo every year and tell of repeated attacks by Albanians.

The first sign that the Serbs might be winning came when a Belgrade newspaper today quoted a Politburo member as saying that when the Politburo meets next month to examine the Serb-Albanian crisis, some members may be sacked. The Serbian Communist Party boss, Slobodan Milosevic, is seeking more power over Kosovo to protect his people there (→25).

Yugoslavia's Serbs march for freedom in Kosovo province.

US Anglicans elect first woman bishop

Sept 24. More trouble in the Church of England over women priests is certain after the election tonight of the first woman bishop in the US Anglican Church. The Rev. Barbara Harris was elected on the eighth ballot. She said she hoped to use "her peculiar gifts as a black woman and as a woman priest".

The Church of England is walking a tightrope, moving slowly towards women priests while trying to keep clergy who dislike the idea within the church. The prospect of a woman bishop may well stir up their opposition.

First of her kind: Barbara Harris.

100 shot dead in fresh Burma demo

Sept 19. The Burmese army, which seized power yesterday, has clamped a heavy hand on Rangoon. Protesters are being met with gunfire and at least 100 people have been shot dead. So many have been hurt that the Burmese Red Cross today asked western embassies for vehicles to carry them to hospital.

One eye-witness said: "There are bodies everywhere. Sometimes it is hard to know who is dead and who is alive." The protesters are refusing to give up, despite their casualties, and tonight General Maung, the leader of the new regime, said grimly: "It is going to be a war of attrition." (→27)

Identikit Europeans are folly, says PM

No to a European federation.

Sept 21. Mrs Thatcher, on a brief continental tour, today continued her personal offensive against a federalist Europe. She told a Luxembourg audience: "A centralised European government would be a nightmare." And in Bruges last night she said: "It would be folly to fit us all into the same sort of identikit European personality."

Mrs Thatcher was asked if she minded being compared for awkwardness with the late President de Gaulle. The Prime Minister replied: "I believe that he was quite a formidable figure." (→18/10)

Sept 20. Roy Kinnear dies after an accident. His bluster, fluster and dogged optimism have left their mark on British comedy.

Johnson leads the Olympic gold rush

Sept 24. Ben Johnson is the world's fastest human being. He scorched down the 100 metre track at the Seoul Olympics today in 9.79 seconds, shattering not only his own world record but also the hopes of America's Carl Lewis. The 1984 champion was second, with Linford Christie of Britain third.

Johnson's emphatic victory was all the more remarkable because he had seemed below his best form this season, even finishing only third in a second-round heat on Thursday. Last year, when he beat Lewis in the World championships, his electric reactions to the starter's gun prompted some to say he had got a flyer. Today, however, there appeared to be no doubts and Lewis was the first to congratulate the Jamaican-born athlete who now wears the Canadian vest.

For Christie, too, the race was a triumph: a bronze medal and the honour of becoming the first European to run the 100 metres in less than ten seconds (see full results on pages 82-83). For Britain, his success went some way to mitigate the disappointment caused by the failure of Steve Cram and Tom McKean to qualify in the heats of the 800 metres.

With the athletics events only just beginning, other sports have dominated the first week of the Olympics. For Britain, there has been no shortage of heroes with gold medals for Adrian Moorhouse in the 100 metres breaststroke, marksman Malcolm Cooper in the small-bore rifle competition and rowers, Steve Redgrave and Andrew Holmes in the coxless pairs.

In global terms, the stars of the first week have been the swimmers Kristen Otto from East Germany (five golds) and Matt Biondi from America (four golds with one event still to come). New Zealand's Mark Todd retained the individual title in the three-day event competition on the aptly-named Charisma, while Greg Louganis of the United States became the first person to retain an Olympic springboard diving title.

For Louganis the competition required courage as well as skill. In one dive, he hit a board on his descent into the water. The injury required stitches, but Louganis came back to win the gold (→30).

Britain's Adrian Moorhouse celebrates his victory in the breaststroke.

Andrew Holmes and Steve Redgrave row to a gold in the coxless pairs.

L. to r.: Johnson, Christie and Lewis run for glory in the men's 100 metres. Johnson is confident his record will not be broken for fifty years.

September

1988

Su	Mo	Tu	We	Th	Fr	Sa
				1	2	3
4	5	6	7	8	9	10
11	12	13	14	15	16	17
18	19	20	21	22	23	24
25	26	27	28	29	30	

25. Yugoslavia: Serbians stage mass demonstrations against Albanians (→5/10).

25. US: George Bush and Michael Dukakis meet in the first televised debate of the presidential campaign (→5/10).

26. Poland: Mieczyslaw Rakowski is appointed Prime Minister (→31).

27. UK: Relief greets the news that the balance of payments deficit last month was only £1,300 million (→28).

27. Gibraltar: The inquest hears a claim that it was impossible for the IRA squad to detonate a bomb by radio (→30).

27. Seoul: Ben Johnson fails a second drugs test and is stripped of his gold medal. →

27. Wales: A little old lady attempts to rob a shop at gunpoint.

28. UK: Chancellor Nigel Lawson admits his current account deficit this year will approach £12,000 million (→4/10).

28. UK: Doctors blame a shortage of intensive care cots for the death of 2,000 babies a year.

28. Paris: Police use tear gas to disperse demonstrations against the opening of *The Last Temptation of Christ*.

29. Oslo: The United Nations peacekeeping forces win this year's Nobel Peace Prize.

29. UK: The serious fraud squad launches an inquiry into the takeover of Harrods by the Al-Fayed brothers (→4/10).

29. UK: An initial inquiry concludes that human error caused the Piper Alpha explosion in July.

30. UN: Britain and Iran resume full diplomatic relations.

30. Burma: At least 425 people have now been killed since General Maung staged his coup a fortnight ago (→4/10).

30. UK: Cattle in the West Country are threatened by the disease, bovine spongiform encephalopathy.

Inquest decides IRA gang lawfully killed

Sept 30. The SAS soldiers who shot and killed three IRA members in Gibraltar last March acted lawfully, the inquest jury decided tonight. The verdict was greeted with relief in Whitehall where the jury's eight hours of deliberations had caused some nervousness, particularly when it emerged that the 11-man jury was split. In the end, the verdict of lawful killing was upheld by a majority of nine to two.

The inquest had lasted 19 days, during which the Crown contended that the soldiers believed the IRA trio — Mairead Farrell, Daniel McCann and Sean Savage — had already planted a bomb. Giving evidence behind screens to protect their identities, the soldiers said they feared the three could set off the bomb by remote control. They also believed, wrongly as it turned out, that they were armed.

In fact, there was no bomb, although explosives were later found in Spain and the IRA admitted the three were part of an "active service unit". Lawyers for the families argued that there was a conspiracy to shoot them dead rather than try to arrest them. There was conflicting evidence as to whether warnings were given (→3/10).

Gromyko goes as Gorbachev wields axe

Gromyko (bottom centre) looks on as his colleagues vote him off.

Sept 30. At a hastily called meeting of the Soviet Communist Party's 300-member Central Committee, Mr Gorbachev today rid himself of remnants of Brezhnev's "era of stagnation", and demoted two prominent critics of his reforms. The President (and former Foreign Minister) Andrei Gromyko, a relic of Stalin's times, went into retirement.

Yegor Ligachev, the Politburo's arch-conservative, lost the key ideology job and was given the unpopular agriculture portfolio. Viktor Chebrikov, sacked as KGB chief, was made chairman of a new law commission. The meeting took place with Ligachev absent on holiday; it lasted less than an hour and votes were unanimous (→1/10).

"Discovery" puts US back in space race

Sept 29. The space shuttle *Discovery* soared in to orbit today, putting America back into the space race after a gap of nearly three years following the *Challenger* disaster in which seven astronauts died.

The launch of *Discovery* from Cape Canaveral went almost with-

out a hitch, apart from a surge in the pressure inside the cabin shortly before lift off which almost led to a postponement. The success of the launch is a profound relief to NASA. "It's good to back in space," commented its director, James Fletcher.

Burma's strongman is back in power

He's back: General Ne Win.

Sept 27. Uneasy peace has settled over Burma with the military government consolidating its hold throughout the country. Western diplomats see the hand of the former dictator General Ne Win behind last week's coup in which 500 died. Ne Win ruled Burma with eccentric ruthlessness for 26 years before his resignation in July after months of street protests against his rule. Now it seems that he is back in power, but most observers believe that opposition to the regime has become so strong that he will not be able to return to the bad old days. The Burmese have had a taste of democracy and will not give it up without a struggle (→30).

Democrats: a new name, a new aim

Sept 29. Paddy Ashdown made a fierce attack on "Thatcherist greed" in his first keynote speech as leader of the Social and Liberal Democrats today.

He told his party conference at Blackpool that their first aim must be to replace Labour as the main challenger to the Tories. Also they must shun coalitions and compromises. Mr Ashdown cried: "We are not rootless vagabonds. We are on our way to power."

Earlier the conference adopted "Democrats" as the new party's short title. Many old Liberals were upset about that.

Seoul '88: drug scandal tarnishes Olympic dream

Gold turned to ashes: Johnson passes through New York's JFK airport.

Disgraced Johnson stripped of gold

Sept 30. Ben Johnson, acclaimed as a hero when he set a world record winning the 100 metres last Saturday, is now the villain of world athletics. The fastest man on earth has been stripped of his gold medal after being found guilty of using drugs. Johnson has flown home to Canada in disgrace, but the scandal of drug-taking in sport has not ended with his departure.

Nine athletes have been disqualified from the Olympics in Seoul after failing drug tests. Among them is Britain's Kerrith Brown, who today lost his judo bronze medal. There was almost a tenth. Linford Christie, Britain's best-ever sprinter, had failed an initial test, but was cleared because laboratory analysts were unsure about the properties of ginseng, a herbal tonic, which he had been taking.

Ironically, Christie had gained from Johnson's disqualification since his bronze in the 100 metres final now becomes a silver. Some other athletes have also said that, ultimately, sport will gain from the exposure of those who cheat by taking drugs.

But never has anyone as famous as Johnson previously been caught in what are now routine drug tests for medallists. And never has a champion fallen so dramatically from glory to shame. Johnson, aged 26, has lost not only his gold medal but also the prospect of lucrative commercial deals which would have made him a dollar millionaire.

His world turned upside down within the space of 72 hours. Last Saturday he won the gold medal and set a world record of 9.79 seconds. In the afternoon he produced a urine sample. On Sunday the International Olympic Committee (IOC) was told that the test had revealed traces of Stanozol, an anabolic steroid which increases strength at the price of long-term risks to liver, kidneys and lungs. A second test on Monday confirmed this finding and, after consultations with the Canadian authorities, Johnson was stripped of his medal in the early hours of Tuesday morning. He now faces a life ban. →

Britain's Kerrith Brown failed a dope test and lost his judo bronze.

"Flo-Jo" becomes the new star as old heroes are eclipsed

Sept 30. The shadow of drugs and Ben Johnson dogged even the innocent in Seoul this week. Florence Griffith-Joyner, the American sprinter who won both the 100 and 200 metres, was greeted with rumours about drugs which were rebutted by tests. "Flo-Jo" won the 100 metres in a time which would have beaten the men in the 1952 Games.

If Flo-Jo was the brightest of the new stars, Seoul also saw the eclipse of older stars. Ed Moses failed to win the 400 metres hurdles and Daley Thompson could finish only fourth in the decathlon. Carl Lewis added the long jump to the 100 metres he won through Johnson's disqualification, but he was second in the 200 metres and watched in dismay as the US relay team was disqualified in a heat.

For Britain, there have been no golds as yet in the athletics stadium. Liz McColgan, Fatima Whitbread and Colin Jackson won silvers, though, and there were bronzes for Yvonne Murray and Mark Rowland. For golds, Britain had to look to Mike McIntyre and Bryn Vaile in the Star class yachting. Oarsmen Redgrave and Holmes added a bronze to the gold which they won last week (→2/10).

Flo-Jo: black, beautiful and fast.

Liz McColgan in the 10,000 metres.

Mike McIntyre and Bryn Vaile sail to a win in the Star class yachting.

October

1988

Su	Mo	Tu	We	Th	Fr	Sa
						1
2	3	4	5	6	7	8
9	10	11	12	13	14	15
16	17	18	19	20	21	22
23	24	25	26	27	28	29
30	31					

1. USSR: Mikhail Gorbachev is appointed president (→2).

1. UK: Barristers are warned that their monopoly will soon be over.

2. Tallinn: The Estonian . Popular Front meets for the first time and demands independence from the USSR (→9).

3. Belfast: Republican gunmen shoot dead an alleged police informer.

4. UK: Nine million workers are earning less than the European Commission's minimum decent wage (→6).

4. UK: The government orders Kuwait to cut its stake in British Petroleum from 21.6 per cent to 9.9 per cent (→5).

4. Rangoon: Troops shoot 12 people dead as unrest continues.

5. UK: 35,000 illegal firearms have been handed in during an arms amnesty.

5. UK: The Monopolies Commission is to investigate petrol pricing and retailing.

6. UK: British Steel is to be privatised next month (→23/11).

6. UK: House prices have risen 34 per cent in the last 12 months (→27).

7. London: A quarter of the capital's active homosexuals are now HIV-positive, and could develop AIDS.

7. West Bank: Israelis shoot 4 dead and injure 27 (→14).

7. UK: A £1.7 million project is announced for research into the world "greenhouse effect".

DEATHS

1. British writer Sir Sacheverell Sitwell (*15/11/1897).

2. British car designer Sir Alexander Arnold Constantine Issigonis (*18/11/06).→

3. West German statesman Franz Josef Strauss (*6/9/15).

4. British writer Geoffrey Edward West Household (*30/11/1900).

8. British magazine publisher Sir Edward George Warris Hulton (*29/11/06).

Milosevic champions the Yugoslav Serbs

Striking motor factory workers besiege Belgrade's parliament building.

Oct 5. For the second day in succession, the Yugoslav parliament in Belgrade has been besieged by workers protesting at steeply falling living standards and demanding the resignation of the government. And for the second day also, the angry demonstrators dispersed after a speech by Slobodan Milosevic, the Serbian Communist Party leader, who is increasingly taking centre stage in the national crisis set off by economic chaos and ethnic conflicts. He told the crowds today: "You should have trust that we shall carry out reforms. If we lose your trust, you should turn us out."

In Vojvodina province, in north-central Yugoslavia, a crowd of 100,000 cheered when speakers demanded that Milosevic supporters replace local party leaders.

Labour conference ignores Kinnock

Oct 6. Labour's annual conference today ignored Neil Kinnock's wishes and reaffirmed the party's commitment to unilateral nuclear disarmament. In turn Mr Kinnock and his allies indicated that, if necessary, they will ignore it in framing their next election manifesto.

Labour's leader said: "There is another year of policy review and today's votes were not conclusive." Before delegates leave Blackpool tomorrow he will appeal to them again not to undermine his drive for power by refusing to ditch vote-losing ideas.

Earlier in the week Mr Kinnock thought wrongly that he had the conference behind him when he explained: "The kind of economy we are faced with is going to be a market economy and we have got to make it work better than the Tories."

Socialist hard-liners denounced this as "revisionism and surrender to capitalism". The fight for the soul of the party continues and a bigger split is on the cards for next year's conference.

Britain nets a hockey gold, but Cram misses out on a medal

Oct 2. The 24th Modern Olympiad ended today in Seoul with Italy's Gelindo Bordin breaking Africa's stranglehold on the men's running events by winning the marathon. No such joy for Steve Cram, however: he finished fourth in the men's 1,500 metres behind Kenya's Peter Rono, with Britain's Peter Elliott in second place.

Britain also won a silver in the men's 4 x 100 metres relay with Linford Christie running after being cleared of drug charges. The British men's hockey team went one better by winning the gold medal, beating West Germany by three goals to one. More predictably, Steffi Graf won the women's gold in tennis, an Olympic sport again after a gap of 64 years (→15).

Peter Rono leads Peter Elliott in the men's 1,500 metres final.

Britain win the men's hockey.

Bentsen tells JDQ: you are no JFK

Oct 5. The Democrat, Lloyd Bentsen, was seen as the winner over J. Danforth Quayle in tonight's television debate between the two vice-presidential candidates. But his success is not thought to have done serious harm to the chances of the Republican candidate for the US presidency, George Bush. Bentsen's most effective riposte in the 90-minute debate came when Senator Quayle, countering charges that he lacks experience, said he had served in Congress as long as "Jack Kennedy did when he sought the presidency". "Senator," said Bentsen, "you are no Jack Kennedy." (→ 13)

Debate-winner Lloyd Bentsen.

Rioters smash Algiers in prices protest

Rioters in Algiers rise up against the Bendjedid regime.

Oct 5. Price rises sent young agitators rampaging in protest through the streets of Algiers today. They smashed shop windows and attacked government-owned department stores, while the police looked on, taking no action.

Black smoke rose over the city as schoolboys and university students set fire to cars. The offices of Lufthansa and the Czech airline CSA were wrecked.

Government sources said that the rioters had been manipulated into a state of revolt, but the source of the trouble lies in the food shortages, rising prices and austerity measures introduced by the government of President Chadli Bendjedid. Algeria has been hit badly by the slump in oil prices but, instead of attempting to reschedule its debts, estimated by foreign bankers to be as high as $23 billion, the government has slashed imports.

The official APS news agency reported this week: "It is only by more stringent austerity measures and greater rigour in spending and increased management efficiency that the country will attain its aims." This may make economic sense, but it does not help the poor people of Algiers who cannot afford to buy bread and meat — if they can find a shop selling them. The situation is explosive and full of danger for the Chadli government (→ 12).

Chile election votes Pinochet out

Oct 6. General Augusto Pinochet, the Chilean strongman, has been defeated in his attempt to win another eight years of power and tonight the capital, Santiago, is full of people celebrating the end of 15 years of military dictatorship.

The cabinet resigned this morning and when the news spread a flag-waving, chanting crowd marched past the presidential palace where President Salvador Allende made his last stand against the military and which has since been the seat of the junta's power. It remains to be seen if General Pinochet will respect the voters' decision.

The junta gets the thumbs down.

Issigonis, inventor of the Mini, dies

Oct 2. Sir Alec Issigonis, whose creations for Morris Motors revolutionised British motoring in the post-war decades, died today.

The Morris Minor, launched in 1948 and still a cult car, was typical of his approach: "I designed the whole car myself — even the little knob that opens the glove box," he said. But he will be remembered above all for the Mini, launched in 1959 and still in production today, several million models later. Huge space savings were made by combining the engine and gearbox, then mounting them sideways under the bonnet. He scorned the sceptics: "An expert is someone who tells you why you can't do something," he said.

Sir Alec Issigonis poses with his famous and well-loved creation.

Three hundred die in Pakistan riots

Oct 2. Violent clashes have again erupted in Karachi and Hyderabad between local Sindhis and the Muhajir people who have their origins in India. The trouble broke out again when masked Sindhi gunmen opened fire on a crowd in Hyderabad; then it spread to Karachi, where troops were called out.

At the height of the disturbances rioters of both communities attacked each others' homes, set ambulances on fire and ransacked shops. Gunmen fired from rooftops in Hyderabad at people buying food during a brief break in the curfew. It is feared that as many as 300 people have been killed.

Angry Sara Keays stops Tebbit's book

Oct 7. Sara Keays won a temporary injunction in the high court today, banning publication of certain passages in the autobiography of Norman Tebbit, the ex-cabinet minister.

These relate to Mr Tebbit's comments about a settlement between Miss Keays and Cecil Parkinson, now the energy secretary, the father of her daughter Flora, aged four. Mr Parkinson, a former chairman of the Conservative Party, resigned from the cabinet in 1983 when he was industry secretary.

1988 Seoul

Men Athletics

100m
1. Carl Lewis USA 9"92
2. Linford Christie GBR 9"97
3. Calvin Smith USA 9"99

200m
1. Joe DeLoach USA 19"75
2. Carl Lewis USA 19"79
3. Robson Da Silva BRA 20"04

400m
1. Steven Lewis USA 43"87
2. Butch Reynolds USA 43"93
3. Danny Everett USA 44"09

800m
1. Paul Ereng KEN 1'43"45
2. Joaquim Cruz BRA 1'43"90
3. Said Aouita MOR 1'44"06

1,500m
1. Peter Rono KEN 3'35"96
2. Peter Elliott GBR 3'36"15
3. Jens-Peter Herold GDR 3'36"21

5,000m
1. John Ngugi KEN 13'11"70
2. Dieter Baumann FRG 13'15"52
3. Hans Joerg Kunze GDR 13'15"73

10,000m
1. M. Brahim Boutaieb MOR 27'21"46
2. Salvatore Antibo ITA 27'23"55
3. Kipkemboi Kimeli KEN 27'25"16

3,000m Steeplechase
1. Julius Kariuki KEN 8'05"51
2. Peter Koech KEN 8'06"79
3. Mark Rowland GBR 8'07"96

110m Hurdles
1. Roger Kingdom USA 12"99
2. Colin Jackson GBR 13"28
3. Tony Campbell USA 13"38

400m Hurdles
1. Andre Phillips USA 47"19
2. El Hadj Dia Ba SEN 47"23
3. Edwin Moses USA 47"56

High Jump
1. Guennadi Adveienko URS 2,38m
2. Hollis Conway USA 2,36m
3. Rudolf Povarnitsine URS 2,36m
Patrick Sjoeberg SWE 2,36m

Long Jump
1. Carl Lewis USA 8,72m
2. Mike Powell USA 8,49m
3. Larry Myricks USA 8,27m

Pole Vault
1. Serguei Bubka URS 5,90m
2. Rodion Gatauline URS 5,85m
3. Grigori Yevgorov URS 5,80m

Triple Jump
1. Christo Markov BUL 17,61m
2. Igor Lapchine URS 17,52m
3. Alexandre Kovalenko URS 17,42m

Shotput
1. Ulf Timmermann GDR 22,47m
2. Randy Barnes USA 22,39m
3. Werner Gunthoer SUI 21,99m

Discus
1. Jurgen Schult GDR 68,82m
2. Romas Ubartas URS 67,48m
3. Rolf Danneberg FRG 67,38m

Hammer
1. Serguei Litvinov URS 84,80m
2. Youri Sedykh URS 83,76m
3. Youri Tamn URS 81,16m

Javelin
1. Tapio Korjus FIN 84,28m
2. Jan Zelezny TCH 84,12m
3. Seppo Raty FIN 83,26m

Marathon
1. Gelindo Bordin ITA 2 h 10'32"
2. Douglas Wakihuru KEN 2 h 10'47"
3. Ahmed Salah DJI 2 h 10'59"

Decathlon
1. Christian Schenk GDR 8 488 pts
2. Torsten Voss GDR 8 399 pts
3. Dave Steen CAN 8 328 pts

4 x 100m Relay
1. URS 38"19 (Bryzguin, Krylov, Mouraziev, Savin)
2. GBR 38"28 (Bunney, Regis, McFarlane, Christie)
3. FRA 38"40 (Marie-Rose, Sangouma, Queneherve, Moniere)

4 x 400m Relay
1. USA 2'58"16 (Everett, S. Lewis, Robinzine, Reynolds)
2. JAM 3'00"30 (Davis, Morris, Graham, Cameron)
3. FRG 3'00"56 (Dobeleit, Itt, Vaihinger, Luebke)

20km Walk
1. Jozef Pribilinec TCH 1 h 19'57"
2. Ronald Weigel GDR 1 h 20'00"
3. Maurizio Damilano ITA 1 h 20'14"

50km Walk
1. Vlasheslav Ivanenko URS 3 h 38'29"
2. Ronald Weigel GDR 3 h 38'56"
3. Hartwig Gauder GDR 3 h 39'45"

Women Athletics

100m
1. Florence Griffith-Joyner USA 10"54
2. Evelyne Ashford USA 10"83
3. Heike Drechsler GDR 10"85

200m
1. Florence Griffith-Joyner USA 21"34 (world rec.; prev. rec. 21"71 by Koch and by Drechsler)
2. Grace Jackson JAM 21"72
3. Heike Drechsler GDR 21"95

400m
1. Olga Brysguina URS 48"65
2. Petra Mueller GDR 49"45
3. Olga Nazarova URS 49"90

800m
1. Sigrun Wodars GDR 1'56"10
2. Christine Wachtel GDR 1'56"64
3. Kim Gallagher USA 1'56"91

1,500m
1. Paula Ivan ROM 3'53"96
2. Lailoute Baikauskaite URS 4'00"20
3. Tatiana Samoilenko URS 4'00"24

3,000m
1. Tatiana Samoilenko URS 8'26"53
2. Paula Ivan ROM 8'27"15
3. Yvonne Murray GBR 8'29"02

10,000m
1. Olga Bondarenko URS 31'05"21
2. Elizabeth McColgan GBR 31'08"34
3. Helena Joupieva URS 31'19"82

100m Hurdles
1. Jordanka Donkova BUL 12"38
2. Gloria Siebert GDR 12"61
3. Claudia Zaskiewicz FRG 12"75

400m Hurdles
1. Debbie Flintoff-King AUS 53"17
2. Tatiana Ledovskaia URS 53"18
3. Helen Fiedler GDR 53"84

High Jump
1. Louise Ritter USA 2,03m
2. Stefka Kostadinova BUL 2,01m
3. Tamara Bykova URS 1,99m

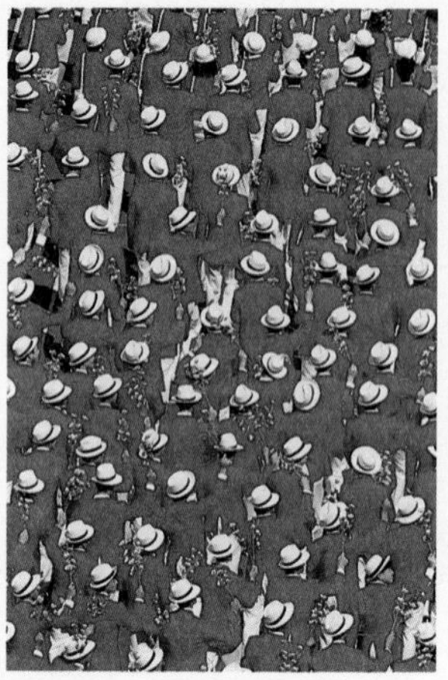

Opening ceremony.

Long Jump
1. Jackie Joyner-Kersee USA 7,40m
2. Heike Drechsler GDR 7,22m
3. Galina Tchistyakova URS 7,11m

Shotput
1. Natalia Lissovskaia URS 22,24m
2. Kathrin Neimke GDR 21,07m
3. Meisu-li CHN 21,06m

Discus
1. Martina Hellman GDR 72,30m
2. Diana Gansky GDR 71,88m
3. Tzvetanka Hristova BUL 69,74m

Javelin
1. Petra Felke GDR 74,68m
2. Fatima Whitbread GBR 70,32m
3. Beate Koch GDR 67,30m

4 x 100m Relay
1. USA 41"98 (Brown, Echols, Griffith-Joyner, Ashford)
2. GDR 42"09 (Moller, Behrendt, Lange, Gohr)
3. URS 42"75 (Kondratieva, Maltschugina, Jirova, Pomochtchnikova)

4 x 400m Relay
1. URS 3'15"18 World rec.; prev. rec. 3'15"92 (Ledovskaia, Nazarov, Piniguina, Bryzguina)
2. USA 3'15"51 (Howard, Dixon, Brisco, Griffith-Joyner)
3. GDR 3'18"29 (Neubauer, Emmelmann, Busch, Muller)

Heptathlon
1. Jackie Joyner-Kersee USA 7 291 pts (World rec.; own prev. rec. 7 215 pts)
2. Sabine John GDR 6 897 pts
3. Anke Behmer GDR 6 858 pts

Marathon
1. Rosa Mota POR 2 h 25'40"
2. Lisa Martin NZL 2 h 25'53"
3. Kathrin Doerre GDR 2 h 26'21"

Men Rowing

Sculls
1. Thomas Lange GDR 6'49"86
2. Peter-Michael Kolbe FRG 6'54"77
3. Eric Verdonck NZL 6'58"66

Coxed Pairs
1. G. Abbagnale, C. Abbagnale ITA 6'58"79
2. M. Streit, D. Kirch GDR 7'00"63
3. S. Redgrave, A. Holme GBR 7'01"95

Double Sculls
1. R. Florijn, N. Rienks HOL 6'21"13
2. B. Schwerzmann, U. Bodenmann GDR 6'22"59
3. A. Martchenko, V. Iakoucha URS 6'22"87

Coxless Pairs
1. A. Holmes, S. Redgrave GBR 6'36"94
2. D. Neagu, D. Dobre ROM 6'38"06
3. B. Presern, S. Mujkic YUG 6'41"01

Coxless Fours
1. GDR 6'10"74 (K. Schmeling, B. Niezecke, B. Eichwurzel, F. Flawonn)
2. ROM 6'13"58 (V. Tomoiaga, V. Robu, I. Snep, D. Popescu)
3. NZL 6'15"78 (I. Whight, G. Johnston, C. White, G. Keys)

Quadruple Sculls (Coxed)
1. ITA 5'53"37 (A. Abbagnale, D. Tizzano, G. Farina, P. Poli)
2. NOR 5'55"08 (A. Hansen, R. Rhorsen, V. Vinjer, L. Bjonness)
3. GDR 5'56"13 (J. Koeppen, H. Habermann, S. Zuehlke, S. Bogs)

Quadruple Sculls (Coxless)
1. GDR 6'03"11 (O. Foerster, R. Brudel, T. Greiner, R. Schroeder)
2. USA 6'05"53 (R. Kennelly, D. Krmpotich, T. Bohrer, R. Rodriguez)
3. FRG 6'06"22 (V. Grabow, J. Puttlitz, G. Grabow, N. Kesslau)

Eights
1. GDR 5'46"05 (T. Moellenkamp, M. Mellinghaus, E. Schultz, A. Wessling, A. Eichholz, T. Domian, W. Maenning, B. Rabe)
2. URS 5'48"01 (V. Bout, N. Komarov, V. Tikhanov, A. Doumtchev, P. Gourkovski, V. Didouk, V. Omelianovitch, A. Vassiliev)
3. USA 5'48"26 (M. Teti, J. Smith, T. Patton, J. Rusher, P. Nordell, J. McLaughlin, D. Burden, J. Pescatore)

Women Rowing

Sculls
1. Jutta Behrendt GDR 7'47"19
2. Anne Marden USA 7'50"28
3. Magdalena Gueorguieva BUL 7'53"65

Coxless Pairs
1. O. Homeghi, R. Arba ROM 7'28"13
2. L. Berberova, R. Stoyanova BUL 7'31"95
3. L. Hannen, N. Payne NZL 7'35"68

Double Sculls
1. M. Schroeter, B. Peter GDR 7'00"48
2. V. Coeanu, E. Lipa ROM 7'04"36
3. S. Madina, V. Ninova BUL 7'06"03

Coxed Fours
1. GDR 6'56"00 (M. Walther, G. Doberschuetz, C. Hornig, B. Siech)
2. CHN 6'58"78 (S. Zhou, X. Yang, Y. Hu, X. Zhang)
3. ROM 7'01"13 (D.L. Balan, H. Anitas, V. Necula, M. Trasca)

Quadruple Sculls (Coxless)
1. GDR 6'21"06 (J. Sorgers, B. Schramm, K. Mundt, K. Foerster)
2. URS 6'23"47 (A. Doumtcheva, I. Frolova, S. Mazyi, I. Kalimbet)
3. ROM 6'23"81 (E. Lipa, V. Cogeanu, A. Minea, A. Balan)

Eights
1. GDR 6'15"17 (A. Strauch, J. Zeidler, K. Haacker,, U. Wild, A. Kluge, B. Schroer, R. Balthasar, U. Stange)
2. ROM 6'17"44 (D.L. Balan, M. Trasca, V. Necula, H. Anitas, A. Bazon, M. Armasescu, R. Arba, O. Homeghi)
3. CHN 6'21"83 (X. Zhou, Y. Zhang, Y. He, Y. Han, X. Zhang, S. Zhou, X. Yang)

Basketball

Men	Women
1. Soviet Union	1. United States
2. Yugoslavia	2. Yugoslavia
3. United States	3. Soviet Union

Boxing

48kg
1. Ivailo Hristov BUL
2. Michael Carbajal USA
3. Robert Isaszegi HON
Leopoldo Serantes PHI

51kg
1. Kwang-Sun Kim KOR
2. Andreas Tews GDR
3. Timofei Skriabin URS
Mario Gonzalez MEX

54kg
1. Kennedy McKinney USA
2. Alexandar Hristov BUL
3. Phajol Moolsan THA
Jorge Julio Rocha COL

57kg
1. Giovanni Parisi ITA
2. Daniel Dumitrescu ROM
3. Abdelhack Achik MOR
Lee Jae-hyuk KOR

60kg
1. Andreas Zuelow GDR
2. George Cramne SWE
3. Nerguy Enkhbat MGL
Romallis Ellis USA

63.5kg
1. Viatcheslav Janovski URS
2. Graham Cheney AUS
3. Lars Myrberg SWE
Reiner Gies FRG

67kg
1. Robert Wangila KEN
2. Laurent Boudouani FRA
3. Jan Dydak POL
Kenneth Gould USA

71kg
1. Park Si-Hun KOR
2. Roy Jones USA
3. Raymond Downey CAN
Richard Woodhall GBR

75kg
1. Henry Maske GDR
2. Egerton Marcus CAN
3. Chris Sande KEN
Hussain Shad Syed PAK

81kg
1. Andrew Maynard USA
2. Nourmagomed Chanavazov URS
3. Henryk Petrich POL
Damir Skaro YUG

91kg
1. Ray Mercer USA
2. Baik Hyun-Man KOR
3. Arnold Vanderlijde HOL
Andrzej Golota POL

More than 95kg
1. Lennox Lewis CAN
2. Riddick Bowe USA
3. Janusz Zarenkiewicz POL
Alexandre Mirochnitchenko URS

Men Canoeing

Canadian-1 (500m)
1. Olaf Heukrodt GDR 1'56"42
2. Mikhail Slivinskii URS 1'57"26
3. Martin Marinov BUL 1'57"27

Canadian-2 (500m)
1. V. Reineski, N. Jouravski URS 1'41"77
2. M. Dopierala, M. Lbik POL 1'43"61
3. P. Renaud, J. Bettin FRA 1'43"81

Canadian-1 (1,000m)
1. Ivan Klementiev URS 4'12"78
2. Joerg Schmidt GDR 4'15"83
3. Nikolai Boohlov BUL 4'18"94

Canadian-2 (1,000m)
1. V. Reineski, N. Jouravski URS 3'48"36
2. O. Heukrodt, I. Spelly GDR 3'51"44
3. M. Dopierala, M. Lbik POL 3'54"33

Kayak-1 (500m)
1. Zsolt Gyulay HUN 1'44"82
2. Andreas Staehle GDR 1'46"38
3. Paul McDonald NZL 1'46"46

Kayak-2 (500m)
1. I. Ferguson, P. McDonald NZL 1'33"98
2. I. Nagaev, V. Denissov URS 1'34"15
3. A. Abraham, F. Csipes HUN 1'34"32

Kayak-1 (1,000m)
1. Greg Barton USA 3'55"27
2. Grant Davies AUS 3'55"28
3. André Wohllebe GDR 3'55"55

Kayak-2 (1,000m)
1. G. Barton, N. Bellingham USA 3'32"42
2. I. Ferguson, P. McDonald NZL 3'32"71
3. P. Foster, K. Graham AUS 3'33"76

Kayak-4 (1,000m)
1. HUN 3'00"20 (Z. Gyulay, F. Csipes, S. Hodosi, A. Abraham)
2. URS 3'01"40 (A. Motouzenko, S. Kirsanov, I. Nagaev, V. Denissov)
3. GDR 3'02"37 (K. Bluhm, A. Wohllebe, A. Staehle, H.-J. Bliesener)

Women Canoeing

Kayak-1 (500m)
1. Vania Guecheva BUL 1'55"19
2. Birgit Schmidt GDR 1'55"31
3. Izabella Dylewska POL 1'57"38

Kayak-2 (500m)
1. B. Schmidt, A. Nothnagel GDR 1'43"46
2. V. Guecheva, D. Paliiska BUL 1'44"06
3. A. Derckx, A. Cox HOL 1'46"00

Kayak-4 (500m)
1. GDR 1'40"78 (B. Schmidt, A. Nothnagel, R. Portwitch, H. Singer)
2. HUN 1'41"88 (E. Geczi, E. Meszaros, E. Rakusz, R. Koban)
3. BUL 1'42"63 (V. Guecheva, D. Paliiska, O. Petkova, B. Ivanova)

Men Cycling

100km Team Time Trial
1. GDR 1 h 57'47" (U. Ampler, M. Kummer, M. Landsmann, J. Schur)
2. POL 1 h 57'54" (J. Halupczok, Z. Jaskula, M. Lesniewski, A. Sypytkowski)
3. SWE 1 h 59'47" (B. Johansson, J. Karlsson, M. Lafis, A. Jarl)

Team Pursuit
1. URS 4'13"31 (V. Ekimov, A. Kaspoutis, D. Melubine, G. Umaras)
2. GDR 4'14"09 (S. Blochwitz, R. Hennig, D. Meier, C. Wolf)
3. AUS 4'16"02 (B. Dutton, S. McGlede, W. McCarney, D. Woods)

Sprint
1. Lutz Hesslich GDR
2. Nikolai Kovch URS
3. Gary Neiwand AUS

1,000m
1. Alexandre Kiritchenko GDR 1'04"499
2. Martin Vinnicombe AUS 1'04"784
3. Robert Lechner FRG 1'05"114

Individual Pursuit
1. Giantauras Umaras URS
2. Dean Woods AUS
3. Bernd Dittert GDR

30km Points Race
1. Dean Frost DEN
2. Leo Peelen HOL
3. Marat Ganeev URS

Individual Road Race
1. Olaf Ludwig GDR 4 h 32'22"
2. Bernd Groene FRG
3. Christian Henn FRG

Women Cycling

Sprint
1. Erika Salumiae URS
2. Christa Rothenburger-Luding GDR
3. Connie Paraskevin-Young USA

Individual Road Race
1. Monique Knol HOL 2 h 52'
2. Jutta Niehaus FRG
3. Laina Zilporitie URS

Equestrian Sports

Grand Prix Jumping Individual
1. Pierre Durand/"Jappeloup" FRA 1,25 pts
2. Greg Best/"Gem Twist" USA 4 pts
3. Karsten Huck/"Neponuk" FRG 4 pts

Grand Prix Jumping Team
1. FRG 17,25 pts (Beerbaum, Brinkmann, Hafemeister, Sloothaak)
2. USA 20,50 pts (Best, Jacquin, Kursinski, Fargis)
3. FRA 27,50 pts (Bourdy, Cottier, Robert, Durand)

Individual Dressage
1. Nicole Uphoff/"Rembrandt" FRG 1,521 pts
2. Margitt Otto-Crépin/"Corlandus" FRA 1,462 pts
3. Christine Stueckelberger/"Gauguin de Lulle" SUI 1,417 pts

Team Dressage
1. FRG 4,302 pts (Klimke, Linsenhoff, Theodorescu, Uphoff)
2. SUI 4,164 pts (Hofer, Stueckelberger Ramseier, Schatzmann)
3. CAN 3,969 pts (Ishoy, Pracht, Smith, Nicoll)

Three-day event (Individual)
1. Mark Todd/"Charisma" NZL 42,60 pts
2. Ian Stark/"Sir Wattie" GBR 52,80 pts
3. Virginia Leng/"Master Craftsman" GBR 62,00 pts

Three-day event (Team)
1. FRG 225,95 pts (Erhorn, Baumann, Kaspareit, Ehrenbrink)
2. GBR 256,80 pts (Phillips, Straker, Leng, Stark)
3. NZL 271,20 pts (Todd, Knighton, Bennie, Pottinger)

Men Fencing

Foil Individual
1. Stefano Cerioni ITA
2. Udo Wagner GDR
3. Alexandre Romankov URS

Sabre Individual
1. Jean-François Lamour FRA
2. Janusz Olech POL
3. Giovanni Scalzo ITA

Epée Individual
1. Arnd Schmitt FR[illegible]
2. Philippe Riboud FR[illegible]
3. Andrei Chouvalov UR[illegible]

Foil Team
1. URS (Romankov, Mamedov, A ptsiaouri, Ibraguimov, Koretski)
2. FRG (Gey, Weidner, Behr, Schreck, Endres)
3. HUN (Ersek, Szekeres, Szelei, Gatai, Busa)

Sabre Team
1. HUN (Nebald, Szabo, Consgradi, Bujdoso, Gedeovari)
2. URS (Mindirgassov, Bourtsev, Pogosov, Alchan, Koriakine)
3. ITA (Cavaliere, Scalzo, Marin, Dalla barba, Meglio)

Epée Team
1. FRA (Lenglet, Srecki, Riboud, Henry Delpha)
2. FRG (Borrmann, Fischer, Gerull, Pusch, Schmitt)
3. URS (Chouvalov, Tichko, Kolobkov, Reznitchenko, Tikhomirov)

Women Fencing

Foil Individual
1. Anja Fichtel FR[illegible]
2. Sabine Bau FR[illegible]
3. Zita Funkenhauser FR[illegible]

Foil Team
1. FRG (Fichtel, Funkenhauser, Bau, Weber, Klug)
2. ITA (Vaccaroni, Zalaffi, Traversa, Gandolfi, Bortolozzi)
3. HUN (Janosi, Stefanek, Szocs, Kovacs Tuschak)

Soccer

1. Soviet Union
2. Brazil
3. Federal Republic of Germany

Men Gymnastics

All-round Individual Competition
1. Vladimir Artemov URS 119,125 p[illegible]
2. Valeri Lioukine URS 119,025 p[illegible]
3. Dimitri Bilozertchev URS 118,975 p[illegible]

All-round Team Competition
1. URS 593,35 pts (Nouvikov, Gogoladze, Bilozertchev, Lioukine, Artemov, Charkov)
2. GDR 588,45 pts (Kroll, Tippelt, Buchner, Behrendt, Hoffmann, Wecker)
3. JPN 585,60 pts (Yukio, Mizushima, Sato, Konishi, Yamada)

Horizontal Bar
1. Valeri Lioukine URS 19,900 p[illegible]
Vladimir Artemov URS 19,900 p[illegible]
3. Holger Behrendt GDR 19,800 p[illegible]
Marius Gherman ROM 19,800 p[illegible]

Horse
1. Dimitri Bilozertchev URS 19,950 p[illegible]
Zsolt Borkai BUL 19,950 p[illegible]
Lubomir Gueraskov URS 19,950 p[illegible]

Rings
1. Dimitri Bilozertchev URS 19,925 p[illegible]
Holger Behrendt GDR 19,925 p[illegible]
3. Sven Tippelt GDR 19,875 p[illegible]

Vault
1. Lou Yun CHN 19,875 p[illegible]
2. Sylvio Kroll GDR 19,862 p[illegible]
3. Park Jong-Hoon KOR 19,775 p[illegible]

Parallel Bars
1. Vladimir Artemov URS 19,925 p[illegible]
2. Valeri Liouкine URS 19,900 p[illegible]
3. Sven Tippelt GDR 19,750 p[illegible]

Floor Exercise
1. Sergei Kharkov URS 19,925 p[illegible]
2. Vladimir Artemov URS 19,900 p[illegible]
3. Lou Yun CHN 19,850 p[illegible]
Yukio Iketani JPN 19,850 p[illegible]

Women Gymnastics

All-round Individual Competition
1. Elena Chouchounova URS 79,662 p[illegible]
2. Daniela Silivas ROM 79,637 p[illegible]
3. Svetlana Boginskaia URS 79,400 p[illegible]

All-round Team Competition
1. URS 395,475 pts (Baitova, Chevtchenko, Straieva, Lachtchenova)
2. ROM 394,125 pts (Voinea, Golea, Popa, Potorac, Dobre)
3. GDR 390,875 pts (Jentsch, Schieferdecker, Fahnrich, Klotz, Kersten, Thummler)

Vault
1. Elena Boguinskaia URS 19,905 p[illegible]
2. Gabriela Potorac ROM 19,830 p[illegible]
3. Daniela Silivas ROM 19,818 p[illegible]

Floor Exercise
1. Daniela Silivas ROM 19,937 p[illegible]
2. Svetlana Boguinskaia URS 19,887 p[illegible]
3. Diana Doudeva BUL 19,850 p[illegible]

Beam
1. Daniela Silivas ROM 19,924 p[illegible]
2. Elena Chouchounova URS 19,875 p[illegible]
3. Phoele Mills USA 19,837 p[illegible]
Gabriela Potorac ROM 19,837 p[illegible]

Asymetric Bars
1. Daniela Silivas ROM 20,000 p[illegible]
2. Dagmar Kersten FRG 19,987 p[illegible]
3. Elena Chouchounova URS 19,962 p[illegible]

Apparatus
1. Lobatch URS 60,000 p[illegible]
2. Dounavska BUL 59,950 p[illegible]
3. Timoshenko URS 59,875 p[illegible]

Rhythmic Competition
1. Lobatch URS 60,000 p[illegible]
2. Dounavska BUL 59,950 p[illegible]
3. Timoshenko URS 59,875 p[illegible]

Weightlifting

52kg
1. Sevdalin Marinov BUL 270,0k[illegible]
2. Chun Byung-Kwan KOR 260,0k[illegible]
3. He Zhuoqiang CHN 257,5k[illegible]

56kg
1. Oksen Mirzoian URS 292,5k[illegible]
2. He Yinqiang CHN 287,5k[illegible]
3. Liu Shoubin CHN 267,5k[illegible]

1988 Seoul

60kg
1. Naim Suleymanoglou TUR 342,5kg
2. Stefan Topourov BUL 312,5kg
3. Ye Huanming CHN 287,5kg

67.5kg
1. Joachim Kunz GDR 340,0kg
2. Israel Militosian URS 337,5kg
3. Li Jinhe CHN 325,0kg

75kg
1. Borislav Guidikov BUL 375,0kg
2. Ingo Steinhoefel GDR 360,0kg
3. Alexander Varbanov BUL 357,5kg

82.5kg
1. Israil Arsamakov URS 377,5kg
2. Istvan Messzi HUN 370,0kg
3. Lee Hyung-Kun KOR 367,5kg

90kg
1. Anatoli Khrapatyi URS 412,5kg
2. Nail Moukhamediarov URS 400,0kg
3. Slawomir Zawada POL 400,0kg

100kg
1. Pavel Kouznetsov URS 425,0kg
2. Nicu Vlad ROM 402,5kg
3. Peter Immesberger FRG 395,0kg

110kg
1. Youri Zakharevitch URS 455,0kg
2. Jozsef Jacso HUN 427,5kg
3. Ronny Weller GDR 425,0kg

More than 110kg
1. Alexandre Kourlovitch URS 462,5kg
2. Manfred Nerlinger FRG 430,0kg
3. Martin Zawieja FRG 415,0kg

Handball

Men	Women
1. Soviet Union	1. South Korea
2. South Korea	2. Norway
3. Yugoslavia	3. Soviet Union

Hockey

1. Great Britain	1. Australia
2. Federal Republic of Germany	2. South Korea
3. Netherlands	3. Netherlands

Judo

60kg
1. Kim Jae-Yup KOR
2. Kevin Asano USA
3. Shinji Hosokawa JPN
Amiran Totikachvili URS

65kg
1. Lee Kyung-Keun KOR
2. Janusz Pawlowski POL
3. Bruno Carabetta FRA
Yosuke Yamamoto JPN

71kg
1. Marc Alexandre FRA
2. Sven Loll GDR
3. Gueorgui Tenadze URS
Michael Swain USA

78kg
1. Waldemar Legien POL
2. Frank Wieneke FRG
3. Torsten Brechot GDR
Bachir Varaev URS

Olympic flame.

86kg
1. Peter Seisenbacher AUT
2. Vladimir Chestakov URS
3. Akinobu Osako JPN
Ben Spijkers HOL

95kg
1. Aurelio Miguel BRA
2. Marc Meiling FRG
3. Robert Van de Walle BEL
Dennis Stewart GBR

More than 95kg
1. Hitoshi Saito JPN
2. Henry Stoehr GDR
3. Cho Yong-Chul KOR
Grigori Veritchev URS

Graeco-Roman Wrestling

48kg
1. Vincenzo Maenza ITA
2. Andrzej Glab POL
3. Bratan Tzenov BUL

52kg
1. Jon Ronningen NOR
2. Atsuji Miyahara JPN
3. Lee Jae-sute KOR

57kg
1. Andras Sike HUN
2. Stoyan Balov BUL
3. Charalambos Holidis GRE

62kg
1. Kamandar Madjidov URS
2. Jivko Vanguelov BUL
3. An Dae-hyun KOR

68kg
1. Levon Djoufalakian URS
2. Kim Sung-moon KOR
3. Tapio Sipilae FIN

74kg
1. Kim Young-nam KOR
2. Daoulet Tourlykhanov URS
3. Jozef Tracz POL

82kg
1. Mikhail Mamiachvili URS
2. Tibor Komaromi HUN
3. Kim Sang-kyu KOR

90kg
1. Atanas Komchev BUL
2. Harri Kosteka FIN
3. Vladimir Popov URS

100kg
1. Andrzej Wronski POL
2. Gerhard Himmel FRG
3. Dennis Koslowski USA

130kg
1. Alexandre Kareline URS
2. Ranguel Guerovski BUL
3. Tomas Johansson SWE

All-In Wrestling

48kg
1. Takashi Kobayashi JPN
2. Ivan Tzonov BUL
3. Serguei Karamchatzov URS

52kg
1. Mitsuru Sato JPN
2. Saban Trstena YUG
3. Vladimir Togouzov URS

57kg
1. Sergei Beloglazov URS
2. Mohammadian IRN
3. Noh Kyung-sun KOR

62kg
1. John Smith USA
2. Stephan Sarkissian URS
3. Simeon Chterev BUL

68kg
1. Arsen Fadzaev URS
2. Park Jang-soon KOR
3. Nate Carr USA

74kg
1. Kenneth Monday USA
2. Adlan Varaev URS
3. Rakhmad Sofiadi BUL

82kg
1. Han Myung-woo KOR
2. Nemci Gencalp TUR
3. Joseph Lohyna TCH

90kg
1. Makharbek Khardartsev URS
2. Akira Ota JPN
3. Kim Tae-woo KOR

100kg
1. Vasile Puscasu ROM
2. Leri Khabelov URS
3. Bill Scherr USA

130kg
1. David Gobedjichvili URS
2. Bruce Baumgartner USA
3. Andreas Schroeder GDR

Men Swimming

50m - Freestyle
1. Matt Biondi USA 22"14
(world rec.; prev. rec. 22"23 by Jager)
2. Tom Jager USA 22"33
3. Guennadi Prigoda URS 22"71

100m - Freestyle
1. Matt Biondi USA 48"63
2. Christopher Jacobs USA 49"08
3. Stephan Caron FRA 49"62

200m - Freestyle
1. Duncan Armstrong AUS 1'47"25
(world rec., prev. rec. 1'47"44 by Gross)
2. Anders Holmertz SWE 1'47"89
3. Matt Biondi USA 1'47"99

400m - Freestyle
1. Uwe Dassler GDR 3'46"95
(world rec.; prev. rec. 3'47"38 by Wojdat)
2. Duncan Armstrong AUS 3'47"15
3. Artur Wojdat POL 3'47"34

1 500m - Freestyle
1. Vladimir Salnikov URS 15'00"40
2. Stephan Pfeiffer GDR 15'02"69
3. Uwe Dassler GDR 15'06"15

100m - Backstroke
1. Daichi Suzuki JPN 55"05
2. David Berkoff USA 55"18
3. Igor Polianski URS 55"20

200m - Backstroke
1. Igor Polianski URS 1'59"37
2. Frank Baltrusch GDR 1'59"60
3. Paul Kingsman NZL 2'00"48

100m - Butterfly
1. Anthony Nesty SUR 53"00
2. Matt Biondi USA 53"01
3. Andy Jameson GBR 53"30

200m - Butterfly
1. Michael Gross FRG 1'56"94
2. Benny Nielsen DEN 1'58"24
3. Anthony Mosse NZL 1'58"28

100m - Breaststroke
1. Adrian Moorhouse GBR 1'02"04
2. Karoly Guttler HUN 1'02"05
3. Dmitri Volkov URS 1'02"20

200m - Breaststroke
1. Josef Szabo HUN 2'13"52
2. Nick Gillingham GBR 2'14"12
3. Sergio Lopez ESP 2'15"21

200m - Individual Medley
1. Tamas Darnyi HUN 2'00"17
(world rec.; own prev. rec. 2'00"56)
2. Patrick Kuehl GDR 2'01"61
3. Vadim Tarotchouk URS 2'02"40

400m - Individual Medley
1. Tamas Darnyi HUN 4'14"75
(world rec.; own prev. rec. 4'15"42)
2. David Wharton USA 4'17"36
3. Stefano Battistelli ITA 4'18"01

4 x 100m Medley Relay
1. USA 3'16"53 (Jacobs, Dalbey, Jager Biondi, world rec.; prev. rec. 3'17"08)
2. URS 3'18"33 (Prigoda, Bachkatov, Evteev, Tkachenko)
3. GDR 3'19"82 (Richter, Fleming, Minneburg, Zesner)

4 x 200m Medley Relay
1. USA 7'12"51 (Dalbey, Cetlinski, Gertsen, Biondi, world rec.; prev. rec. 7'13"10)
2. GDR 7'13"68 (Dassier, Lodziewski, Fleming, Zesner)
3. FRG 7'14"35 (Hochstein, Fahrner, Hentzel, Gross)

4 x 100m Freestyle Medley
1. USA 3'36"93 (Berkoff, Schroeder, Biondi, Jacobs)
2. CAN 3'39"28 (Tawesbury, David, Ponting, Goss)
3. URS 3'39"96 (Polianski, Volkov, Yarochtchouk, Prigoda)

Water-Polo

1. Yugoslavia
2. United States
3. Soviet Union

Women Swimming

50m - Freestyle
1. Kristin Otto GDR 25"49
2. Yang Wenyi CHN 25"64
3. Katrin Meissner GDR 25"71
Jill Sterkel USA 25"71

100m - Freestyle
1. Kristin Otto GDR 54"93
2. Zhuang Yong CHN 55"47
3. Catherine Plewinski FRA 55"49
(France rec.; own prev. rec. 55"53)

200m - Freestyle
1. Heike Friedrich GDR 1'57"65
2. Sylvia Poll CRC 1'58"67
3. Manuela Stellmach GDR 1'59"01

400m - Freestyle
1. Janet Evans USA 4'03"85
2. Heike Friedrich GDR 4'05"94
3. Anke Moehring GDR 4'06"62

800m - Freestyle
1. Janet Evans USA 8'20"20
2. Astrid Strauss GDR 8'22"09
3. Julie MacDonald AUS 8'22"93

100m - Backstroke
1. Kristin Otto GDR 1'00"89
2. Krisztina Egerszegi HUN 1'01"56
3. Cornelia Sirch GDR 1'01"57

200m - Backstroke
1. Krisztina Egerszegi HUN 2'09"29
2. Kathrin Zimmermann GDR 2'10"61
3. Cornelia Sirch GDR 2'11"45

100m - Butterfly
1. Kristina Otto GDR 59"00
2. Birte Weigang GDR 59"34
3. Qiuan Hong CHN 59"45

200m - Butterfly
1. Katleen Nord GDR 2'09"29
2. Birte Weigang GDR 2'09"91
3. Mary T. Meagher USA 2'10"80

100m - Breaststroke
1. Tania Dangalakova BUL 1'07"95
2. Antoaneta Frankeva BUL 1'08"74
3. Silke Hoerner GDR 1'08"83

200m - Breaststroke
1. Silke Hoerner GDR 2'26"71
2. Huang Xiaomin CHN 2'27"49
3. Antoaneta Frankeva BUL 2'28"34

200m - Individual Medley
1. Daniela Hunger GDR 2'12"59
2. Helena Dendeberova URS 2'13"31
3. Noemi Lung ROM 2'14"85

400m - Individual Medley
1. Janet Evans USA 4'37"76
2. Noemi Lung ROM 4'39"46
3. Daniela Hunger GDR 4'39"76

4 x 100m Medley Relay
1. GDR 3'40"53
(Otto, Meissner, Hunger, Stellmach)
2. HOL 3'43"39
(Ma. Muis, Mi. Muis, Van Bentum, Brienesse)
3. USA 3'44"25
(Wayte, Kremer, Walker, Torres)

4 x 100m Individual Medley
1. GDR 4'03"73 (Otto, Hoerner, Weigang, Meissner)
2. USA 4'07"90 (Barr, McFarlane, Jorgensen, Wayte)
3. CAN 4'10"49 (Melien, Higson, Kerr, Nugent)

Synchronized Swimming Individual
1. Carolyn Waldo CAN 200,150 pts
2. Tracie Conforto Ruiz USA 197,633 pts
3. Mikako Kotani JPN 191,850 pts

Synchronized Swimming Duet
1. Canada 197,717 pts
2. United States 197,284 pts
3. Japan 190,159 pts

Men Diving

Springboard Diving
1. Greg Louganis USA 730,80 pts
2. Tan Liangde CHN 704,88 pts
3. Li De Liang CHI 665,28 pts

High Diving
1. Greg Louganis USA 638,61 pts
2. Xiong Ni CHN 637,47 pts
3. Jesus Mena MEX 594,39 pts

Women Diving

Springboard Diving
1. Gao Min CHN 580,23 pts
2. Li Qing CHN 534,33 pts
3. Kelly McCormick USA 533,19 pts

High Diving
1. Xu Yannei CHN 445,20 pts
2. Michele Mitchell USA 436,95 pts
3. Wendy Williams USA 400,44 pts

Modern Penthatlon

Individual
1. Janos Martinek HUN 5 404 pts
2. Carlo Massullo ITA 5 379 pts
3. Vakhtang Iagorachvili URS 5 367 pts

Team
1. Hungary 15 886 pts
2. Italy 15 571 pts
3. Great Britain 12 276 pts

Tennis

Men:s Singles
1. Miloslav Mecir TCH
2. Tim Mayotte USA
3. Stefan Edberg SWE
Brad Gilbert USA

Men:s Doubles
1. Ken Flach, Robert Seguso USA
2. Emilio Sanchez, Sergio Casal ESP
3. Stefan Edberg, Anders Jarryd SWE
Miloslav Mecir, Milan Srejber TCH

Daley Thompson.

Women's Singles
1. Steffi Graf FRG
2. Gabriela Sabatini ARG
3. Manuela Maleeva BUL
Zina Garrison USA

Women's Doubles
1. Pam Shriver, Zina Garrison USA
2. Jana Novotna, Helena Sukova TCH
3. Steffi Graf, Claudia Kohde Kilsch FRG
Elizabeth Smylie, Wendy Turnbull USA

Table Tennis

Men's Singles
1. Yoo Nam-Kyu KOR
2. Kim Ki-Taik KOR
3. Erik Lindh SWE

Men's Doubles
1. Chen Long Can, Wei Quingguang CHN
2. Ilija Lupulescu, Zoran Primorac YUG
3. Ahn Jae Hyung, Yoo Nam Kyu KOR

Women's Singles
1. Chen Jing CHN
2. Li Huifen CHN
3. Jiao Zhimin CHN

Women's Doubles
1. Hyun Jung Hwa, Yang Young-ja KOR
2. Chen Jing, Jiao Zhimin CHN
3. Jazna Fazlic, Gordana Perkucin YUG

Men Shooting

Free Pistol
1. Sorin Babii ROU 660 pts
2. Ragnar Skanaker SWE 657 pts
3. Igor Bassinski URS 657 pts

Rapid-Fire Pistol
1. Afanasi Kouzmine URS 698 pts
(world rec.)
2. Ralf Schumann GDR 696 pts
3. Zoltan Kovacs HUN 693 pts

Airgun
1. Taniou Kiriakov BUL 687,9 pts
2. Erich Buljung USA 687,9 pts
3. Xu Maifeng CHN 684,5 pts

Small-Bore Rifle, Prone
1. Miroslav Varga TCH 703,9 pts
2. Cha Young-Chul KOR 703,8 pts
3. Attila Zahonyi HUN 701,9 pts

Airgun, 10m
1. Goran Maksimovic YUG 695,6 pts
2. Nicolas Berthelot FRA 694,2 pts
3. Johann Riederer FRG 694 pts

Small-Bore Rifle, 3 positions
1. Malcolm Cooper GBR 1279,3 pts
2. Alister Allan GBR 1275,6 pts
3. Kirill Ivanov URS 1275 pts

Moving Target
1. Tor Heiestad NOR 689 pts
2. Huang Shiping CHN 688 pts
3. Guennadi Avramenko URS 686 pts

Trap Shooting
1. Dimitri Monakov URS 222 pts
2. Miroslav Bednarik TCH 222 pts
3. Frans Peeters BEL 219 pts

Skeet
1. Axel Wegner GDR 222 pts
2. Alfonso De Izuarrizaga CHI 221 pts
3. Jorge Guardiola ESP 220 pts

Women Shooting

Airgun, 10m
1. Jasna Sekaric YUG 489,5 pts
2. Nino Saloukvadze URS 487,9 pts
3. Marina Dobranicheva URS 485,2 pts

Sport Pistol
1. Nino Saloukvadze URS 690 pts
2. Tomoko Hasegawa JPN 686 pts
3. Jasna Sexaric YUG 686 pts

Small-Bore Rifle, 3 positions
1. Silvia Sperber FRG 685,6 pts
2. Vessela Letcheva BUL 683,2 pts
3. Valentina Tcherkassova URS 681,4 pts

Airgun
1. Irina Chilova URS 498,5 pts
2. Silvia Sperber FRG 497,5 pts
3. Anna Maloukhina URS 495,5 pts

Men Archery

Individual
1. Jay Barrs USA 338 pts
2. Park Sung-Soo KOR 336 pts
3. Vladimir Echeev URS 335 pts

Team
1. South Korea 986 pts
2. United States 972 pts
3. Great Britain 968 pts

Women Archery

Individual
1. Kim Soo-Nyung KOR 344 pts
2. Wang Hee-Kyung KOR 332 pts
3. Yun Young-Sook KOR 327 pts

Team
1. South Korea 982 pts
2. Indonesia 952 pts
3. United States 952 pts

Men Yachting

Finn Class
1. Jose Luis Doreste ESP 36,1 pts
2. Peter Holmberg VI 40,4 pts
3. John Cutler NZL 45 pts

470 Class
1. Thierry Peponnet- Luc Pillot FRA 34,7 pts
2. Tynou et Thomas Tyniste URS 46 pts
3. John Shadden-Charlie McKee USA 49 pts

Flying Dutchman Class
1. DEN 31,4 pts (Jorgen Bojsen Moller, Christian Gronborg)
2. NOR 37,4 pts (Olepetter Pollen, Erik Bjorkum)
3. CAN 48,4 pts (Frank McLaughlin, John Willen)

Soling Class
1. GDR 11,7 pts (Jochen Schuemann, Thomas Flach, Bernt Jaekel)
2. USA 11,4 pts (John Kostecki, William Baylis, Robert Billingham)
3. DEN 52,7 pts (Jesper Bank, Jan Mathiasen, Steen Secher)

Tornado Class
1. FRA 16 pts (Jean-Yves Le Deroff, Nicolas Henard)
2. NZL 35,4 pts (Christopher Timms, Rex Sellers)
3. BRA 40,1 pts (Lars Grael, Clinio Freitas)

Windsurfing
1. Bruce Kendall NZL 35,4 pts
2. Jan D. Boersma ANE 42,7 pts
3. Michael Gebhardt USA 48 pts

Star Class
1. GBR 45,4 pts (Michael McIntyre, Philippe Vaile)
2. USA 48 pts (Mark Reynolds, Hal Haenel)
3. BRA 50 pts (Torban Grael, Nelson Falcao)

Women Yachting

470 Class
1. USA 26,7 pts (Allison Jolly, Lynne Jewell)
2. SWE 40 pts (Marit Soderstrom, Brighitta Bengtsson)
3. URS 45,4 pts (Larissa Moskalenko, Irina Tchounikavskaia)

Volleyball

Men	Women
1. United States	1. Soviet Union
2. Soviet Union	2. Peru
3. Argentina	3. China

FINAL LIST OF MEDALS

Country		Gold	Silver	Bronze	Total
Soviet Union	(URS)	55	31	46	132
German Democratic Republic	(GDR)	37	35	30	102
Unites States	(USA)	36	31	27	94
South Korea	(KOR)	12	10	11	33
Federal Republic of Germany	(FRG)	11	14	15	40
Hungary	(HUN)	11	6	6	23
Bulgaria	(BUL)	10	12	13	35
Rumania	(ROM)	7	11	6	24
France	(FRA)	6	4	6	16
Italy	(ITA)	6	4	4	14
China	(CHN)	5	11	12	28
Great Britain	(GBR)	5	10	9	24
Kenya	(KEN)	5	2	2	9
Japan	(JPN)	5	3	7	14
Australia	(AUS)	3	6	5	14
Yugoslavia	(YUG)	3	4	5	12
Czechoslovakia	(TCH)	3	3	2	8
New Zealand	(NZL)	3	2	8	13
Canada	(CAN)	3	2	5	10
Poland	(POL)	2	5	9	16
Norway	(NOR)	2	3	0	5
Netherlands	(HOL)	2	2	5	9
Denmark	(DEN)	2	1	1	4
Brazil	(BRA)	1	2	3	6
Spain	(ESP)	1	1	2	4
Finland	(FIN)	1	1	2	4
Turkey	(TUR)	1	1	0	2
Morocco	(MOR)	1	0	2	3
Austria	(AUT)	1	0	0	1
Portugal	(POR)	1	0	0	1
Surinam	(SUR)	1	0	0	1
Sweden	(SWE)	0	4	7	11
Switzerland	(SUI)	0	2	2	4
Jamaica	(JAM)	0	2	0	2
Argentina	(ARG)	0	1	1	2
Netherlands Antilles	(ANE)	0	1	0	1
Chile	(CHI)	0	1	0	1
Costa Rica	(CRC)	0	1	0	1
Virgin Islands	(VI)	0	1	0	1
Indonesia	(INS)	0	1	0	1
Iran	(IRN)	0	1	0	1
Peru	(PER)	0	1	0	1
Senegal	(SEN)	0	1	0	1
Belgium	(BEL)	0	0	2	2
Mexico	(MEX)	0	0	2	2
Colombia	(COL)	0	0	1	1
Djibouti	(DJI)	0	0	1	1
Greece	(GRE)	0	0	1	1
Mongolia	(MGL)	0	0	1	1
Pakistan	(PAK)	0	0	1	1
Philippines	(PHI)	0	0	1	1
Thailand	(THA)	0	0	1	1
Total		**241**	**234**	**264**	**739**

October
1988

9. UK: Imprisoned jockey Lester Piggott is to get parole this month (→24).

9. Iran: Ayatollah Khomeini appoints his son Ahmad as his successor.

9. UK: The BBC announces a new channel, Radio Five, to broadcast sport and schools programmes (→27).

10. Winchester: A suspected IRA hit squad is charged with plotting to murder Northern Ireland Secretary Tom King (→27).

10. UK: Mrs Thatcher pledges there will be no cover-up on the Barlow Clowes crash (→20).

10. Wentworth: Sandy Lyle wins the World Matchplay golf championship.

11. UK: The government imposes its pay package on the nurses after talks break down.

11. London: The inquest into the King's Cross tube fire deaths returns a verdict of accidental death (→10/11).

12. Brazil: The government announces measures to halt the destruction of the tropical rain forest.

12. USSR: The Kremlin offers $600 million "reparations" to Afghanistan (→13).

12. UK: The organisers of *Sport Aid* go into liquidation, with debts of £2.3 million.

13. Peking: Premier Deng Xiao-ping announces a summit with President Gorbachev.

13. UK: The Queen sues the *Sun* newspaper for breach of copyright after it prints one of her private photographs.

14. US: President Reagan stops shipping arms to the Contra rebels in Nicaragua.

14. Israel: The death toll in the Palestinian uprising is 297 Arabs and six Israelis (→18).

15. North Sea: The accommodation module at the Piper Alpha rig is raised.

15. Seoul: The Paralympic Games open.

DEATH

13. British actress Mary Morris (*13/12/15).

Mysterious Turin Shroud is mediaeval fake, say carbon-dating scientists

Oct 13. Modern science has exposed one of most revered relics which has brought Catholic pilgrims to Turin for centuries. The Turin Shroud was believed to have come from Christ's tomb and to contain his imprint. Today Cardinal Anastasio Ballestrero confirmed that the carbon-dating tests at Oxford University and elsewhere all dated the linen of the shroud between 1260 and 1390AD.

Fakes of religious relics were quite common then, but even the scientists cannot explain how this piece of mediaeval linen contained the bloodstained image of a crucified man like a modern photographic negative. No known mediaeval process could do anything like that.

Fake — but still a mystery.

Latvian Popular Front demands self-rule

Oct 9. Over 2,000 Latvians packed the Lutheran cathedral in the capital of Riga today for the first mass held there for 30 years. Afterwards, delegates to a grassroots nationalist congress voted to form a Popular Front movement committed to loosening ties with Moscow and gaining economic and cultural self-determination.

The Front is committed to supporting Mr Gorbachev's reform policies but, like similar movements in the neighbouring Baltic republics of Estonia and Lithuania, is inspired by a yearning to regain the independence enjoyed for 20 years between the two world wars. In 1940 Stalin annexed the three republics, banned the display of the national flags and tried to destroy the national identities by flooding the republics with Russian immigrants.

Under Gorbachev the pressures have been eased, and communist officials are seeking to work with the popular fronts, while warning that nationalist excesses and "anti-Russian racism" will not be tolerated (→17).

After weeks of uncertainty, Jean-Michel Jarre's spectacular concerts in London's Docklands went ahead, complete with lasers and fireworks.

Algeria referendum to follow the riots

Oct 12. The Algerian government announced today that a referendum will be held on November 3 on the package of political reforms proposed by President Chadli in the wake of the riots which left 170 people dead as young demonstrators clashed with armoured troops. Chadli promises greater democracy and a reorganisation of government structure.

The riots were sparked by food shortages and price rises, but the root of the trouble is Algeria's need to shed the Islamic-Socialist dreams of the men who won the war of independence against the French and build an efficient modern state. The riots may, in fact, have helped Mr Chadli by focusing attention on Algeria's problems.

Geordie soccer king "Wor Jackie" dies

Jackie Milburn in the 1950s.

Oct 14. Traffic was brought to a halt in Newcastle today by the funeral of Jackie Milburn, the footballer, who died last Sunday of cancer, aged 64. "Wor Jackie" was a Tyneside legend and the crowds came in their thousands, standing along the funeral route as once they had stood on the terraces at St James's Park. Many remembered Milburn's great goals which had won the FA Cup in the 1950s, others praised his sportsmanship. "He was quite simply a smashing lad," said nephew Jack Charlton.

"Spycatcher" ban ends

Vindicated: former MI5 agent Peter Wright (left) and his lawyer.

Oct 13. The government's long legal battle to prevent any mention in the British media of *Spycatcher*, the memoirs of the former MI5 officer Peter Wright, finally failed today when the House of Lords ruled unanimously against it. Last year's injunctions against the *Guardian*, the *Observer* and the *Sunday Times* are now lifted. The judgement, however, was based on the narrow ground that the book was so widely published elsewhere that further publication in Britain could not cause harm. The argument that evidence of serious wrongdoing by MI5 justified publication was rejected.

Naguib Mahfouz is Arabic Nobel winner

Oct 14. This year's surprise choice for the Nobel literature prize is an Egyptian novelist little known in Europe, Naguib Mahfouz. He is the first writer in Arabic to win the prize. The Swedish Academy ranked his descriptions of Cairo alongside Dickens's London or Zola's Paris. "The Arabic novel is not even a century old and has largely been created by Mahfouz," said one of them (→17).

Mahfouz, whose writing is "rich in nuance" and "evocatively ambiguous".

Dukakis doomed by Bush TV debate win

Oct 13. Michael Dukakis, the Democratic challenger for the US presidency, failed to take advantage of the second and last television debate with his Republican opponent, Vice-President George Bush, who was generally judged to have drawn the first.

The extent to which Dukakis's liberal instincts are at odds with the prevailing mood in the United States was revealed in his answer to the very first question.

If someone raped and killed his wife, Kitty (who was sitting in the audience), a journalist asked Mr Dukakis, would he favour the death penalty for the murderer? No, said Dukakis bravely.

Mr Bush, in contrast, said that some crimes were "so heinous, so brutal, so outrageous" that he did favour the death penalty. Dukakis

It's going well for George Bush.

failed to shake the impression Bush has sought to give of him — that he is out of touch with mainstream American beliefs. Bush has now opened up a lead of five points in the polls which Dukakis will find hard to close (→30).

Paisley yells abuse at "Antichrist" Pope

Oct 11. In an astonishing outburst today, the Reverend Ian Paisley, the Northern Ireland MP, interrupted the speech to the European Parliament by Pope John Paul II. He jumped to his feet as soon as the Pope began to speak, waving a banner with the slogan "John Paul Antichrist". He shouted out "I renounce you as the Antichrist" several times before Lord Plumb, the Parliament's president, had him thrown out.

The Pope gave strong support in his speech for European unity. Mr Paisley's outburst was a reminder that in Ulster, at least, the ancient European split between Catholics and Protestants is still as wide as ever (→16).

Ian Paisley says his piece.

Tight security for Tories at Brighton

Oct 14. Euphoric grassroot Tories chanted "Ten more years!" after Mrs Thatcher indicated at their party conference this afternoon that she is ready to stay in the leadership that long. The conference — back in Brighton for the first time since the IRA narrowly failed to assassinate the cabinet in 1984 — was protected by the tightest-ever security measures.

John Smith suffers a heart attack

Oct 9. John Smith, Labour's shadow chancellor and strongly fancied as a future party leader, had a major heart attack today. He was lucky. It happened when he was in an Edinburgh hospital for a check-up after chest pains. An hour later and he would have been flying to London. Doctors have told him to lose three stones. He expects to be convalescent until the New Year.

October

1988

Su	Mo	Tu	We	Th	Fr	Sa
						1
2	3	4	5	6	7	8
9	10	11	12	13	14	15
16	17	18	19	20	21	22
23	24	25	26	27	28	29
30	31					

16. Vatican: The Pope celebrates ten years in office.

17. USSR: Conservative Yegor Ligachev is demoted from the important post of Second Secretary (→21).

17. Brussels: The trial of 26 British soccer fans, alleged to be responsible for riots at the Heysel stadium, begins.

17. UK: A survey says that over a thousand bird species are in danger of extinction worldwide, compared with 290 ten years ago.

18. Cheltenham: The government sacks all trade unionists still employed at the intelligence-gathering unit, GCHQ.

18. Brussels: German chancellor Helmut Kohl opposes Mrs Thatcher by backing a common European economic policy (→26).

18. Israel: Meir Kahane's racist Kach party is banned from the forthcoming Knesset elections (→22).

19. India: 164 people die in two separate aeroplane crashes.

19. Europe: England draw 0-0 with Sweden in a World Cup qualifying round. In other matches Wales and Finland draw 2-2, Scotland and Yugoslavia draw 1-1, and Hungary beat Northern Ireland 1-0.

19. Gulf: Britain's Armilla Patrol is to cease escorting merchant ships through the Straits of Hormuz.

20. France: Public service workers strike and march for pay increases.

21. USSR: Lithuanians send a hated Soviet official back to Moscow. →

22. Nicaragua: Hurricane Miriam kills at least 87 people.

22. Aqaba: King Hussein of Jordan and President Mubarak of Egypt meet PLO leader Yasser Arafat for talks.

DEATHS

17. British cartoonist Michael Ffolkes (Brian Davis) (*6/6/25).

20. British aviatrix Sheila Scott (*27/4/27).

Children missing after cruise ship sinks

Oct 21. Nine adults and five British schoolchildren are missing after their cruise ship, the *Jupiter,* sank in the Aegean Sea. The ship, on a half-term cruise round the Mediterranean with 472 children and teachers on board, collided with an Italian freighter just after leaving the Greek port of Piraeus.

Crew members said there was a great noise, and then the ship started to sink. "We had no time to reach the rescue boats ... the young kids were crying hysterically," said one. Dozens of teenagers were hurled into the water as the ship went down, and survivors alleged that lifejackets were not available and that some of the crew had abandoned ship before the passengers.

Small ships, lifeboats and helicopters were used for the rescue operation, with children ferried to hospital in a fleet of ambulances. Most were suffering from shock or

The children come ashore.

minor injuries. The Greek authorities have arrested Flavio Caminale, the Italian freighter's captain, on a possible charge of manslaughter. It appears he may have rammed the *Jupiter* which was lying stationary in the harbour when the incident took place (→23).

Talks could end South Africa sports ban

Oct 17. In another bid to end the sports boycott of South Africa, four officials of the National Soccer League flew from Johannesburg to Lusaka, Zambia, tonight to meet leaders of the African National Congress, the black nationalist organisation banned in South Africa. Last week South African rugby officials met ANC representatives in Zimbabwe to talk about

getting South Africa back into world rugby by organising teams on non-racial lines. Other South African sporting bodies are also planning meetings with the ANC.

But there is also opposition. In London Sam Ramsamy, leader of the South African Non-Racial Olympic Committee, said: "We will continue with our campaign to isolate South Africa in sport."

Briton wins a Nobel Prize for medicine

Oct 17. The British scientist Sir James Black has been awarded the 1988 Nobel Prize for medicine for developing drugs which help millions of sufferers from stomach ulcers and heart disease.

Black's approach in his drug research was to analyse the workings of the body in great detail and then to design drugs on the basis of that knowledge. It led to the highly successful Inderal for heart disease and high blood pressure, and Tagamet for stomach ulcers.

Black shares the Prize with two Americans, Gertrude Elion and George Hitchings, who pioneered the development of some important anti-cancer drugs.

Sir James in his laboratory.

The world watches as rescuers race to save Alaskan whales

Oct 20. The fate of the three grey whales stranded in a frozen plain at Barrow Point, Alaska, lies in the balance today as a giant ice-smashing barge inches towards them. The world has been watching on television as the two adults, named Siku and Poutu, and baby Kannick fight for air through two small holes kept clear by chainsaws and de-icing machinery.

Scientists hope that the barge, which is being towed by helicopter, will cut a channel to the open sea, enabling the trapped whales to swim south to warmer seas, but it is making painfully slow progress. Meanwhile, President Reagan has told the would-be rescuers his thoughts are with them (→28).

Rescuers struggle to keep the whales' hole from freezing over.

Government ends legal "right of silence"

Demonstrators gag themselves to protest against the media ban.

Oct 20. The criminal suspect's right of silence — it cannot be interpreted as evidence of guilt — is to be abolished. The courts will in future attach whatever significance they consider proper to the fact that someone has remained silent when questioned.

This change was announced by the government tonight. Opposition MPs and civil liberty organisations attacked it as undermining a cornerstone of British justice: the presumption of innocence.

The move, aimed at IRA terrorists, came just 24 hours after the government banned interviews by broadcasters with members of terrorist organisations or their supporters. The BBC and ITV protested. The government said that there is a war on.

Beethoven's "Tenth" bemuses audiences

Oct 19. Part of Beethoven's unfinished Tenth Symphony, which he was writing for the Royal Philharmonic Society of London when he died in 1827, was premiered at a concert given by the society last night in London. Sketches left by Beethoven have recently been identified by Dr Barry Cooper of Aberdeen, who reconstructed the first movement. He filled in the gaps in the jigsaw with his impressions of what Beethoven intended. The audience was only mildly enthused.

Oct 18. Jaguar's new prototype, the XJ220, is unveiled at the Motor Show. If it goes into production, it will cost £350,000 and do 0-100 in 8 seconds.

Lithuania joins Baltic chorus for self-rule

Oct 22. Patriotic songs that have been banned for almost 50 years were sung again in the streets of Lithuania's capital of Vilnius tonight as 200,000 people joined in celebrating the rebirth of their national, Catholic identity. The Lithuanian Reform Movement, launched three months ago ostensibly to back Mr Gorbachev's *perestroika*, became a full-blooded nationalist movement when its first congress was held here this week and demands for self-government, with a Lithuanian currency and a national army, were voiced. In the Catholic cathedral of Vilnius, restored to the Church only yesterday after having been a picture gallery for 40 years, a mass was held today ($\rightarrow$ 26).

Pressure mounts in the Baltic.

Dutiful Diana puts heat on "Fergie"

Oct 18. Launching a new look for the children's charity Barnardo's, the Princess of Wales today praised stable family life. She said that marriage is not always easy, but caring parents could save children from the risk of drugs, prostitution and homelessness. Her speech, long planned, came at a time when many newspapers had carried criticisms of her sister-in-law, the Duchess of York (or "Fergie" as they call her), for neglecting her family by leaving her daughter, Princess Bea, at home while she visited Australia.

Irish golfers win the Dunhill Cup

Oct 16. Ireland, seeded eighth out of 16 nations, today confounded the form book to win golf's Dunhill Cup at St Andrew's. The Irish trio of Des Smyth, Ronan Rafferty and Eamonn Darcy — drawn from north and south of the border — beat Australia by two games to one.

The United States and Scotland had both gone out at the quarterfinal stage. Australia knocked out Spain in the semi-finals, while Ireland conquered England in a contest suspended overnight when mist halted play with one hole to go.

Minister under fire after City firm crashes

Oct 20. The government was under growing pressure tonight to recognise a moral responsibility towards 18,000 investors who lost savings in the collapse of investment firm, Barlow Clowes International.

Lord Young, the trade and industry secretary, was roughly treated at a private meeting of Tory backbenchers when he denied responsibility and said there were no grounds for paying compensation.

Sir Anthony Barrowclough, the Parliamentary Ombudsman, is considering whether to investigate possible mistakes by Lord Young's department, which allowed Barlow Clowes to continue investment operations while under suspicion.

Taking none of the blame for BCI.

Su	Mo	Tu	We	Th	Fr	Sa
						1
2	3	4	5	6	7	8
9	10	11	12	13	14	15
16	17	18	19	20	21	22
23	24	25	26	27	28	29
30	31					

23. Piraeus: Two British people, including a schoolgirl, are still missing after Friday's sinking of the *Jupiter*.

23. Reading: Steve Davis wins the Rothmans Grand Prix snooker championship.

24. Suffolk: Lester Piggott is freed from Highpoint Prison after serving 12 months of a three year sentence.

25. Bradford: Tories push through £5.8 million of cuts in a stormy council meeting.

25. Chelmsford: A 13-year-old boy is convicted of murdering two-year-old Sharona Joseph.

25. UK: Lloyds Bank announces plans to pay interest on current accounts.

26. Strasbourg: Jacques Delors accuses Mrs Thatcher of wrecking progress towards an open European market in 1992.

26. Lebanon: An Israeli air bomb attack kills 15 (→30).

27. UK: The government boosts pensions by 5.9 per cent, but freezes child benefits at their present level.→

27. UK: Ministers propose a "pay-as-you-view" system to pay for the BBC (→7/11).

28. UK: British Rail announces a 21 per cent increase in rail fares.

28. Alaska: Two of the trapped whales reach the open sea.

30. US: Michael Dukakis admits to being a liberal.

30. West Bank: Three people die in a patrol attack on a bus.

31. Poland: The authorities announce the closure of the Lenin shipyard in Gdansk.

31. UK: A leaked document reveals government plans to scrap free higher education.→

DEATHS

27. British actor Charles Hawtrey (Charles Frederick Joffre Hawtree) (*1914).

28. British broadcaster Jack de Manio (*26/1/14).→

29. Italian artist Pietro Annigoni (7/6/10).→

Oscar and Lucinda help Carey win Booker

Oct 25. The Booker Prize judges took only 25 minutes today to award the annual £15,000 to the Australian writer, Peter Carey, for his novel *Oscar and Lucinda*. It is a story about two passionate gamblers, Oscar, a young vicar, and Lucinda, a Sydney heiress, set in mid-19th-century Australia and England.

Other contenders on the Booker Prize short list, chosen from 103 entries, were Bruce Chatwin, Penelope Fitzgerald, Salman Rushdie, Marina Warner, and David Lodge whose novel *Nice Work* was favourite in the ante-post betting. It is set, as usual, in the university town of Rummidge, reminiscent of Birmingham.

Peter Carey and his book.

BBC radio favourite Jack de Manio dies

Oct 28. Jack de Manio, who presented the *Today* programme on Radio Four for 13 years, has died at the age of 74. He was known and prized for his gaffes, muddling up his scripts or getting the time wrong.

He was the most human of broadcasters. He was outspoken about his betes noires, such as nodding dogs in car rear windows. A critic compared his voice to the purr of a pre-war Bentley ticking over.

Police turn dogs on Prague marchers

Oct 28. When people gathered in Prague's Wenceslas Square today and cried "Long Live Freedom", Czechoslovakia's communist masters sent riot police in with tear gas, dogs and water cannon. It was the 70th anniversary of the country's birth as an independent democratic republic. Crushed by Hitler in 1938, democracy was reborn in 1945, only to be extinguished by a Moscow-inspired coup in 1948.

Cabinet backs new laws for lawyers

Oct 24. The biggest shake-up of the legal profession this century was foreshadowed this afternoon by Lord Mackay, the Lord Chancellor and head of the judiciary.

The cabinet has agreed that the profession is one of the last outposts of privilege and is overdue for greater competition and removal of restrictive practices.

Reforms are likely to include allowing solicitors to appear in the higher courts and ending their near-monopoly of probate, conveyancing and other work. The idea of a "no win, no fee" system of payment by results will also be considered.

TV adverts blamed for "lager louts"

Oct 25. The Hofmeister beer and his ilk have a lot to answer for, according to the *Good Beer Guide*, published today. It alleges that the lovable yobs of the TV adverts turn into the violent lager louts of the real world. "Nobody should be surprised about the lager lout phenomenon. If there is constant suggestion on the television screen that it's a sign of virility to drink lager, what else can you expect?" it asks.

Prince Charles slams modern architecture's "terrible damage"

The inhuman scale of modern architecture offends the Prince.

Oct 28. Prince Charles shocked the modern architecture establishment and won the sympathy of countless laymen tonight with an *Omnibus* television film written and narrated by himself. He showed examples of the "terrible damage" inflicted on Britain's townscapes by architects. He said he had discovered on his travels how many people are "appalled by what we have done to so many of our towns since the war".

Examples of the damage were the British Library — "like an academy for secret police" — the National Theatre — "a nuclear power station in the middle of London" — and the "jostling scrum of skyscrapers" round St Paul's. "Can one imagine the French doing this sort of thing round Notre Dame? When did we lose our vision?" he demanded.

Dissidents may be freed

President Gorbachev welcomes Chancellor Kohl to the Kremlin.

Oct 26. After four days of talks with Mr Gorbachev in Moscow, the West German Chancellor, Helmut Kohl, said today they had achieved results "beyond my expectations". The Soviet leader, he said, had promised to release by the end of the year all those regarded by the West as political prisoners. That represents a substantial — and unprecedented — gesture for a regime which until recently flatly denied that any political prisoners existed.

After Mr Kohl had returned home, doubts began to arise as to how many prisoners would be released. Western estimates of the number of prisoners of conscience vary. The Germans say that over 200 Soviet citizens are held on political or religious grounds.

But the Soviet spokesman Gennady Gerasimov said only "a dozen or two" political prisoners remain in custody. If Mr Gorbachev sticks to that figure then he is unlikely, to say the least, to get Western support for his plan to stage a human rights conference in Moscow in 1991. The West's view is that many Soviet dissidents are being held on trumped-up criminal charges.

Computer hacking comes under fire

Oct 24. After the release of a man who got into sensitive British and American defence systems via a computer terminal in Surrey, MPs today called for legislation to make computer "hacking" a crime. "This man could have blown the entire NATO system and endangered the world yet, incredibly, he has committed no crime whatsoever," said one infuriated politician.

Experts retorted that to make hacking illegal would only push the hackers underground into the criminal underworld, and that it is up to the managers of computer systems to make them more secure.

Annigoni, painter royal, dies at 78

Oct 28. Pietro Annigoni, who died today in Florence, made an international name with his two portraits of Queen Elizabeth II. The first, in 1955, showed her as a romantically young and challenging figure in Garter robes, and 300,000 people flocked to the Royal Academy to see it.

In 1969 he did a second portrait, not only older but more severe, which hangs in the National Portrait Gallery. Although scorned by most art critics as a painter of pastiche Old Masters, Annigoni's pictures gave an image to the Queen's reign which no others did.

IRA death squad guilty of King plot

The IRA squad's target, Mr King.

Oct 27. After being locked in argument for nearly 15 hours, the jury today brought in a majority verdict of conspiracy to murder on three young Irish Sinn Fein supporters. Their main target, apparently, was Tom King, the secretary of State for Northern Ireland. His daughter, Elisa, saw them sitting on his wall when she was out riding last August. The police arrested them and found the numbers of cars belonging to Mr King, and the car numbers and names of other IRA targets, written in tiny writing. Finbar Cullen, John McCann and Marina Shanahan were enthusiastic rather than effective. They got several numbers wrong.

Thatcher runs into child benefit storm

Oct 31. Neil Kinnock today called Mrs Thatcher a cheat and Tory MPs yelled back "You're a disgrace." Mr Speaker forced the opposition leader to withdraw his remark as unparliamentary. Mr Kinnock went off and repeated it tonight on television.

Political tempers are rising as the government continues to review the financing of the social services and the opposition accuses it of starting to dismantle the welfare state.

Today's row centred on the cabinet's decision to freeze weekly child benefit at £7.25 per child for the second year in succession instead of adjusting it in line with inflation. At the same time it is providing more cash for family credit.

Several internal Whitehall inquiries have begun into leaks about government plans for changes in benefits structure. Robin Cook, Labour's spokesman on social services, said that honourable civil servants "are outraged at what they have got to take in".

The government firmly rejects charges of bad faith. Ministers explained that every change under consideration is aimed at giving more help within available resources to people who need it most. They stressed particularly that the basic state pension is untouchable.

Oct 28. Two hundred-ton locomotives crash through their buffers and fall onto a busy London road. The police think vandals let off the brakes.

November

1988

Su	Mo	Tu	We	Th	Fr	Sa
		1	2	3	4	5
6	7	8	9	10	11	12
13	14	15	16	17	18	19
20	21	22	23	24	25	26
27	28	29	30			

1. India: Bomb blasts, blamed on Sikh separatists, kill 23 people.

1. Poland: The Solidarity Trade Union says the Lenin shipyard closure was a political move.→

1. Belfast: Davy Payne, a Loyalist gunman, is jailed for 19 years for murder.

1. S. Africa: The government bans the anti-apartheid newspaper *Weekly Mail*.

1. UK: The British Film Institute records all of today's television for posterity.

2. Paris: The outgoing European Commissioner Lord Cockfield says it is a disgrace that Britain has not joined the European Monetary System.

2. London: Architects hit back at Prince Charles, blaming planners and politicians for disastrous buildings.

3. Seoul: 24,000 police protect ex-president Chun Doo Hwan from a student lynch mob.

3. France: AIDS is declared an official epidemic.

3. Hungary: Party officials urge speedier economic reforms (→10).

3. Algeria: Voting begins on President Chadli Bendjedid's reform package (→4).

4. UK: The coroner gives a verdict of accidental death on Major Hugh Lindsay, who died while skiing with Prince Charles in March.

4. Afghanistan: The USSR suspends her withdrawal due to guerrilla activity.

4. Algeria: 92 per cent of voters in the plebiscite said "yes" to reform.

4. Jerusalem: Palestinians issue the text of their Declaration of Independence.

4. Benidorm: Spanish police ask for British police to help them patrol holiday louts.

5. Twickenham: England beat Australia 28-19 in a rugby international.

5. UK: Police arrest 56 young people in raids on "Acid House" parties.

Likud pips Labour in the Israeli election

President Chaim Herzog (left) starts haggling with Yitzhak Shamir.

Nov 2. Prime Minister Yitzhak Shamir's right-wing Likud party has won the Israeli general election by the smallest of margins, gaining one seat more than Shimon Peres' Labour party. President Chaim Herzog is now expected to ask Mr Shamir to form a government.

It will not be an easy task, for Mr Shamir will not revive his coalition with Mr Peres and must look for support from the ultra religious parties which have made a surprisingly strong showing in the election, increasing their seats in the Knesset from 13 to 18.

There will be much haggling before a deal is struck. The Sephardic Party, Shas, is believed to be demanding the ministries of housing, the interior and education or religious affairs in return for pledging its six members' support to Mr Shamir. It is also understood that in separate negotiations the extreme right-wing Tehiya Party, with five seats, has demanded the important post of deputy defence minister.

These small parties of zealots may be able to demand a commitment from Mr Shamir that he will impose strict religious laws which are against the wishes of most Israelis. Shas, for example, is demanding a return to strict observance of the Sabbath — the day when many Israelis go to the beach.

Meanwhile, the PLO has described the results as "a fatal blow for peace" and said it expected "more intransigence, hate and terrorism with a Likud government".

Church elders punish Lord Chancellor

Nov 4. Lord Mackay of Clashfern, Lord Chancellor and head of the judiciary, was today banned from taking communion and from his post of church elder for six months. His offence — attending the Roman Catholic funeral services of two fellow judges. His church — the tiny Free Presbyterian Church of Scotland which calls the Pope "the anti-Christ son of perdition".

One of its austere courts ruled that Lord Mackay — its most distinguished member — must be punished for "incorrect behaviour". "I went purely to pay respects to dead colleagues," he said. Notice of appeal was lodged.

Punished for offering condolences

Koo Stark wins her tabloid libel case

Nov 3. The *Sunday People* newspaper was today ordered to pay £300,000 in damages to Koo Stark, the actress and photographer. The *People* had published a series of articles which alleged that she had an adulterous affair with Prince Andrew after her marriage to the Green Shield stamps heir Timothy Jeffries.

Miss Stark told the court that her marriage was in difficulties at the time, and that the "cruelly damaging and wholly untrue" stories ruined her attempts at reconciliation. Even so, many are surprised at the size of the award — the fourth largest ever made in Britain.

A spotless reputation regained.

Skegness parents vote to "opt out"

Nov 2. Parents in Skegness today became the first to vote in favour of the local grammar school "opting out" of local authority control, under the terms of the Education Reform Act passed by parliament this year. Four in five of the parents voted, and of them nearly 95 per cent backed the proposal for the school to continue with direct funding from Whitehall. Opting-out is a key element of the reforms introduced by Kenneth Baker, the Education Secretary. Another is city technology colleges, the first of which opens at Solihull this week.

Thatcher presses for Polish freedom

Nov 4. Mrs Thatcher rounded off three whirlwind days in Poland with a visit to Gdansk where shipyard workers cheered her to the echo and chanted "Commies out!". Beside her, the Solidarity leader Lech Walesa beamed his approval as she told the workers that Solidarity was more than a trade union. 'It's an expression and a focus of opposition," she said.

The British Prime Minister took her message of freedom everywhere. At the state banquet in her honour she told the Polish leader, General Wojciech Jaruzelski, to get down to "a real dialogue with representatives of all sections of society, including Solidarity". She responded to appeals for Western credits and investment by saying these would be forthcoming when the Polish government and people had shown their resolve "to break through to success". Just in case the Polish leadership had not got the message, she went on: "Success

Margaret Thatcher meets Solidarity's leader Lech Walesa.

depends on openness and free discussion. We in the West would never have achieved our great technological advance without them."

In reply, Jaruzelski said: "Conditions for broad national conciliation are emerging. A new phase of democratic, humanistic socialism is

emerging." While she was in Warsaw, Mrs Thatcher visited the shrine of the Solidarity priest, Father Jerzy Popieluszko, murdered by secret police in 1984. Afterwards she walked along the crowd barriers responding to cries of "Vivat Thatcher!" (→6).

Harvest failures expose 20 million to risk of famine

Nov 4. China, plagued by droughts and floods and insect pests, has had a disastrous harvest, and an official warning was given today that 20 million peasants face "serious difficulties in feeding themselves". He Kang, the agriculture minister, said the situation was grave and that the supply of fertiliser and insecticides was in chaos.

Mr He said that one of the main problems was that many peasants had given up growing grain and were concentrating on cash crops which they were selling privately. There had also been much building on land which had traditionally been given over to grain.

The authorities insist, however, that while the difficulties are severe they could not be compared with those of the "three difficult years" from 1959 to 1961 when 16 million people died of starvation.

Mercenaries aid Maldives coup attempt

Nov 4. An attempt by 400 Tamil mercenaries to overthrow the government of President Maumoon Abdul Gayoom of the Maldives was thwarted today when the Indian government airlifted a force of paratroops and commandos to Male, the capital of these holiday islands.

The president took refuge in the headquarters of his national security force when the mercenaries landed, seized a number of hostages and began to shoot up the city. They are believed to have killed 25 people

The president, defended by his 100 troops, held out until the Indians landed and rapidly cleared the streets. Reports from the capital say that the mercenaries appeared to be seeking the return to power of Ibrahim Nasir, a former president, who has made two previous attempts to seize the islands by force.

The latest development is that many of the mercenaries have fled on board a freighter, taking their hostages with them. They are being shadowed by ships of the Indian navy. Meanwhile, the 1,000 Western tourists on the islands are continuing their holidays.

A mercenary is arrested.

INDIA

N

Indian Ocean

SRI LANKA

MALDIVES

Revolt fails to save free NHS check-ups

Nov 1. A sudden announcement of an extra £2 billion for the National Health Service failed to quell a major revolt by Tory MPs tonight. The government came closer to parliamentary defeat than at any time since last year's general election: its paper majority of 102 was reduced in the voting lobbies to only eight.

Thirty Tories sided with the opposition parties against new charges for dental check-ups. Many others abstained. There was also a smaller revolt over introduction of eye-test charges. Tory "wets" are restive (→7).

Lawson: a £2 billion sweetener?

Whitehall red light for lead-free petrol

Nov 3. The government's campaign to persuade more motorists to convert their cars to lead-free petrol was undermined today by news that most ministers still drive with lead additives in their fuel. Unleaded petrol gives less air pollution and is cheaper. But the effort and expense of conversion mean only two per cent of motorists use lead-free fuel.

Thatcherite values rebuffed by survey

Nov 3. The annual *British Social Attitudes* report, published today, suggests that despite Tory election successes, few voters agree with the values of Thatcherism. Support for the principles of the NHS is at an all-time high and the survey says industry should place the worker and consumer above the shareholder and quick profits.

Su	Mo	Tu	We	Th	Fr	Sa
		1	2	3	4	5
6	7	8	9	10	11	12
13	14	15	16	17	18	19
20	21	22	23	24	25	26
27	28	29	30			

6. USSR: Moscow warns the Baltic states not to expect too much autonomy.

6. US: A computer "virus" planted by a student has brought down 6,000 systems in the last week.

6. US: A late poll puts Dukakis within five percentage points of Bush.→

6. Poland: Lech Walesa calls for a national strike.

7. UK: Britain and Iran agree to resume diplomatic relations, broken off in 1980.

7. UK: Civil servants stage a 24-hour strike in protest at the GCHQ union ban.

7. UK: The Church of England says it will not recognise women bishops ordained abroad.

8. UK: The known death toll from AIDS has reached 1,002, with 1,862 cases reported.

8. Las Vegas: Sugar Ray Leonard wins boxing's world welterweight title for the fifth time at the age of 32.

9. UK: A White Paper on education proposes freezing student grants, topped up by commercial loans.

9. West Germany: Chancellor Kohl expresses "pain and shame" on the 50th anniversary of *Kristallnacht*.→

9. US: The world's first plutonium-powered heart pacemaker is fitted to a 48-year-old man.

10. Hungary: New legislation legalises rival political parties.

10. Warrington: Eddy Shah launches *The Post*, a new national tabloid newspaper.

11. USSR: Cosmonauts Vladimir Titov and Musa Manarov break endurance records after 326 days on a space station.

11. UK: Relatives of victims of the Piper Alpha disaster reject Occidental Oil's offers of compensation.

DEATH

9. American lawyer John Newton Mitchell, US Attorney General and defendant in the Watergate scandal (*15/9/13).

Nationalists score shock victory in Govan

The bagpipes welcome Govan victor Jim Sillars to Westminster.

Nov 10. The Scottish Nationalists captured Glasgow's Govan constituency today in one of the most sensational by-election upheavals for years. A massive Labour majority of 19,509 in last year's general election was changed to a 3,554 one for the SNP.

So Govan has pushed Scotland's future to the forefront of the United Kingdom's political agenda. The new MP, Jim Sillars, said: "We have lit a bonfire. The Scottish people are on the march again for independence."

The Queen was worried by the nationalist upsurge in the 1970s. Mrs Thatcher and Mr Kinnock assure her now that Govan is not signalling the end of the UK.

Quake hits China: 900 feared dead

Nov 8. Nearly 1,000 people are believed to have died in an earthquake which has destroyed 14 villages in the mountains of China's Yunnan province near the Burmese border. Reports trickling in from the devastated areas speak of survivors being dragged from the ruins of their homes. The rescue operation is being coordinated by the army, and supplies are being airlifted to the emergency teams. The tremor measured 7.6 on the Richter scale.

Safety neglected on Tube, says King's Cross fire report

Nov 10. The inquiry into last year's fire at King's Cross underground station today placed the blame for the 31 deaths partly on the men in charge. Sir Keith Bright chairman of London Regional Transport was criticised for monitoring financial matters to the neglect of safety. Dr Tony Ridley, the director of London Underground, was accused of fostering a corporate culture in which fires were accepted as inevitable. Both men resigned before the inquiry's report was published.

London Underground, said the report, failed to act on repeated warnings from safety experts to improve facilities and staff training to cope with a major fire which should have been foreseen.

Out: Sir Keith Bright.

Pentagon takes wraps off the Stealth fighter radar cannot see

The first picture of the USAF's high-technology F-117A prototype.

Nov 9. The US Air Force today made public the existence of its top-secret new weapon, the Lockheed F-117A "Stealth" fighter. The high-technology planes have been tested under cover of darkness, but the Pentagon must now reveal its secret so that daytime exercises can begin.

The twin-engined fighter is made of radar absorbent materials to enable it to penetrate enemy defences without being spotted. A "Stealth" bomber is also in prototype. The programme is estimated to have cost $7,000 million so far.

George Bush is elected US President

Nov 11. Vice-President George Bush won the American presidential election comfortably today. The Republican candidate carried 40 states against only ten for his Democratic opponent, Governor Michael Dukakis of Massachusetts and his vice-presidential choice, Senator Lloyd Bentsen.

In the electoral college Bush won 426 votes, Dukakis 112. The president-elect and his running-mate, Senator Dan Quayle of Indiana, got 54 per cent of the popular vote.

The Democrats retained control of Congress, and indeed slightly improved their position there. In the Senate they moved up from 54 seats to 56, and in the House of Representatives from 258 to 262.

First reactions in Washington are that the Bush administration will not be very different from the Reagan administration. After running a surprisingly abrasive campaign, the new President can expect a difficult relationship with Congress. Both the Democratic Speaker of the House, Jim Wright, and Republican Senator Robert Dole, whom Bush beat in rough primary campaigns, have made it clear he need expect no favours.

Mr Bush has already appointed his campaign manager and close friend, the former Treasury Secretary, Jim Baker, as his Secretary of State. Mr Bush is known to hope for an early summit with Mikhail Gorbachev.

Mr Bush is expected to retain the Treasury Secretary, Nick Brady. One priority will be to reassure world markets that he can reduce the budget deficit, in spite of an election pledge not to raise taxes.

Bush celebrates a clearcut victory over Michael Dukakis.

HOW THE AMERICANS VOTED - STATE BY STATE

States won by Bush
States won by Dukakis

Hurd offers more choice for viewers

Nov 7. Britain's television and radio face their most radical shake-up since commercial television was introduced more than 30 years ago. Changes announced by the government today include at least one new national TV channel, two new satellite channels, an unspecified number of local TV stations and the possibility of subscriptions replacing the BBC's licence fee.

Douglas Hurd, the Home Secretary, justified his proposals on the grounds of greater choice for the viewer. Many programme-makers in the BBC and ITV companies, however, fear that more will mean worse, with quality suffering as controls are eased.

Jenninger quits in "Nazi" speech row

Nov 11. The President of the West German Bundestag, Phillip Jenninger, resigned today, 24 hours after making an ill-judged speech marking the 50th anniversary of *Kristallnacht* (or "Crystal Night"), when synagogues were burned and Jews murdered or put in concentration camps. Jenninger tried to explain why Germans had admired Hitler before the war. But the speech came out like an excuse for Nazism.

The French, including President Mitterrand, are delighted to welcome the Prince and Princess of Wales for a visit to Paris.

Lawson backtracks after pensions gaffe

Nov 7. MPs were surprised when Nigel Lawson today pledged more cash for needy pensioners "in due course". So were Whitehall officials unaware of the scheme.

The Chancellor is doing a Houdini act to get out of trouble. He briefed journalists and later accused them of concocting stories not squaring with what he told them. The journalists wrote that the government is considering means-testing of pensions and other welfare benefits. Mr Lawson flatly denied saying it.

He challenged them to produce their notebooks. They did. They challenged him to produce a Treasury tape recording of the briefing. Then the Treasury discovered that the tape recorder had somehow not worked. The journalists were cross while Labour suspected Lawson had let the cat out of the bag.

Soccer fans face ID card scheme

Nov 9. Football fans will need an identity card to watch matches in England and Wales, as a result of legislation announced by the government today. Computer checks at the turnstiles will enable police to weed out trouble-makers. Football authorities say the ID cards will drive away casual spectators and force some clubs to close.

November

1988

Su	Mo	Tu	We	Th	Fr	Sa
		1	2	3	4	5
6	7	8	9	10	11	12
13	14	15	16	17	18	19
20	21	22	23	24	25	26
27	28	29	30			

13. Birmingham: A car ploughs into a Remembrance Day parade, injuring 13 children and four adults.

13. Greece: Premier Andreas Papandreou announces a government purge in the wake of a major banking scandal.

13. Sydney: West Indian captain Viv Richards scores his 100th century.

14. New York: A record price of $24.27 million is paid for Picasso's *Maternite*.

14. Israel: Yitzhak Shamir is asked to form the new government.

14. Algiers: The Palestine National Council declares a Palestinian state in Gaza and the West Bank (→30).

15. Pretoria: A white gunman shoots three blacks dead (→17).

15. Geneva: South Africa, Angola and Cuba agree terms under which Namibia will gain its independence.

16. Washington: Mrs Thatcher makes a farewell visit to President Reagan.

16. UK: The *Sun* newspaper agrees to pay £100,000 to charity after printing one of the Queen's private photos.

16. Riyadh: Demands for the resignation of manager Bobby Robson grow as Saudi Arabia hold England to a 1-1 draw.

17. London: Nurses picket hospitals to protest against new pay gradings (→28).

17. S. Africa: The extremist "White Liberation Front" is banned after street shootings in Pretoria (→23).

18. UK: Rupert Murdoch's bid to buy the book publishers, Collins, is resisted by authors.

18. UK: Nearly 300 drinking water supplies in England have an unacceptably high level of pesticides.

19. Murrayfield: The Australian rugby union team beat Scotland 32-13.

DEATHS

16. British politician Baroness (Jennie) Lee of Asheridge (*3/11/04).

19. Greek ship owner Christina Onassis (*11/12/50).

Pakistan poll victory for Benazir Bhutto

Supporters of the candidates in a historic poll parade their allegiances.

Nov 17. A poignant moment in modern politics occurred in Karachi today as Benazir Bhutto claimed victory in the first democratic general election in Pakistan for 11 years. She becomes the first woman to lead a country in the Islamic world, restores democracy after the dictatorship of the late General Zia and avenges the execution of her father.

While not achieving an absolute majority, she only requires the backing of 12 of the 40 independent MPs elected to form a government for her Pakistan People's Party. "Things are looking very good," Miss Bhutto told an ecstatic audience of thousands of supporters at her home town of Larkana in the Punjab before she left for the Pakistani capital.

Miss Bhutto has promised sweeping democratic reforms. She has long been a leader of movements to oust the Zia regime and a symbol of Pakistan's hopes for an end to repression. Her victory is made all the more exciting for Pakistanis, as the odds were stacked against her by the acting government which took over after General Zia was killed in a plane crash in August.

However, Miss Bhutto faces a number of critical problems. The economy is severely depressed, the powerful army remains hostile, and there is widespread corruption, poverty, social imbalance and an urgent need for land reform (→30).

Baker gives schools an English lesson

Nov 15. Children should be taught the essentials of English grammar, the Education Secretary, Kenneth Baker, decided today. He rejected proposals from a working party that spoken English should carry equal weight with reading and writing for 11-year-olds, insisting that there will be greater emphasis on "grammatical structure" when national testing begins in the 1990s.

The working party had expressed fears that too much concern over spelling and grammar could limit creativity in communication. It also addressed the problem of dialects, which it said were not "incorrect".

Nov 14. Prince Charles enjoys the party for his 40th birthday.

Inflation fuelled by mortgage rate rise

Nov 18. The pace of inflation is quickening again, according to official statistics tonight. It was running at 6.4 per cent in the year to October — the highest rate since 1985. Higher mortgage payments are largely responsible.

Nigel Lawson, the Chancellor, is now seen to have been over-optimistic in his forecasts about economic developments. Opposition MPs said that the situation is getting out of control because the latest figures will fuel wage demands. It is expected that interest rates — now 12 per cent — will be kept high well into next year. They are Mr Lawson's main anti-inflation tool.

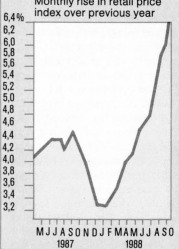

HOW INFLATION HAS RISEN

Monthly rise in retail price index over previous year

Apartheid protest lands four in jail

Nov 18. Four of South Africa's best-known anti-apartheid campaigners are facing long jail sentences today after being found guilty of treason. They were implicated in rioting in black townships in 1983 after rent increases were announced. Seven others were found guilty and 11 acquitted. The four men were Popo Molefe, leader of the United Democratic Front, which the authorities regard as a cover for the banned African National Congress; Tom Manthta; Patrick Lekota; and Moss Chikane. After the sentence Molefe shouted: "Tell our friends to be strong." (→23)

Ethnic unrest challenges unity of Communist world

Estonia: Moscow reforms spurned

Nov 16. In an extraordinary act of defiance, the Estonian assembly in the capital Tallinn today voted unanimously to reject plans by Mr Gorbachev for reforming the Soviet constitution. Instead, the Estonians adopted their own new constitution, which gives them power to reject or change legislation promulgated by Moscow.

While stopping short of demanding outright independence, the assembly insisted on the "sovereignty of Estonia", with human rights guaranteed, private property allowed and all land and natural resources brought under Estonian control. The Gorbachev reforms allow Moscow to retain wide powers over regional economic planning which Estonians complain has dragged down their living standards and ruined the environment of their Baltic republic.

Estonia's communists, led by a Gorbachev ally, Vaino Valjas, have gone along with the burgeoning nationalism. But in an apparent gesture of reassurance to Estonia's sizeable Russian minority (40 per cent of the 1.5 million people), Valjas said recently: "The future of the country is in the hands of us all."

Serbs rally in Belgrade to protest against their treatment in Kosovo.

Serbia: A million rally for independence

Nov 19. Addressing a rally attended by an estimated one million Serbs in Belgrade today, Slobodan Milosevic, the charismatic Serbian Communist Party leader, denounced "secret meetings, agreements made in restaurants and a lot of dirty slyness", which he said were creating obstacles to a solution of the Kosovo crisis. Milosevic said Serbia would be ready to risk military action "if necessary" to stop ethnic Albanians persecuting Serbs in Yugoslavia's Kosovo province.

He was cheered by an audience of well-dressed women, shabbily clad workers and Orthodox Christians with pictures of Serbia's patron saint, St Sava.

In Pristina, the province's capital, tens of thousands of ethnic Albanians continued their demonstrations for the fourth successive day against the sacking of two Kosovo Communist Party officials blamed by Belgrade for allowing xenophobic fever to take hold among them.→

Georgia: Freedom campaign grows

Nov 23. Georgia, in the Soviet Union's Transcaucasian south, has joined the Baltic republics in challenging Mr Gorbachev over his constitutional reforms and demanding greater freedom from Moscow.

While 200,000 demonstrators outside called for an end to the "Russification" of the republic, deputies in the Georgian Supreme Soviet building in Tbilisi endorsed a call for Moscow to "take account of the demands of the Georgian community". Seventy per cent of the 5.3 million people of Georgia are ethnic Georgians.

Georgia, Stalin's native land where he spent the first 20 years of his life, lies between the Black Sea and the Caspian, and has a long history of resisting foreign invaders: Mongols, Persians, Turks and Arabs. A brief spell of independence for the republic came after the Bolshevik revolution; it was crushed by Stalin in 1921. Since then nationalist pressures have surfaced on a number of occasions. In 1978 they erupted in violent and widespread riots when Moscow announced plans for giving Russian equal official status with the Georgian language (→20).

Dubcek speaks out against 1968 invasion

Nov 13. When Alexander Dubcek received an honorary degree from Bologna University today, he made a scathing attack on the repression in 1968 of his "Prague Spring" to give Czechoslovakia socialism with a human face — but he did not actually utter a word of criticism.

Before he spoke he gave reporters copies of the full text of his speech, which referred to his country's trauma 20 years ago, the stifling of reforms and the years of "economic stagnation, sterility and incalculable moral loss". But when he spoke he said none of these things. If he had done, his words would have been broadcast to Czechoslovakia by Western radio, with the risk of angering the Communist diehards in Prague.

Silent in speech, but not in words.

Mappa Mundi may be lost to nation

Nov 15. Hereford Cathedral is to auction off one of Britain's greatest mediaeval treasures, its thirteenth-century "Mappa Mundi". It could fetch up to £7 million to put the Cathedral on a sound financial footing and pay for repairs and building work.

The Mappa is a remarkable representation of the mediaeval world drawn on vellum by a Hereford monk. It shows over 400 cities, together with illustrations of people, plants, animals and events.

The auction sale marks the collapse of negotiations to sell the Mappa to the British Library. Bibliophiles have mounted a campaign to keep the map in Hereford.

Nov 15. The Soviet space shuttle Buran is launched on the back of the Energia booster rocket to make two orbits of the earth.

Su	Mo	Tu	We	Th	Fr	Sa
		1	2	3	4	5
6	7	8	9	10	11	12
13	14	15	16	17	18	19
20	21	22	23	24	25	26
27	28	29	30			

20. Belfast: Nine British soldiers are killed by a 600-pound car bomb.

20. Yugoslavia: Ethnic Albanians stage a mass protest against the forced resignation of their leaders.→

21. Glasgow: The "Committee of 100" is launched to fight against the Scottish poll tax.

21. Paris: Police detain David Evans, wanted in connection with the disappearance of 15-year-old Anna Humphries (→27).

21. Madrid: Police arrest 69 scientologists on suspicion of fraud and embezzlement.

22. London: Sculptor Tony Cragg wins the Turner art prize

22. Ottawa: Brian Mulroney's Conservative party wins the general election.

23. S. Africa: Premier Botha reprieves the Sharpeville Six from the death penalty (→24).

24. S. Africa: The government promises that Nelson Mandela, at present in hospital, will not go back to jail.

25. Harrogate: Markku Alen wins the Royal Automobile Club Lombard rally.

25. London: Peter May resigns as chairman of selectors of the England cricket team.

25. London: A teacher wins civil damages for an alleged rape, despite the absence of a criminal prosecution.

26. London: Welsh extremists are suspected of firebomb attacks on the offices of estate agents.

27. Bridgnorth: Anna Humphries' body is found in the river Severn.

28. UK: British Coal announces the closure of two pits in South Wales.

29. London: "Charter 88", a movement calling for a British Bill of Rights and other reforms, is launched.

30. Newcastle: Eleven people are injured when two trains collide.

30. UK: The Crown Prosecution Service admits that Patrick Ryan's extradition warrants were flawed.

Thatcher fumes as Ryan slips the net

Nov 29. Anglo-Irish relations were plunged into a new crisis tonight as Mrs Thatcher fumed over the government's inability to secure either the extradition from Belgium or the arrest in Ireland of Patrick Ryan, an ex-priest and alleged continental quartermaster of the IRA.

Ryan, a suspected terrorist, was flown from Brussels to Dublin after the Belgian authorities said that a British application for extradition was "vague and flawed". He then slipped away from a Dublin clinic to rest in a religious establishment "somewhere in Ireland".

Mrs Thatcher said that the Irish government's failure to arrest him was "a matter of grave concern". She added: "It is no use governments adopting great declarations and commitments about fighting terrorism if they then lack the resolve to put them into practice." She vowed to have a showdown with Charles Haughey, the Irish prime minister, at a European summit meeting in Rhodes this weekend. In Dublin Mr Haughey reacted angrily. He thought that Mrs Thatcher was behaving as though she forgot she was dealing with another sovereign nation with its own different legal procedures. A British request for Ryan's extradition is still under consideration.

Meanwhile, the European Court of Human Rights today ruled against Britain detaining terrorist suspects for seven days without charge. This has also upset the government (→30).

Freed in Belgium, back in Ireland.

Water and power sell-off top policy list

Nov 22. The privatisation of the water and electricity supplies were the major items in the government's heavy new legislative programme, which was outlined in the Queen's speech opening the parliamentary session today.

Mrs Thatcher said that users will pay more for water and electricity under changed arrangements. She told MPs that this should be acceptable because higher charges will cover the cost of environmental improvements like tackling pollution.

The Commons debate about the new programme began in an atmosphere of rancour. The opposition protested that in many ways the government is relentlessly centralising power and threatening civil liberties. Mrs Thatcher dismissed that as "astonishing rubbish".

The Prime Minister expressed anger over reports that she had advised the Queen not to accept an expected invitation from President Gorbachev to visit Russia.

She snapped: "It has not been discussed in any way at all. It (the invitation) is totally hypothetical." The reports were based on signals which Westminster journalists believed they detected not a million miles from Downing Street.

Bob Hoskins wishes he'd never asked "Who Framed Roger Rabbit".

Gorbachev tackles ethnic unrest

Nov 29. Mr Gorbachev had soothing words for the nationalists of the Baltic republics when he addressed the Supreme Soviet today. He said that criticisms of the rigidity of the Soviet Union's present political structure were justified, and promised that his reforms would "blow up" an "ossified" system and replace it with "people's power". He was asking the Supreme Soviet to endorse his constitutional changes, which his critics say go too far in underpinning the strong unitary state he says must be preserved.

AIDS "could kill 17,000 by 1992"

Nov 30. Up to 50,000 people in Britain today could be HIV-positive, and by the end of 1992 there might be as many as 17,000 deaths from AIDS, says a government-sponsored report published today.

Homosexual men appear to have become less promiscuous, so the figures are lower than earlier projections. Heterosexuals, on the other hand, have made no such changes, and the spread of AIDS remains a serious threat among them. The government has promised extra resources to treat sufferers.

Nurses' action hits London hospitals

Nov 28. Today was a "day of action" by London's nurses protesting against the new grading system operated by the NHS. Twenty hospitals were affected by the protest, but most nurses stayed at work. Managers described the impact on hospital services as "minimal".

Another protest today has made more impact. Forty-four midwives at the North Middlesex hospital resigned en masse because the new grading structure fails to recognise their extra skills and training, putting them on the same level as ordinary nurses. One, Pauline Ducrez, said she "stepped up from general nursing", but that regrading meant her taking a step down again.

Nurses take to the streets again.

Benazir Bhutto (l.), in the prime minister's chair, chats to her mother.

Bhutto takes seat in Pakistan assembly

Nov 30. Benazir Bhutto has taken her place in Pakistan's National Assembly. Officials led her to the prime minister's chair as visitors and members applauded loudly. Today's events are the culmination of Miss Bhutto's nine year battle to replace the late General Zia ul-Haq, who executed her father Zulfikar Ali Bhutto in 1979.

Dressed in Moslem dark clothing, with her hair covered by a veil, Miss Bhutto was accompanied by her mother Nusrat. Her businessman husband Asif Zardari and sister Sanam watched the proceedings. Tomorrow, President Ghulam Ishaq Khan is expected to make a televised speech asking her to form a government. Miss Bhutto's rival, Naraz Sharif, a Zia appointee, has declined to take his seat in the assembly. He has opted to sit in the Punjab local assembly, where he hopes to be elected chief minister, instead. Observers claim that Sharif bribed and threatened members of the National Assembly to win their support.

An electoral college will choose a new president on December 12, and within the next 60 days Miss Bhutto must secure a vote of confidence from the National Assembly. But with her Pakistan People's Party claiming 95 of the 237 seats, and more to come, this will be a mere formality.

US veto on Arafat sparks row in UN

Nov 30. The United States has refused to issue an entry visa for the Palestine Liberation Organisation leader Yasser Arafat to address the United Nations General Assembly in New York. The decision, by the Secretary of State, George Shultz, has been widely condemned.

The US has cited Arafat's links with terrorism as the reason for its refusal, but in a UN vote on a motion to deplore the action only Israel sided with the US, while Britain alone abstained.

While legal arguments continue, UN leaders are preparing to thwart the veto by staging a special session at Geneva — to be addressed by Mr Arafat next month.

Arafat: centre of the storm.

Interest rates jump as trade gap grows

Nov 25. Bank base interest rates were raised again today — to 13 per cent — in a government move to eliminate the growing threat of a 1970s-style inflationary spiral.

Nigel Lawson, the Chancellor, believes that squeezing company profit margins is the best way to force employers to reject big pay demands. The Treasury admits that there is a risk now of recession and strikes, but says it is worth taking.

The rise coincided with the announcement of a huge £2.4 billion trade deficit in October. "The economy is basically sound," said Mr Lawson. "All will be well."

Student loans protest brings central London to a standstill

Nov 24. Mounted police clashed with students demonstrating in London today against government proposals to introduce "top-up" loans instead of grants. MPs interrupted proceedings in parliament to protest against what some claimed was police violence. "Horses were brought in without warning," said Ann Clwyd, a Labour MP.

The violence flared when a minority of 16,000 marchers tried to break away from an agreed route to approach the House of Commons. As protesters blocked Westminster Bridge, London's traffic ground to a halt in what the police said was the capital's worst-ever jam. Over 20 students were hurt.

The police wade in to disperse the student demonstrators.

December
1988

Su	Mo	Tu	We	Th	Fr	Sa
				1	2	3
4	5	6	7	8	9	10
11	12	13	14	15	16	17
18	19	20	21	22	23	24
25	26	27	28	29	30	31

1. Ireland: Patrick Ryan says he would rather starve to death than be extradited to Britain.→

1. Pakistan: Benazir Bhutto is appointed Prime Minister (→8).

1. London: A gunman is shot after taking a hostage in the West End (→14).

2. United Nations: The General Assembly votes for a session in Geneva to allow Yasser Arafat to attend (→14).

3. UK: Edwina Currie warns against eating eggs.→

4. Brazzaville: South Africa walks out of Angola/Namibia peace negotiations with Cuba and Angola (→13).

4. UK: The British Steel flotation is 3.3 times oversubscribed.

5. Iran: Khomeini's regime is reported to be embarking on the systematic execution of all political opponents.

5. UK: The Post Office is to allow stamps to be sold in newsagents, petrol stations and other retail outlets.

6. New York: Boris Becker beats Ivan Lendl in the Masters tennis final.

6. USSR: 31 have died in riots in Azerbaijan.

7. Armenia: An earthquake rocks the area of Spitak.→

7. South Africa: Nelson Mandela is moved to a luxury home in prison grounds.

7. Stockholm: Yasser Arafat says he recognises the existence of the State of Israel (→13).

8. Pakistan: Bhutto releases 1,000 political prisoners.

8. West Germany: A US military plane crashes into a city, killing six.

9. UK: Farmers start to slaughter their chickens as egg sales drop by 60 per cent (→16).

9. UK: The board of Next sacks chief executive George Davies for being "autocratic".

DEATHS

6. American rock 'n' roll singer Roy Orbison (*23/4/36).→

Gorbachev slashes Red Army troops

Dec 7. Mikhail Gorbachev today unwrapped his Christmas present for the world — unilateral troop cuts of 500,000 men or ten per cent of Soviet military strength within the next two years. The troop cuts were the centrepiece of a dramatic speech by President Gorbachev to the United Nations in which he called for "a new world order" in international relations.

It was the first speech by a Russian leader to the UN General Assembly since Khrushchev's shoe-banging appearance in New York in 1960. Today Mikhail Gorbachev used words to surprise his audience which applauded enthusiastically. Not only is the scale of the troop cuts unprecedented, but never before has a Soviet leader embraced so warmly the prospect of international cooperation.

President Reagan, who met his Soviet counterpart for lunch after the UN speech, said he "heartily approved" of the speech. European leaders generally responded positively to Gorbachev's vision of a continent that one day may not be divided into two military blocs.

Nato's chiefs were more wary, pointing out that Warsaw Pact forces would still retain numerical supremacy, despite the cuts. Nor is military unease confined to the West: Marshal Sergei Akhromeyev, the Soviet chief of the general staff, has retired, ostensibly for health reasons, but more likely because of his opposition to Gorbachev's cuts in the armed forces.

Gorbachev challenges the West to take up his call for a peaceful world.

Six tank divisions, with 5,000 tanks based in East Germany, Hungary and Czechoslovakia, will be disbanded, with a further 5,000 tanks taken out of service in the western Soviet Union. Eight hundred combat aircraft and 8,500 artillery systems will also go. In all, one quarter of Soviet tanks and artillery in Europe will be scrapped.

Assault and landing forces will also be reduced, including specialist units for crossing rivers. This heralds a potentially seismic shift in Soviet strategy which until now has been based on offensive capabilities. Nato was formed to counter frontal assaults across the German plain.

Now Mr Gorbachev, too, is talking in terms of defence with the prospect of negotiating further cuts.

Although the troop cuts were the most dramatic element in the Soviet president's speech, it was also a *tour de force* as a review of global problems. He talked about a UN peacekeeping force in Afghanistan, unveiled proposals for tackling Third World debts, and called for new diplomatic initiatives to combat environmental damage. "Our ideal is a world community of states, based on the rule of law," he said. It is a long way from the Cold War, let alone the creed that fuelled the first Russian revolution.

Currie ruffles feathers of egg producers

Dec 5. The hens are insulted. The egg industry is furious. The health ministry is confused and the agriculture ministry is "extremely angry". Britain's egg-lovers are bamboozled.

The cause of this eggy chaos? The junior health minister Edwina Currie's widely-publicised weekend television statement that "most of the egg production in this country sadly is now infected with salmonella". Mrs Currie was referring to a Public Health Laboratory report which implicated eggs in four recent outbreaks of food poisoning.

Reaction was swift and over-whelmingly negative. "Factually incorrect and highly irresponsible," said the Egg Industry Council, who noted that only 26 out of 36,000 reported cases of food poisoning this year involved eggs. "A load of rubbish," said the Egg Producers' Association. "Incomprehensible," complained the National Farmers Union. Egg farmers say their living is now under threat because orders have fallen sharply.

Nevertheless, food poisoning has increased by over 50 per cent since 1982 and the government today announced measures to control the spread of the bacteria (→9).

Dec 6. It's Over: rock star Roy Orbison dies of a heart attack.

Armenian city "wiped off the earth"

Dec 10. The death toll from Wednesday's earthquake near the Turkish border in northern Armenia, the worst ever in the area, is now believed to top 100,000, with nearly half a million left homeless. The quake measured 6.9 on the Richter scale, on which anything over six is considered serious.

The town of Spitak, which normally houses 50,000 people, has been utterly wiped off the face of the earth. An eye-witness said: "People sit at the roadside on mattresses and bundles, their faces hardened with grief."

In Leninakan, a city of 300,000 people, 80 per cent of apartment blocks collapsed completely, burying most of the occupants. Kirovakan and Stepanakan, also near the epicentre of the earthquake, have suffered similar devastation.

Survivors recall how, at 11.41 on Wednesday morning, a brief feeling of giddiness was followed by 40 seconds of violent earth shaking. Another tremor, measuring 5.8, followed four minutes later. Schools, hospitals, apartments, factories and government buildings came crashing down in a shower of girders, concrete and bricks. Rescue workers can still hear faint cries from people trapped in the rubble.

President Gorbachev has cut short his trip to the USA, dropping plans to visit Cuba and Britain, to tour the stricken area. As the Soviet Union today observed a national day of mourning, Gorbachev visited what remains of Leninakan. He told victims that the whole country shared their sorrow. "Now the important thing is to save everyone who can be saved," he said.

The rescue operation is now well under way, with French, Swiss and British specialists at the scene. But workers complain of a shortage of skills, equipment and co-ordination. People are working feverishly, but no one is directing them. Roads and railways are out of action and thick fog is preventing planes carrying aid and rescue workers from landing. Basic services like water, electricity and sewage must be restored.

An international appeal has been launched. Kidney machines, blood supplies, cranes and lifting gear are the main requirements (→11).

Armenia's buildings shook down to the ground, leaving nothing standing.

The people of Leninakan show their grief at losing family and friends.

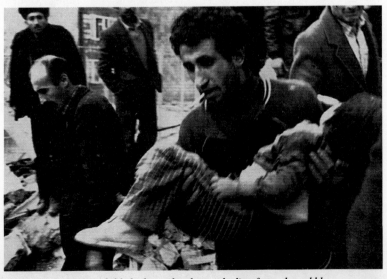

A rescuer carries a child, lucky to be dragged alive from the rubble.

Ryan row disrupts European summit

Dec 3. Britain's anger over its inability to win the extradition of Patrick Ryan, a former priest accused of terrorist offences, is disrupting the European summit in Rhodes. An angry Mrs Thatcher ticked off the Belgian prime minister, Wilfried Martens, for his country's refusal to extradite Ryan, and then complained to Charles Haughey about Ireland's handling of the affair. Both men countered by saying she did not understand their legal systems (→13).

Christmas sack for Wearside and City

Dec 6. Sunderland and the City of London are unlikely partners in gloom today as job losses soured the Christmas spirit. Some 2,400 jobs are to go with the government's closure of North East Shipbuilders, the last remaining shipyard on Wearside which was once the world's largest shipbuilding centre. And in the City 450 jobs are going at merchant bankers Morgan Grenfell in the wake of last year's stock market crash (→15).

Cyclone kills 1,200

Dec 2. Still reeling from the devastating floods in September, officials in Bangladesh met today to assess a new disaster. In the worst storm of the century, a cyclone has brought 110mph winds and rain to a wide area of the country. The death toll has passed 1,200, with 6,000 missing and over 20,000 injured. Five million are believed homeless.

Soviet jet hijacked

Dec 2. Five Russians landed in Israel's main airport tonight in a hijacked Ilyushin-76 plane. At first the Israelis thought they were Jewish refugees, but they turned out to be armed robbers making a long-distance get-away. Israel will send them back. Relations with the Soviet Union have warmed since the incident.

December

1988

Su	Mo	Tu	We	Th	Fr	Sa
				1	2	3
4	5	6	7	8	9	10
11	12	13	14	15	16	17
18	19	20	21	22	23	24
25	26	27	28	29	30	31

11. Armenia: 78 troops die when an aid-carrying jet crashes at Leninakan.

11. Armenia: Five members of the "Karabakh committee" are arrested for fomenting ethnic unrest (→15).

11. UK: A private sector plan to save the Hotol space plane crumbles when the investors fail to agree.

12. US: David Jenkins, a former British 400-metre champion, is jailed for running a steroid drugs ring.

12. UK: The *Sun* newspaper pays £1 million to Elton John for printing untruths about his private life.

12. Mexico: Sixty die when a fireworks stall explodes in a street market.

13. Geneva: Yasser Arafat addresses the United Nations, inviting Israel to attend peace talks. →

13. Brazzaville: South Africa signs an accord which will give Namibia independence.

14. Spain: Eight million workers stage a strike against government economic policies.

14. London: Gunmen wound five in a shoot-out at a Post Office (→16).

15. UK: 450 job losses are announced at the Swan Hunter shipyard on Tyneside.

15. UK: Tory ex-cabinet minister John Biffen speaks in favour of a non-nuclear defence policy.

15. Sweden: Police arrest a man suspected of murdering premier Olof Palme in 1986.

16. UK: British Rail confirms that faulty installation of signalling caused the Clapham Junction crash; a man dies to bring official death toll to 34.

16. Israel: Troops shoot four dead in the West Bank.

16. Surrey: A man is murdered and another stabbed by a violent gang during a county-wide rampage.

17. Warrington: Eddy Shah's *Post* newspaper closes, after printing 33 issues and losing £9 million.

US to open historic dialogue with Arafat

Dec 14. After years of refusing to deal with the Palestine Liberation Organisation, the United States is now ready to start a "substantive dialogue" with them, following a press announcement by PLO chairman Yasser Arafat.

Reading from a prepared statement, Arafat removed all barriers to peaceful negotiations by renouncing "totally and absolutely ... all forms of terrorism including individual, group and state terrorism". He also accepted United Nations resolutions 242 and 338, recognising Israel's right to exist within secure borders.

The US secretary of state, George Shultz, said he regarded Arafat's statement as a major step towards direct negotiations between Israel and the Palestinians, but insisted that the United States did not recognise last month's unilateral declaration of a Palestinian state in the West Bank and Gaza.

Israeli reaction, somewhat confused because of the parties' continuing negotiations for a coalition,

Arafat: V for victory?

was horrified and disappointed. A spokesman for the prime minister said the US was fooled by Arafat's "cheap words". The PLO leader claims he can do nothing to stop the Palestinian uprising ("intifada") in the West Bank (→16).

Violence rocks run-up to Sri Lanka poll

Dec 16. Two bombs exploded in Sri Lanka tonight at the final rally of Mrs Sirimavo Bandaranaike, the leader of the main opposition party to the government in next week's presidential election. Crowds fled in panic, and at least 20 people were injured, as Mrs Bandaranaike was hustled to safety by bodyguards.

The explosion came towards the end of an election campaign dominated by violence. Fighting between Sinhalese extremists and paramilitary government forces has killed about 20 people a day, mostly in the south of the country where

support for Mrs Bandaranaike, a former prime minister, is strongest. Ironically, the heartland of the Tamil separatists in the north and east of Sri Lanka has been relatively calm, not least because 50,000 Indian troops are patrolling there.

Mrs Bandaranaike has drawn larger crowds than Ranasinghe Premadasa, the prime minister and candidate of the ruling United National Party. Despite fears of further disruption, it appears likely that the poll — Sri Lanka's first since a general election in 1977 — will go ahead on Monday.

Armenia counts the cost of catastrophe

Dec 17. Rescuers are winding up their search for survivors in the rubble of Armenia. The clear-up operation is about to start, and then the rebuilding process. But with 55,000 corpses to bury, many lives have been permanently shattered. And the ethnic unrest in Gorbachev's tragic republic goes on.

Currie quits over storm in egg cup

Dec 16. Edwina Currie, the junior health minister, has resigned after a health warning that infuriated Britain's egg producers and which could cost the taxpayer over £10 million in buying up unsold eggs.

Her statement that most eggs were infected with salmonella was the last in a long line of remarks which often seemed calculated to offend. In the world according to Currie, northerners die of "ignorance and crisps", cervical cancer is the result of "being far too sexually active — nuns don't get it", "good Christian people ... will not catch AIDS", and people should "postpone that second holiday and use the money for an operation".

It is ironic that her fatal blunder was perhaps her least misleading one. Microbiologists confirm that Britain is facing its worst-ever outbreak of salmonella, with eggs a prime suspect. Her real mistake may have been to upset Britain's powerful farming lobby.

Goodbye, Edwina.

Thatcher snubbed over Ryan extradition

Dec 13. Ireland today refused to extradite Patrick Ryan, the former priest accused of terrorist offences, on the grounds that he would not receive a fair trial in Britain. Mrs Thatcher said this decision was a "great insult" to the British people.

In Dublin John Murray, the Irish Attorney General, said that attacks on Ryan in the British parliament and press had created "irredeem-

able" prejudice. In London Neil Kinnock, the Labour Party leader, blamed Mrs Thatcher for poisoning the atmosphere by her remarks which, he argued, had led to today's refusal to extradite Ryan.

The Irish authorities invited Britain to use Irish law to prosecute Ryan in the Republic. This is now receiving lukewarm consideration in Whitehall.

Signal failure blamed for rail disaster at Clapham

Firemen, doctors, police and ambulancemen join forces in an attempt to rescue injured passengers from the wreckage of three trains.

Dec 12. Thirty-six people are feared to have died today when a packed commuter train piled into the back of another just outside Clapham Junction, the world's busiest railway junction, in south-west London. Seconds later an empty train ploughed into the wreckage, and only quick thinking by its guard prevented a fourth train joining the pile-up.

It was Britain's worst railway disaster for more than 20 years, with more than 100 people injured in addition to those who died. Tonight, as rescue workers salvage personal belongings such as brief cases strewn over the track, signal failure appeared to be the most likely cause of the tragedy. British Rail admitted that "the fail safe mechanism did not work".

The accident occurred at 8.13 this morning when the 6.30 train from Bournemouth crashed into the rear of the 7.18 from Basingstoke to Waterloo. The Bournemouth train sheared into the air and onto its side in a cloud of flying glass and metal, only to crash into an empty train travelling south on the adjoining track. It was the guard of this train who ran back to stop a fourth train, packed with passengers, joining the wreckage. Survivors spoke later of the devastating moment of impact.

"We were flung into the air and our train was pushed sideways and crushed against the banking. I landed on top of people," said Graham Winston who was in the Basingstoke train. Mike Clarke, in the buffet car of the Bournemouth train, described how it "just disintegrated". He added: "The roof split open and the bogeys came up through the floor. Everything went dark and furniture and debris flew around."

Rescue workers were hampered by the location of the crash in a deep cutting. "Bodies were ripped apart and the trains tangled together," said Chris Fitzgerald, a fireman. Many people were trapped in the wreckage, unable to move. As rescue workers prised open the enmeshed trains, doctors crawled towards them to give lifesaving transfusions and painkilling drugs. Less seriously injured survivors sat on the trackside, bloodied and wrapped in blankets.

More than 1,000 people were on the trains and overcrowding, as well as the signal failure, will be examined at a public inquiry (→16).

Red for danger: the worst crashes

MAY 1915: 227 people killed in a collision between a troop train and a passenger train near Gretna Green in the Scottish Borders.

OCTOBER 1952: 112 people killed and 340 injured at Harrow and Wealdstone station when a Perth to Euston express ran into another train, with a Manchester express then hitting the wreckage.

DECEMBER 1957: 92 people killed and 173 injured when two trains collided in fog under a bridge which then collapsed at Lewisham.

NOVEMBER 1967: 49 people killed and 78 injured when a Hastings to Charing Cross train was derailed at Hither Green, south London.

December
1988

Su	Mo	Tu	We	Th	Fr	Sa
				1	2	3
4	5	6	7	8	9	10
11	12	13	14	15	16	17
18	19	20	21	22	23	24
25	26	27	28	29	30	31

18. UK: Neil Kinnock says he backs electoral reform, but not proportional representation.

18. Israel: Three Palestinians are shot dead in the occupied territories (→19).

19. UK: The government announces £20 million worth of intervention in the egg market.

19. Israel: The Labour and Likud parties agree to form a coalition.

19. London: Twelve men are arrested, suspected of being the gang which rampaged through Surrey last week.

20. UK: Vickers wins a contract to prove their ability to make the British Army's next tank, Challenger 2.

20. West Midlands: Three senior police officers receive firebombs in the mail.

20. Ramsgate: A cross-channel ferry catches fire, with 500 people on board.

20. UK: Salmonella infection is found in a quarter of all plants supplying poultry feed.

20. London: Princess Beatrice is baptised.

21. London: Police uncover an IRA bomb factory in Clapham.

21. London: Christine Mason and Roy Aston are jailed for 12 years for murdering their baby Doreen.

21. USSR: Soviet cosmonauts Musa Manarov and Vladimir Titov return from a record 365 days in space.

21. Seville: Spain beats Northern Ireland 4-0 in a World Cup qualifying match.

22. UK: New Zealand cancels the planned tour by the England cricket team.

23. Lockerbie: A hundred bodies remain missing; the "black boxes" fail to give any clue to what caused the crash.

23. New York: Ex-Miss America Bess Myerson is cleared of attempting to corrupt a judge.

24. UK: The Queen changes her Christmas speech, mentioning Armenia, Clapham and Lockerbie.

Policeman shot dead by Coventry gunman

The siege started after a police car (left) rammed the getaway car.

Dec 19. A policeman was shot dead and another seriously injured today after armed robbers held up a bank in Coventry. Two men were being chased by police after the theft of £600 from a branch of Midland Bank in the town.

One of the thieves shot at a police car, killing the driver, PC Gavin Carlton, aged 29. A detective who took up the chase, DC Leonard Jakeman, was later shot in the stomach during a scuffle with the men. He is now reported to be stable after surgery.

The men then fled across a golf course, taking refuge in a house in Stoneleigh Avenue. One man eventually gave himself up to the police. The other shot himself dead.

Nations agree peace for southern Africa

Dec 22. Eight months of intense diplomatic activity reached a climax today in New York, where South Africa, Cuba and Angola signed treaties for the phased withdrawal of Cuban troops from Angola. Agreements for the eventual independence of Namibia, the south-west African state occupied by South Africa, were also signed. Any peace that comes to the area is likely to be uneasy, however. South Africa will continue to support Unita, the rebel army waging war in Angola, which shelters and gives aid to about 6,000 African National Congress fighters, who seek black rule in South Africa.

Department stores hit by firebombs

Dec 20. Millions of pounds' worth of damage was caused to department stores around Britain today when they were attacked by firebombs. By far the most seriously hit was Dingles in Plymouth which was gutted by the worst fire in the city since the Second World War. Police suspect animal rights extremists are behind the attacks which included incendiary devices at Harrods and Selfridges in London, and Howell's in Cardiff. The offices of the *Fur Trade Review* and the home of a Cambridge physiology professor were also targets.

RUC must testify at inquest, rules court

Dec 20. The Northern Ireland Appeal Court today ordered three officers of the Royal Ulster Constabulary to give evidence to a fresh inquest into the deaths, six years ago, of three unarmed men at the hands of an undercover RUC squad. The ruling is a setback for the British authorities, who have tried to restrict the scope and powers of inquests in Northern Ireland.

A new inquest will now look into one of the so-called Stalker-Sampson incidents, in which the RUC is alleged to have operated a "shoot to kill" policy. The government is likely to appeal against the decision.

Premier wins poll, but protest looms

Dec 20. Sri Lanka's prime minister, Ranasinghe Premadasa, has edged to victory in the presidential election held yesterday. He won exactly half of the votes cast, defeating Mrs Bandaranaike who had 45 per cent of the vote.

Intimidation by Sinhalese extremists, who waged a campaign of terror in the lead-up to the poll, meant an unusually low turnout of 55 per cent. Sixty-five polling stations stayed closed because of left-wing threats. Mrs Bandaranaike is therefore challenging the result.

Dec 19. Villagers greet a truckload of Vietnamese soldiers returning from Cambodia. 18,000 troops are involved in the withdrawal operation.

Jumbo jet crashes on Scottish town: 270 killed

Blazing houses light up a chunk of wreckage from the doomed airliner.

The nose section, with the crew dead inside, landed three miles away.

Dec 22. A Pan American jumbo jet crashed on to the town of Lockerbie in the Scottish Borders last night, killing all 259 passengers on board and at least 11 people on the ground to make it Britain's worst air disaster. As accident investigators began examining the wreckage, it emerged today that US embassies had received a warning that a Pan Am flight would be a terrorist target for a bomb.

The plane, flying from Heathrow to New York, broke up in mid-air so suddenly that the crew was unable to send any message and so dramatically that wreckage was scattered over large areas of Lockerbie and the surrounding countryside. As dawn broke over the small market town, the devastation caused by the crash of Pan Am flight 103 was there for all to see.

Bodies were strewn around the town and fields, often mutilated beyond recognition. Twisted fragments of metal littered streets and gardens. On a hillside three miles away lay the nose of the aircraft, largely intact, while in the town a wing had gouged a deep crater, totally destroying half a dozen houses in Sherwood Crescent.

Flight 103 had originated in Frankfurt and then, after a stop at London's Heathrow airport, took off 25 minutes late at 6.25pm for New York. The plane — the 15th Boeing 747 to be built and now 19 years old — was at its cruising height of 31,000 feet and crossing the Scottish border towards the North

Atlantic when, at 7.19pm, it disappeared from radar screens. There were high winds, but no other aircraft was in the area at the time.

Minutes later what eyewitnesses described as a "fireball" fell from the sky over Lockerbie. "The whole sky lit up and it was virtually rain-

"The sky lit up ... it was raining fire"

ing fire," said Mike Carnahan. "The plane was trailing flames when it went over and there was a terrible explosion. The crash was very close to the centre of the town in a residential area."

What later turned out to have been a wing of the doomed plane gouged a crater out of Sherwood Crescent, a small street adjoining the main A74 Glasgow-England

road. Several houses here were simply vaporised by the explosion and others were gutted by fire. Cars on the road were burnt out and for a time there were fears that a petrol station would also explode.

One resident of Sherwood Crescent said: "I just heard this thin screaming sound. The ground shook. It felt like an earthquake." Another added: "There were cars ablaze on the road and the houses were blazing like an inferno."

As the Fire Brigade battled to control dozens of fires, RAF helicopters flew medical teams to Lockerbie, a market town with a population of 2,500. Today they have been joined by soldiers as well

as policemen who are combing the area not only for bodies but also clues to the cause of the disaster. The Prime Minister, the Duke of York and the American ambassador were among visitors to the scene; the Queen and President Reagan sent messages of sympathy.

Most of the passengers were American, flying home for Christmas reunions with their families. They included servicemen and 38 students from Syracuse University in New York state. Distraught relatives gathered at New York's Kennedy airport. If it is proved that a bomb caused the tragedy, the crash is bound to focus renewed attention upon airport security. MPs expressed concern that Heathrow was not told of the threat to Pan American flights which was circulated by US authorities (→23).

A huge crater and charred houses mark the scene of the Pan Am tragedy.

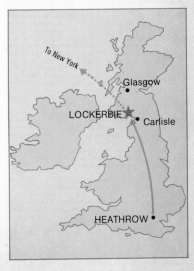

To New York · Glasgow · LOCKERBIE · Carlisle · HEATHROW

December

1988

Su	Mo	Tu	We	Th	Fr	Sa
				1	2	3
4	5	6	7	8	9	10
11	12	13	14	15	16	17
18	19	20	21	22	23	24
25	26	27	28	29	30	31

25. Vatican: The Pope appeals for help for AIDS sufferers worldwide.

25. S. Africa: Twelve people die in violence in Natal townships.

25. Paris: The Paris-Dakar motor rally starts.

26. Kempton: Desert Orchid wins the King George VI steeplechase.

26. India: Nineteen people die in riots following the murder of a local politician.

26. UK: Junior doctors launch a campaign to protest against their dangerously long working hours (→28).

27. Dhaka: 250 people are missing, feared drowned, when a river ferry sinks.

27. Armenia: Four hundred bodies are still buried under rubble as the clearing-up operation gets under way.

27. Honolulu: Ex-president Marcos of the Philippines goes into hospital with heart problems.

28. Australia: A commission calls for new rules to halt the high death toll of Aborigines in police custody.

28. UK: Health minister David Mellor says some junior doctors exaggerate the number of hours they work.

29. Armenia: The estimated death toll in the earthquake is reduced to 25,000.

29. UK: A leading building society and bank announce mortgage increases to bring interest rates up to 13.75 per cent.

29. Melbourne: West Indian Malcolm Marshall becomes the ninth cricketer ever to take 300 Test wickets.

30. Moscow: Yuri Churbanov, Brezhnev's son-in-law, is jailed for 12 years on corruption charges.

30. USA: Colonel Oliver North subpoenas President Reagan and George Bush to testify in the Iran-Contra trial due to start next year.

31. Rio de Janeiro: A hundred people are feared dead when a pleasure-boat sinks.

International hunt begins for jet bombers

Dec 30. Scottish detectives are flying to Germany today as an international hunt begins for the bombers responsible for last week's crash of a Pan Am jumbo jet at Lockerbie. The US president-elect George Bush said: "We will seek hard and punish firmly and decisively those who did this."

Calls for revenge have swelled in America since it was announced on that "conclusive" evidence of sabotage had been found by Ministry of Defence scientists on two parts of a metal luggage pallet.

"The explosive's residues recovered from the debris have been positively identified and are consistent with the use of a high-performance plastic explosive. This led directly to the plane's destruction," said Michael Charles, who is heading the British accident investigation team.

First suspicions have focussed upon extremist Arab groups, such as the Popular Front for the Liberation of Palestine led by Ahmed

Terror suspect: Ahmed Jebril.

Jebril, which opposes the recent diplomatic initiative of Yasser Arafat, who has offered to help British and American police hunting the bombers. The final death toll is 270, but the search continues for many missing bodies.

Drifting tanker cuts North Sea oil flow

Dec 26. Three North Sea oilfields shut down completely today when a storage vessel broke free from its moorings in gale-force winds. The shut-down — automatic if vessels are adrift near oil installations — could lead to severe disruptions in British oil output and add to Britain's growing balance of payments deficit. Shell, one of the operators affected, said it could take months to re-open the closed platforms.

Homelessness "has doubled in 1980s"

Dec 29. The number of homeless people in Britain has doubled between 1979 and 1987, according to Shelter's annual report on homelessness. Official statistics show over 370,000 homeless, but the true figure is in the millions, says the housing charity. New social security rules, spiralling house prices and rents, and the end of council house-building have forced people onto the streets, it says.

Europe beefs about US meat hormones

Dec 28. A trade war between the European Community and the US loomed larger today when European Commission president Jacques Delors threatened to match stiff taxes which Washington has said it will put on some luxury foods from Europe.

The growing row stems from an EC ban on imports of hormone-treated meat. The EC says that the ban, effective from January 1 1989, is needed because five particular types of hormone are feared to have links with child deformities. The import ban extends to meat from all sources, of which US meat accounts for no more than £170m each year. However, the US has threatened to levy 100 per cent taxes on some EC goods, such as tinned tomatoes and ginger beer, if the measures go through. Alfred Kingon, US ambassador to the EC, claimed the ban was based on "irrational scientific grounds".

Bhutto and Gandhi seal nuclear treaty

Dec 31. India and Pakistan signed their first agreements for 16 years today at the end of a historic meeting in Islamabad, the Pakistani capital, between prime ministers Rajiv Gandhi and Benazir Bhutto.

The deal is the first diplomatic coup for Miss Bhutto since she was elected as Pakistan's first woman premier in November, and marks the beginning of what she called at a press conference "a momentum for peace" between the traditionally hostile neighbours. It is the first time in nearly 30 years that an Indian leader has officially visited Pakistan.

The pact hinges on a pledge by both sides not to attack each other's nuclear establishments. This will be of greater importance to Pakistan than to India, as the Pakistanis are believed to be near to possessing their own nuclear bomb.

Making friends: Pakistan's Benazir Bhutto and India's Rajiv Gandhi.

Tehran frees Briton jailed for two years

Dec 29. Nicholas Nicola, aged 23, returned to London on Tuesday after serving two years in a Tehran jail. Nicola's crime was to stray into Iran while touring the Pakistani border. His release has helped the steadily-improving relationship between Britain and Iran. But there is still no sign of release for British businessman Roger Cooper, jailed for longer on a slimmer pretext.

There was more good news today when the Valente sisters, aged six and seven, returned to their native France. The girls spent over a year as hostages in Lebanon by the Abu Nidal terrorist group, accused of spying for Israel.

Government falls in Yugoslavia

Dec 30. The government of Yugoslavia, rocked all year by ethnic unrest in Serbia, today bowed to economic troubles and resigned. It is the first time that an entire government has collapsed since the Communists came to power in 1945. Branko Mikulic, the prime minister, announced his resignation after parliament had failed to approve a budget for 1989 and a package of economic reforms designed to curb soaring inflation and to end a wave of strikes.

Dec 31. Actress Penelope Keith is among those mentioned in the New Year's honours list. Miss Keith is awarded an OBE.

Arts: Salome unveils in year of Tempest

Bated breath all round as this Picasso fetches a cool £20.9m.

The most discussed opera of the year was Covent Garden's production of *Salome* in which **Sir Peter Hall** directed his wife, **Maria Ewing**. Physically as well as vocally striking, she removed all seven veils and bared herself completely to the audience as well as to Herod.

It was not long afterwards that Lady Hall informed the public that their marriage was over, although they continued to fulfil joint engagements. Hall meanwhile was busy directing Shakespeare's *The Tempest*, whose near-naked Caliban, streaked with dirt, was judged suitable for inspection by the Queen on her 25th anniversary visit to the National Theatre.

This was only one of four productions of *The Tempest* in a boom year for Shakespeare. The National and RSC had the hot competition of **Kenneth Branagh's** Renaissance Company's sell-out season in the West End, **Jonathan Miller's** Old Vic company and **Derek Jacobi's** *Richard II*. By the end of the year Peter Hall was directing **Vanessa Redgrave** in the first production of the non-subsidised Peter Hall Company.

David Hockney's owlish high profile ensured big attendances for his retrospective at the Tate Gallery. Is he rivalling his idol Picasso in versatility? asked critics. Not yet anyway in price — a Tokyo department store paid £20.9 million at Christie's for *Acrobat and Young Harlequin*. But then Sotheby's had demonstrated the unreality of auction prices by obtaining £780,000 for paintings by the rank amateur, **Sir Noel Coward**.

To judge by the coverage you would conclude that **Joan Collins** was the most significant new novelist this year except perhaps for **Tom Wolfe**, observer of New York's Vanity Fair. Biographers buzzed over memories of **Richard Burton** — his brother, his widow and, with great brouhaha, **Melvyn Bragg**, who seemingly attained mystical identification with him. Bernard Shaw, to whom **Michael Holroyd** devoted 15 years' study, seemed minor in comparison.

On television a revival of the 30-year-old "Face to Face" with **John Freeman** made today's interviews look positively vapid.

Alan Bennett as Anthony Blunt in his own play "Single Spies".

Things they said in the year 1988 …

What's wrong with being a boring kind of guy ?
George Bush

I have no regrets.
Edwina Currie

I don't think a prostitute is more moral than a wife, but they are doing the same thing.
The Duke of Edinburgh

All the evidence I see so far is that the present level of interest rates is adequate.
Nigel Lawson (in November)

There is no such thing as collective guilt.
Kurt Waldheim

Senator, you are no Jack Kennedy.
Lloyd Bentsen (to Dan Quayle)

I am fed up with being humiliated.
Denzil Davies

I know a little more this time.
Eddie Shah

I don't think modesty is the outstanding characteristic of contemporary politics.
Edward Heath

Loadsamoney !
Harry Enfield

I want to be a good sailor's wife.
The Duchess of York

The use or threat of force can no longer be an instrument of foreign policy.
Mikhail Gorbachev

The hits of the year

TOP FILMS
Fatal Attraction; Crocodile Dundee II; Three Men and a Baby.

TOP SINGLES
The Only Way is Up (Yazz/Plastic Population); I Should Be So Lucky (Kylie Minogue); Mistletoe and Wine (Cliff Richard).

TOP HARDBACK FICTION
Rivals (Jilly Cooper); Rock Star (Jackie Collins); To Be the Best (Barbara Taylor Bradford).

TOP HARDBACK NON-FICTION
Guinness Book of Records; Moonwalk (Michael Jackson); A Brief History of Time: from the Big Bang to Black Holes (Stephen Hawking).

(Sources: Screen International, Sunday Times/MRIB, Bookseller.)

The World's Nations

This section gives brief updated facts on each nation's geographical location, population, area, language, religion, political status, and membership in international organizations. The head of state and head of government are also named. Figures provided for Gross National Product (GNP) and population are the latest available. Currency values are based on May 30, 1988, indicative rates. The texts provide a short summary of the main events of 1988. A list of abbreviations used is provided on page 123.

Afghanistan

Central Asia
251,773 sq. mi
Pop: 8-10m.
UN

Capital: Kabul (Pop: 2m.)
Official languages: Pushtu, Dari (Persian)
Religion: Moslem (Shiah, Sunni)
Political status: People's republic
Head of state: Najibullah (since 1987)
Head of government: Sultan Ali Kishtmand (since 1981)
GNP per capita: $250 (1985)
Currency: afghani (£1 = 99.25)

The signing in Geneva on April 14 of a U.S. and Soviet-guaranteed peace agreement did not lead to an end of the bloodshed in war-torn Afghanistan. The historic peace accord marked the start of the process of withdrawal of the 115,000 Soviet troops which had rolled into Afghanistan in December 1979. Under the terms of the accord, all Soviet forces must be out by February 15, 1989. Soviet losses during the war against the Western-backed Afghan rebels, or mujahedeen, are estimated at more than 20,000 men. Well over a million Afghans died in a war that spilled over into Pakistan, soured superpower relations and blocked significant improvement of links between Moscow and Beijing. The Soviet pullout was marked by an upsurge in rebel attacks on Soviet and Afghan army positions, particularly in Kabul. Bomb and rocket attacks increased during the summer. The Soviet Union, citing repeated mujahedeen violations of the U.N.-sponsored Geneva accord, "temporarily halted" its troop pullout in November. This prompted the United States to call on Afghan rebels to refrain from attacks on Soviet troops.

Albania

Southeastern Europe
11,101 sq. mi
Pop: 3.08m.
UN, Warsaw Pact

Capital: Tirana (Pop: 206,000)
Official language: Albanian
Religion: officially atheist
Political status: Socialist people's republic
Head of state: Ramiz Alia (since 1982)
Head of government: Adil Carçani (since 1982)
GNP per capita: $930 (1986)
Currency: lek (£1 = 9.97)

Albania, isolated from the outside world for decades, in 1988 further opened up. In June, a party of 100 students was allowed to visit Yugoslavia, while in October Hungary said it was ready to start talks on an exchange of ambassadors with Albania.

Algeria

North Africa
919,595 sq. mi
Pop: 22.6m.
UN, AL, OAU, OPEC

Capital: Algiers (Pop: 1,721,607)
Official language: Arabic
Religion: Sunni Moslem
Political status: Socialist republic
Head of state: Chadli Bendjedid (since 1979)
Head of government: Kasdi Merbah (since 1988)
GNP per capita: $2,430 (1984)
Currency: Algerian dinar (£1 = 9.24)

President Chadli Bendjedid in November appointed Health Minister Kasdi Merbah, 50, as premier, a month after violent rioting led to a referendum in which voters approved broad reforms. According to official figures, 176 people died in the riots.

Andorra

Southern Europe
180 sq. mi
Pop: 42,712

Capital: Andorre la Vieille
Official language: Catalan
Religion: Roman Catholic
Political status: Principality
Heads of state: The Spanish Bishop of Urgel, Mgr. Joan Marti y Alanis, and French President François Mitterrand
Head of government: Josef Pintat Solans (since 1986)
GNP per capita: $9,000
Currencies: French franc and Spanish peseta

A medieval necropolis containing about 100 skeletons of people who died between the 12th. and 15th. centuries was discovered in August near the Sant Joan de Casselles chapel.

Angola

Southwestern Africa
481,351 sq. mi
Pop: 8.96m.
UN, OAU

Capital: Luanda (Pop: 960,000)
Official language: Portuguese
Religions: Roman Catholic 55%, Protestant 9%, animist 34%
Political status: Socialist people's republic
Head of state: José Eduardo dos Santos (since 1979)
GNP per capita: $500 (1985)
Currency: kwanza (£1 = 52.77)

Following lengthy talks with the United States, South Africa and Cuba, Angola agreed in November to a plan calling for the phased withdrawal of some 55,000 Cuban troops sent to help Angola fight South African-backed rebels.

Antigua and Barbuda

Caribbean
171 sq. mi
Pop: 81,500
UN, OAS, Caricom, CW

Capital: St John's (Pop: 30,000)
Official language: English
Religion: Christian (mostly Anglican)
Political status: Constitutional monarchy
Head of state: Queen Elizabeth II
Head of government: Vere C. Bird (since 1981)
GNP per capita: $1,990 (1984)
Currency: Eastern Caribbean dollar (£1 = 4.79)

The 13 leaders of the English-speaking Caribbean Community in October agreed to abolish nearly all trade barriers between their nations, thus establishing a free-trade zone in the economically-buffeted region.

Argentina

South America
1,073,358 sq. mi
Pop: 31.06m.
UN, LAIA, OAS

Capital: Buenos Aires (Pop: 9,927,404)
Official language: Spanish
Religion: Roman Catholic 92%
Political status: Federal republic
Head of state: Raul Alfonsin (since 1983)
GNP per capita: $2,470 (1984)
Currency: austral (£1 = 10.77)

In October, the government set elections for May 1989. The poll will mark the first time a presidential term has been completed in the last 36 years. Earlier, a court sentenced three former members of the military junta to 12 years in jail for their role in the 1982 war with Britain over the Falklands. In April, a U.S. court ordered a former Argentine general to pay damages of 21 million dollars to a man he allegedly tortured. Rebel army troops in December seized the country's largest military base.

Australia

South Pacific
2,966,200 sq. mi
Pop: 15.97m.
UN, ANZUS, CW, OECD

Capital: Canberra (Pop: 286,000)
Official language: English
Religions: Anglican 36%, other Protestant 25%, Roman Catholic 33%
Political status: Federal constitutional monarchy
Head of state: Queen Elizabeth II
Head of government: Robert Hawke (since 1983)
GNP per capita: $11,172 (1984)
Currency: Australian dollar (£1 = 2.46)

Britain's Queen Elizabeth II in April attended ceremonies marking the 200th. anniversary of British settlement in the former convict colony. It was the Queen's 12th. official visit to Australia and was followed by several other British royal visits. In September, a Darwin court quashed the convictions of an Australian couple for the 1980 death of their baby daughter, closing the book on the celebrated "dingo murder" case as a miscarriage of justice. In November, it was announced that AIDS has killed 525 Australians, 24 of them women. In the same month, Australia and China signed a major five-year agreement to cooperate in space technology. This was seen by Canberra as a big boost for Australia's fledgling space industry.

Austria

Western Europe
32,376 sq. mi
Pop: 7.57m.
UN, EFTA, OECD

Capital: Vienna (Pop: 1,481,399)
Official language: German
Religions: Roman Catholic 84.3%, Protestant 5.6%
Political status: Federal parliamentary republic
Head of state: Kurt Waldheim (since 1986)
Head of government: Franz Vranitsky (since 1986)
GNP per capita: $12,297 (1986)
Currency: schilling (£1 = 21.03)

Chancellor Franz Vranitsky firmly condemned in November the "fanatics of Vienna" who took part in the 1938 "Crystal Night" Nazi wave of pogroms during which 30 Austrian Jews were massacred.

Bahamas

Caribbean
5,353 sq. mi
Pop: 235,000
UN, OAS, CW, Caricom

Capital: Nassau (Pop: 135,437)
Official language: English
Religions: Baptist 29%, Anglican 23%, Roman Catholic 22%
Political status: Constitutional monarchy
Head of state: Queen Elizabeth II
Head of government: Sir Lynden O. Pindling (since 1967)
GNP per capita: $7,950 (1984)
Currency: Bahamian dollar (£1 = 1.77)

The long-running investigation of premier Lynden Pindling for alleged drug trafficking dragged on. The Bahamian attorney general said a drug runner's claim that Mr. Pindling had accepted bribes was "incredible".

Bahrain

Middle East
265.5 sq. mi
Pop: 416,275
UN, AL, GCC

Capital: Manama (Pop: 121,986)
Official language: Arabic
Religion: Moslem 85%, Christian 7.3%
Political status: Emirate
Head of state: Isa bin Sulman Al-Khalifa (since 1961)
Head of government: Khalifa bin Sulman Al-Khalifa (since 1973)
GNP per capita: $11,708 (1985)
Currency: Bahrain dinar (£1 = 0.669)

Bahrain in November became the 138th. signatory to the international nuclear non-proliferation treaty. In October, Bahrain and Qatar agreed to end a border dispute over the tiny Gulf island of Fasht al-Dibel.

Bangladesh

Southern Asia
55,598 sq. mi
Pop: 104.1m.
UN, CW

Capital: Dhaka (Pop: 3,440,147)
Official language: Bangla
Religions: Moslem 80%, Hindu, Buddhist, Christian
Political status: Presidential republic
Head of state: Hossain Mohammad Ershad (since 1983)
Head of government: Moumoud Ahmed (since 1988)
GNP per capita: $140 (1986)
Currency: Taka (£1 = 54)

The ruling Jatiya Party won a huge majority in a March 3 parliamentary vote. In September, Bangladesh's worst floods in living memory killed some 2,000 people, with 29 million people being made homeless. A December cyclone left at least 1,500 dead and 16,000 people missing.

Barbados

Caribbean
166 sq. mi
Pop: 253,055
UN, CW, OAS, Caricom

Capital: Bridgetown (Pop: 7,466)
Official language: English
Religions: Anglican 70%, Methodist, Moravian, Roman Catholic
Political status: Constitutional monarchy
Head of state: Queen Elizabeth II
Head of government: Erskine Sandiford (since 1987)
GNP per capita: $4,560 (1984)
Currency: Barbados dollar (£1 = 3.57)

An alert was issued in October following the arrival in Barbados of grass-hoppers which posed a threat to crops. The insects had migrated across the Altantic after causing devastation in many parts of Africa.

Belgium

Western Europe
11,778 sq. mi
Pop: 9.86m.
UN, EEC, NATO, OECD

Capital: Brussels (Pop: 973,499)
Official languages: French, Dutch, German
Religion: mostly Roman Catholic
Political status: Constitutional monarchy
Head of state: King Baudouin I (since 1951)
Head of government: Wilfried Martens (since 1981)
GNP per capita: $7,870 (1984)
Currency: Belgian franc (£1 = 62.50)

In May, Belgian premier Wilfried Martens named a center-left cabinet, ending more than six months of life without a government. A major row erupted with Britain in December over Belgium's refusal to extradite an Irish priest sought by London for suspected terrorist links.

Belize

Central America
8,866 sq. mi
Pop: 171,000
UN, Caricom, CW

Capital: Belmopan (Pop: 3,500)
Official language: English
Religions: Roman Catholic 62%, Protestant 28%
Political status: Constitutional monarchy
Head of state: Queen Elizabeth II
Head of government: Manuel Amadeo Esquivel (since 1985)
GNP per capita: $1,200 (1985)
Currency: Belize dollar (£1 = 3.55)

Belize and Guatemala agreed in May to set up a permanent commission with British participation to work out a treaty ending a long-time territorial dispute between the two Central America nations.

Benin

West Africa
43,483 sq. mi
Pop: 4.15m.
UN, OAU

Capital: Porto Novo (Pop: 208,258)
Official language: French
Religions: Mainly animist, Christian, Moslem
Political status: Socialist people's republic
Head of state: Ahmed Kerekou (since 1972)
GNP per capita: $250 (1983)
Currency: franc CFA (£1 = 507)

Benin celebrated in October the 16th. anniversary of the 1972 revolution, amid a continuing economic crisis. In May, the United States expressed concern about an increasing Libyan presence in the country.

Bhutan

South Asia
18,000 sq. mi
Pop: 1.3m.
UN

Capital: Thimphu (Pop: 15,000)
Official languages: Dzongkha, Lhotsam (Nepali), English
Religions: Buddhist 75%, Hindu 25%
Political status: Monarchy
Head of state: Jigme Singye Wangchuk (since 1972)
Head of government: Council of ministers
GNP per capita: $140 (1984)
Currency: Ngultrum (£1 = 22.90)

The young ruler of the tiny Himalayan kingdom, King Jigme Singye Wangchuck, in October formally wed four sisters whom he had privately married nine years ago and with whom he has had eight children.

Bolivia

South America
424,165 sq. mi
Pop: 6.25m.
UN, LAIA, OAS

Capital: Sucre (legal), La Paz (de facto; pop: 881,404)
Official languages: Spanish, Quechua, Aymara
Religion: Roman Catholic 95%
Political status: Presidential republic
Head of state: Victor Paz Estensoro (since 1985)
GNP per capita: $400 (1985)
Currency: boliviano (£1 = 3.92)

In August, U.S. Secretary of State George Shultz escaped an assassination attempt in La Paz. A self-styled "nationalist commando" later claimed responsibility for placing a powerful bomb close to Mr. Shultz's motorcade. He had earlier strongly condemned the effects of the international traffic in Bolivian cocaine. The U.S. in October sent military helicopters to help Bolivia stamp out the drug trade. The extreme-left "Shining Path" terrorist group in 1988 continued its attacks on government and civilian targets.

Botswana

Southern Africa
220,000 sq. mi
Pop: 1.13m.
UN, CW, OAU

Capital: Gaborone (Pop: 96,000)
Official languages: English, Setswana
Religions: Bahai, Moslem, Hindu, Christian
Political status: Presidential republic
Head of state: Quett Ketumile Joni Masire (since 1980)
GNP per capita: $920 (1983)
Currency: pula (£1 = 2.97)

During a September visit, Pope John Paul II said Botswana was "an island of peace in a troubled sea". Tensions with South Africa remained very high in 1988, as Botswana denounced apartheid policies.

Brazil

South America
3,286,487 sq. mi
Pop: 141.3m.
UN, LAIA, OAS

Capital: Brasilia (Pop: 411,305)
Official language: Portuguese
Religion: Roman Catholic 89%, Protestant 6.6%, Spiritualist
Political status: Federal republic
Head of state: José Sarney (since 1985)
GNP per capita: $1,740 (1986)
Currency: cruzado (£1 = 173.96)

President Sarney in March scored a political victory when the National Assembly approved a U.S.-style presidential system. After some 20 months of bargaining, the National Congress in October put a new constitution into effect, a step hailed as crucial in the country's transition to democracy. But the economic crisis raged on, with 1988 inflation approaching 800 per cent. An October wave of strikes halted work in 17 of the government's 26 departments. In November municipal elections, Mr. Sarney's Brazilian Democratic Movement Party suffered a major set-back when leftist parties won control of a number of Brazil's most important cities, including Sao Paulo, the country's largest and wealthiest.

Brunei

Southeast Asia
2,226 sq. mi
Pop: 221,900
UN, CW, ASEAN

Capital: Bandar Seri Begawan (Pop: 63,868)
Official languages: Malay, Chinese
Religions: Moslem 63%, Buddhist 14%, Christian 10%
Political status: Sultanate
Head of state: Sultan Muda Hassanal Bolkiah Mu'izzadin Waddaulah (since 1967)
GNP per capita: $15,989 (1985)
Currency: Brunei dollar (£1 = 3.56)

In July, thirty four political prisoners, mostly foreign students, were freed after swearing allegiance to Sultan Hassanal Bolkiah. In August, oil-rich Brunei offered billions of dollars in aid to the Philippines.

Bulgaria

Southeastern Europe
42,823 sq. mi
Pop: 8.95m.
UN, CMEA, Warsaw Pact

Capital: Sofia (Pop: 1,114,962)
Official language: Bulgarian
Religions: mostly Orthodox, Moslem 7%
Political status: Socialist people's republic
Head of state: Todor Zhivkov (since 1971)
Head of government: Georgi Atanasov (since 1986)
GNP per capita: $6,460
Currency: lev (£1 = 1.52)

Bulgarians elected 25.87 per cent of non-party candidates in March local elections, while the Communist Party had a 60.78 share of the poll. A multiple choice of candidates was being offered to voters for the first time since the communists came to power at the end of World War II. Bulgaria, previously regarded as one of the most conservative communist bloc countries, in 1988 was in the forefront of socialist states adopting policies linked to Soviet leader Mikhail Gorbachev's economic and social reforms, or "perestroika".

Burkina Faso

Western Africa
105,839 sq. mi
Pop: 8.33m.
UN, OAU

Capital: Ouagadougou (Pop: 442,223)
Official language: French
Religions: animist 45%, Moslem 43%, Christian 12%
Political status: Presidential republic
Head of state: Blaise Compaoré (since 1987)
GNP per capita: $160 (1984)
Currency: franc CFA (£1 = 507.00)

Burkina Faso's President, Captain Blaise Compaoré, in October lashed out at the "anarchy" among the ranks of the country's armed forces, vowing to reform the army set up by his predecessor Thomas Sankara.

Burma

Southeast Asia
261,228 sq. mi
Pop: 37.85m.
UN

Capital: Rangoon (Pop: 2,458,712)
Official language: Burmese
Religion: Buddhist
Political status: Socialist people's republic
Head of state: U San Yu (since 1981)
Head of government: Saw Maung
GNP per capita: $180 (1983)
Currency: kyat (£1 = 11.15)

General Ne Win, who had seized power in a military coup in 1962, stepped down on July 23 amid rising discontent with his rule. On September 18, the military seized power after two months of often violent mass demonstrations and strikes against 26 years of authoritarian one-party rule by the Burma Socialist Program Party. Western experts set the death toll at around 400. Before being ousted, the government of President Maung Maung ordered all members of the military and state employees to quit the BSPP. A military government led by General Saw Maung said in late September that it would hold multi-party elections, but only after law and order had been restored.

Burundi

Central Africa
10,759 sq. mi
Pop: 4.92m.
UN, OAU

Capital: Bujumbura (Pop: 272,000)
Official languages: Kirundi, French
Religions: Roman Catholic 60%, traditional tribal beliefs 32%
Political status: Presidential republic
Head of state: Pierre Buyoya (since 1987)
Head of government: Adrien Sibomana (since 1988)
GNP per capita: $250 (1984)
Currency: Burundi franc (£1 = 208.87)

Massacres between Hutu and Tutsi tribesmen in August left 5,000 dead, according to government figures. Diplomats said up to 50,000 may have died. On October 19, Adrien Sibomana became premier.

Cambodia

Southeast Asia
69,898 sq. mi
Pop: 6.23m.
UN

Capital: Phnom Penh (Pop: 500,000)
Official language: Khmer
Religions: Theravada Buddhism, Roman Catholic and Moslem minorities
Political status: People's republic
Head of state: Heng Samrin (since 1979)
Head of government: Hun Sen (since 1985)
GNP per capita: no accurate estimate available
Currency: riel (£1 = 170)

The year saw considerable progress in diplomatic efforts to settle the Cambodian conflict, with Vietnam promising to withdraw 50,000 of its estimated 120,000 troops by the end of the year. Hanoi also announced in May that all the Vietnamese troops which invaded Cambodia in 1978 would be repatriated by the end of 1990 at the latest. Foreign observers were to be allowed to witness the pullout in December. This was conducted by land, sea and river routes. Vietnam said in June its intervention in Cambodia had cost the lives of some 25,000 Vietnamese troops. In October, President Reagan met with Cambodia's resistance leader Prince Norodom Sihanouk, who was ousted in a 1970 U.S.-backed coup. Mr. Reagan echoed Prince Sihanouk's call for an international peace conference on the Cambodian issue.

Cameroon

Western Central Africa
179,558 sq. mi
Pop: 9.88m.
UN, OAU

Capital: Yaoundé (Pop: 435,892)
Official languages: French, English
Religions: animist 39%, Roman Catholic 21%, Moslem 22%, Protestant 18%
Political status: Presidential republic
Head of state: Paul Biya (since 1982)
GNP per capita: $800 (1983)
Currency: franc CFA (£1 = 507)

President Paul Biya celebrated the sixth anniversary of his November 6, 1982 rise to power, calling on the population to continue its efforts aimed at overcoming the country's severe economic crisis.

Canada

North America
3,553,357 sq. mi
Pop: 25.4m.
UN, NATO, OECD, CW

Capital: Ottawa (Pop: 819,263)
Official languages: English, French
Religions: Roman Catholic, Protestant
Political status: Parliamentary monarchy
Head of state: Queen Elizabeth II
Head of government: Martin Brian Mulroney (since 1984)
GNP per capita: $12,940 (1984)
Currency: Canadian dollar (£1 = 2.24)

Canada's conservative Prime Minister Brian Mulroney won a clear-cut parliamentary majority in hotly-contested November 21 elections. The election was essentially fought on the issue of a free trade agreement with the United States. After his victory, Mr. Mulroney said he would call parliament back in December to enact the pact. He vowed to implement the trade accord on schedule on January 1, 1989. Opponents of the accord said it would reduce Canada to being an "economic colony" of the United States. Canada's business community strongly supported the pact, which will, over the next decade, eliminate almost all hindrances to the flow of trade between Canada and the U.S. In September, the U.S. Senate approved the free trade accord in an 83 to 9 vote. Following the success of the 1988 Winter Olympics in Calgary, Victoria was awarded in September the 1994 Commonwealth Games. In June, relations with Moscow took a turn for the worse, when a wave of tit-for-tat expulsions of diplomats broke out. In September, Mr. Mulroney signed an agreement making the Indian Dene tribe the biggest private landowners in North America. It was to recover rights lost in 1899. In October, Canada authorised a U.S. ship to navigate the contested Northwest Passage.

Cape Verde

Atlantic
1,557 sq. mi
Pop: 350,000
UN, OAU

Capital: Praia (Pop: 37,676)
Official language: Portuguese
Religion: Roman Catholic 98%
Political status: Republic
Head of state: Aristides Maria Pereira (since 1975)
Head of government: Pedro Verona Rodrigues Pires (since 1975)
GNP per capita: $320 (1983)
Currency: escudo Caboverdiano (£1 = 130.21)

In September, Justice Minister Jose Araujo stepped down, citing bad health. In October, the government began a wide-ranging review of the trouble-plagued and increasingly criticised state-run health service.

Central African Republic

Central Africa
240,324 sq. mi
Pop: 2.78m.
UN, OAU

Capital: Bangui (Pop: 473,817)
Official language: French
Religions: animist beliefs 57%, Roman Catholic 20%, Protestant 15%, Moslem 8%
Political status: Presidential republic
Head of state: André Kolingba (since 1981)
GNP per capita: $280 (1984)
Currency: franc CFA (£1 = 507)

The government in November categorically denied reports that it had allowed several thousand tons toxic waste from Western Europe to be dumped in the country in exchange for pay-offs to senior officials.

Chad

Central Africa
495,752 sq. mi
Pop: 5.24m.
UN, OAU

Capital: N'Djaména (Pop: 511,700)
Official languages: French, Arabic
Religions: Moslem 44%, animist 38%, Christian 17%
Political status: Presidential republic
Head of state: Hissène Habré (since 1982)
GNP per capita: $88 (1984)
Currency: franc CFA (£1 = 507)

Chad and its northern neighbour Libya in October restored full diplomatic ties after a six-year break. Both sides pledged to respect a late 1987 cease-fire which ended a drawn out and violent border dispute.

Chile

South America
284,520 sq. mi
Pop: 12.07m.
UN, LAIA, OAS

Capital: Santiago (Pop: 4,318,305)
Official language: Spanish
Religions: Roman Catholic, Protestant, Jewish
Political status: Presidential republic under a military regime
Head of state: Augusto Pinochet Ugarte (since 1974)
GNP per capita: $1,590 (1984)
Currency: Chilean peso (£1 = 432.73)

General Augusto Pinochet lost an October bid to remain in power until 1997 after 54.68 per cent of voters said "no" to eight more years of power for the President. However, General Pinochet refused to step down right away, although the Chilean leader is constitutionally bound to hold open presidential elections by December 1989 at the latest. The plebiscite was marred by arrests and violent police reprisals against Chileans opposed to Gen. Pinochet's continued rule. The election results led to widespread celebration after 15 years of military rule. In mid-October, Chile rejected a U.S. request for $12 million in compensation for the killing of Orlando Letelier, a Chilean exile leader assassinated in Washington in 1976.

China

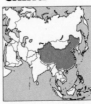

East Asia
3,682,131 sq. mi
Pop: 1,072.2m.
UN

Capital: Beijing (Peking; pop: 5.86m.)
Official language: Chinese
Religions: officially atheist; Confucianism, Buddhism, Taoism
Political status: People's republic
Head of state: Li Xiannian (since 1983)
Head of government: Li Peng (since 1987)
GNP per capita: $250 (1986)
Currency: Renminbi yuan (£1 = 6.58)

A new and younger government, featuring reformists close to senior leader Deng Xiaoping, took the reins of power in China in April. There were growing calls for the retirement of Mr. Deng, who despite his 84 years and pledges to step down continued to run the country. Faced with record inflation and potential social unrest, Chinese leaders found themselves divided over what road to take, with the most cautious demanding that political stability be put ahead of reforms. In March, the United States said it would resume sales of high technology to China, thus ending a five-month embargo, because Washington was satisfied that Beijing was not selling Silkworm anti-ship missiles to Iran. In November, the government said there will be as many as 1.27 billion Chinese in the year 2000, some 70 million more than officially predicted in 1980. China's first-ever sex-education exhibition was held in Shanghai in October. A devastating November earthquake in southwestern China killed about 750 people and seriously injured 3,400 others. More than 700,000 houses were destroyed and damage was estimated at well over £65 million.

Colombia

South America
440,829 sq. mi
Pop: 29.5m.
UN, LAIA, OAS

Capital: Bogota (Pop: 4,185,174)
Official language: Spanish
Religion: Roman Catholic
Political status: Democratic presidential republic
Head of state: Virgilio Barco Vargas (since 1986)
Head of government: Cesar Gaviria Trujillo
GNP per capita: $1,129 (1986)
Currency: peso (£1 = 483.52)

Police in May raided what was probably the biggest cocaine processing plant in the country, seizing 6,000 pounds of the drug. In October, government and opposition leaders agreed on constitutional reforms.

Comoros

Indian Ocean
719 sq. mi.
Pop: 422,500
UN

Capital: Moroni (Pop: 20,112)
Official languages: French, Arabic
Religions: Moslem (Sunni) 99%, Christian
Political status: Federal Islamic republic
Head of state: Ahmed Abdallah Abderemane (since 1978)
GNP per capita: $290 (1985)
Currency: Comorian franc (£1 = 507)

The Islamic republic celebrated the 13th. anniversary of its independence in July amid a deep economic crisis. The World Bank in October said it would increase its credits to the impoverished island nation.

Congo

Central Africa
132,046 sq. mi
Pop: 2.18m.
UN, OAU

Capital: Brazzaville (Pop: 595,102)
Official language: French
Religions: Roman Catholic 54%, Protestant 24%, animist 19%, Moslem 3%
Political status: People's republic
Head of state: Denis Sassou-Nguesso (since 1979)
Head of government: Ange-Edouard Poungui (since 1984)
GNP per capita: $1,140 (1984)
Currency: franc CFA (£1 = 507)

A delegation of U.S. businessmen and congressional leaders visited Brazzaville in November to discuss U.S. investment possibilities. The government meanwhile pressed ahead with its austerity measures. In October, the wages of 15,000 ruling party officials were cut by ten per cent as part of the regime's austerity drive.

Costa Rica

Central America
19,730 sq. mi
Pop: 2.66m.
UN, OAS

109

Capital: San José (Pop: 241,464)
Official language: Spanish
Religion: Roman Catholic
Political status: Democratic republic
Head of state: Oscar Arias Sanchez (since 1986)
Head of government: Rodrigo Arias Sanchez
GNP per capita: $1.280 (1984)
Currency: colone (£1 = 130.26)

The hurricane Joan hit Costa Rica in October, killing at least 25 people and leaving a trail of devastation behind. Earlier, Costa Rica accused a group of Panamanian soldiers of having illegally crossed the border.

Cuba

Caribbean
44,206 sq. mi
Pop: 10.19m.
UN, CMEA, OAS

Capital: Havana (Pop: 2,014,800)
Official language: Spanish
Religions: Roman Catholic, Methodist, Baptist
Political status: Socialist republic
Head of state: Fidel Castro Ruz
GNP per capita: $2,696 (1981)
Currency: peso (£1 = 1.342)

The Pentagon in March acknowledged that Cuban forces possessed some Frog-7 nuclear-capable missiles, but stressed none had been equipped with nuclear warheads. In June, the worst flooding in 25 years killed more than 20 people and ended 10 years of drought. A Cuban gunboat in October seized the ship carrying New Zealand's America's Cup entry. In September, relations with Britain soured after a Cuban diplomat was expelled from London in a bizarre incident in which he shot an alleged deserter from Cuba's secret service. Calling it an act of U.S. provocation, Mr. Castro decorated the diplomat.

Cyprus

Southern Europe
3,572 sq. mi
Pop: 673,100
UN, CW

Capital: Nicosia (Pop: 163,700)
Official languages: Greek, Turkish
Religions: Greek Orthodox 80%, Moslem 19%
Political status: Republic
Head of state: George Vassiliou (since 1988)
GNP per capita: $5.703 (1986)
Currency: Cyprus pound (£1 = 0.804)

Independent candidate George Vassiliou won February presidential elections. Despite some progress, hopes for an early reunification of Cyprus faded in November.

Czechoslovakia

Central Europe
49,383 sq. mi
Pop: 15.5m.
UN, CMEA, Warsaw Pact

Capital: Prague (Pop: 1,194,000)
Official languages: Czech, Slovak
Religion: Roman Catholic 24%
Political status: Federal socialist republic
Head of state: Gustav Husak (since 1975)
Head of government: Ladislav Adamec (since 1988)
GNP per capita: $8.700 (1985)
Currency: Czech koruna (£1 = 16.10)

In a major October government reshuffle, Ladislav Adamec replaced Lubomir Strougal as premier. The 70th. anniversary of Czechoslovakia's founding was celebrated for the first time in decades in late October.

Denmark

Northern Europe
16,631 sq. mi
Pop: 5.12m.
UN, EEC, NATO, OECD

Capital: Copenhagen (Pop: 622,275)
Official language: Danish
Religion: Lutheran 90%
Political status: Constitutional monarchy
Head of state: Queen Margrethe II (since 1972)
Head of government: Poul Schlueter (since 1982)
GNP per capita: $7,533 (1985)
Currency: krone (£1 = 11.44)

Conservative Prime Minister Poul Schlueter formed a new coalition government in June following inconclusive elections focusing on Denmark's role in NATO and its decision to ban nuclear ships from Danish ports.

Djibouti

Northeastern Africa
8,960 sq. mi
Pop: 470,000
UN, AL, OAU

Capital: Djibouti (Pop: 250,000)
Official languages: French, Arabic
Religion: mostly Moslem
Political status: Presidential republic
Head of state: Hassan Gouled Aptidon (since 1977)
Head of government: Barkat Gourad Hamadou (since 1978)
GNP per capita: $760 (1984)
Currency: Djibouti franc (£1 = 313)

Western aid was rushed to Djibouti in October to help it fight the spread of crop-ravaging locusts. In Novem-

ber, a man was arrested for a two-month long wave of bomb attacks on power stations and government offices. His motives were not clear.

Dominica

Caribbean
290 sq. mi
Pop: 94,191
UN, CW, 0AS, Caricom

Capital: Roseau (Pop: 20,000)
Official language: English
Religion: Roman Catholic 80%
Political status: Republic
Head of state: C.A. Seignoret (since 1983)
Head of government: Mary Eugenia Charles (since 1980)
GNP per capita: $970 (1983)
Currencies: French franc, £ sterling and East Caribbean dollar (£1 = EC$4.79)

Dominica's leaders in July objected to U.S. government attempts to indict Panamanian strongman General Manuel Antonio Noriega on charges of drug trafficking.

Dominican Republic

Caribbean
18,700 sq. mi
Pop: 6.6m.
UN, OAS

Capital: Santo Domingo (Pop: 1,313,172)
Official language: Spanish
Religion: Roman Catholic
Political status: Presidential republic
Head of state: Joaquin Balaguer (since 1986)
GNP per capita: $1,090 (1984)
Currency: peso oro (£1 = 8.81)

President Joaquin Balaguer, blind and aged 80, seeemed set to seek a sixth term in office in the 1990 elections. In September, Hurricane Gilbert left five dead in its wake.

Ecuador

South America
104,505 sq. mi
Pop: 9.64m.
UN, LAIA, OAS, OPEC

Capital: Quito (Pop: 1,110,248)
Official languages: Spanish, Quechua
Religion: Roman Catholic
Political status: Presidential republic
Head of state: Leon Febres Cordero (since 1984)
GNP per capita: $1,160 (1985)
Currency: sucre (£1 = 638.27)

Ecuador's annual inflation rate hi a record of 77.4 percent in 1988, while the foreign debt stood at over $11 billion. In October, the president of the High Court was assassinated by an unknown assailant.

Egypt

North Africa
386,900 sq. mi
Pop: 49.28m.
UN, AL, OAU

Capital: Cairo (Pop: 6,205,000)
Official language: Arabic
Religions: Sunni Moslem 90%, Coptic Christian 7%
Political status: Presidential republic
Head of state: Hosni Mubarak (since 1981)
Head of government: Atef Mohamed Naguib Sidki (since 1986)
GNP per capita: $466 (1984)
Currency: Egyptian pound (£1 = 3.96)

Egyptian novelist and short story writer Naguib Mahfouz was awarded the 1988 Nobel Prize for Literature in October. In November, the U.S. and Egypt agreed to co-produce the M-1 tank in a further tightening of U.S.-Egyptian military ties.

El Salvador

Central America
8,236 sq. mi
Pop: 5.48m.
UN, OAS

Capital: San Salvador
Official language: Spanish
Religion: Roman Catholic
Political status: Presidential republic
Head of state: José Napoléon Duarte (since 1984)
GNP per capita: $880 (1985)
Currency: colon (£1 = 8.85)

President José Napoléon Duarte fought a losing battle with terminal cancer. Presidential elections were set for March 19, 1989, as the war with leftist rebels, which has already claimed 65,000 lives, dragged on. The leftist alliance named former exile Guillermo Ungo as its candidate.

Equatorial Guinea

West Africa
10,831 sq. mi
Pop: 384,000
UN, OAU

Capital: Malabo (Pop: 10,000)
Official language: Spanish
Religions: mostly Roman Catholic, Protestant
Political status: Presidential republic
Head of state: Teodoro Obiang Nguema Abasogo (since 1979)
GNP per capita: $420 (1983)
Currency: franc CFA (£1 = 507)

This former Spanish colony celebrated the 20th. anniversary of its independence in October. A worldwide drop in cocoa prices had a severe effect on the hard-hit economy, forcing the country to look for aid.

Ethiopia

Northeastern Africa
471,800 sq. mi
Pop: 46m.
UN, OAU

Capital: Addis Abada (Pop: 1,412,575)
Official languages: Amharic, Galla
Religions: Moslem 45%, Ethiopian Orthodox 40%
Political status: People's democratic republic
Head of state: Mengistu Haile Mariam (since 1977)
Head of government: Fikre-Selassie Wogderess (since 1987)
GNP per capita: $110 (1984)
Currency: birr (£1 = 3.64)

Already facing a violent, 27-year-old rebellion in the province of Eritrea, continued nationwide famine and a devastating plague of locusts, Ethiopia in 1988 was hit by its worst epidemic of malaria in 25 years. In November, the government launched a major economic and agricultural reform programme aimed at the country's ailing economy.

Fiji

South Pacific
7,076 sq. mi
Pop: 714,000
UN

Capital: Suva (Pop: 71,255)
Official language: English
Religions: Christian 42%, Hindu 33%, Moslem 6%
Political status: Republic
Head of state: Ratu Sir Penaia Ganilau (since 1987)
Head of government: Ratu Sir Kamisese Mara (since 1987)
GNP per capita: $1,700 (1985)
Currency: Fiji dollar (£1 = 2.57)

The discovery in June of a cache of Soviet arms led the government to step up security measures. Fijian leader Sitiveni Rabuka and premier Ratu Sir Kamisese Mara vowed to fight subversion. In September, Australia threatened to cut aid after tension rose between Canberra and Suva.

Finland

Northern Europe
117,615 sq. mi
Pop: 4.93m.
UN, NC, OECD, EFTA

Capital: Helsinki (Pop: 487,581)
Official languages: Finnish, Swedish, Lappish
Religion: Lutheran 89.2%, Greek Orthodox 1.1%
Political status: Democratic parliamentary republic
Head of state: Mauno Koivisto (since 1982)
Head of government: Harri Holkeri (since 1987)
GNP per capita: $14,302 (1986)
Currency: Finnmark (£1 = 7.22)

President Mauno Koivisto, a Social Democrat, on March 1 began his second six-year term. He had failed to win an absolute majority in the elections held the previous month.

France

Western Europe
211,968 sq. mi
Pop: 55.62m.
UN, EEC, OECD,

Capital: Paris (Pop: 2,188,918)
Official language: French
Religion: Roman Catholic 76%, Moslem 4.5%, Protestant 1.4%
Political status: Parliamentary republic
Head of state: François Mitterrand (since 1981)
Head of government: Michel Rocard (since 1988)
GNP per capita: $9,280 (1985)
Currency: French franc (£1 = 10.14)

France's voters had a particularly busy year: they were called to the polls seven times. In May, Socialist candidate François Mitterrand defeated conservative presidential hopeful Jacques Chirac. The extreme-right National Front led by Jean Marie Le Pen was the chief victim of June legislative elections. It secured just one seat of the 32 it had held in the previous National Assembly. In May, three French hostages in Beirut returned to an emotional welcome in Paris. The three, a journalist and two diplomats, had been held hostage for three years. Also in May, 19 Melanesian separatist militants died on the French South Pacific territory of New Caledonia when French troops attacked to free hostages they had been holding in a cave. In June, pro-independence and loyalist leaders on New Caledonia signed accords designed to restore peace to the archipelago. The pact was approved by a majority of voters in a referendum held in France in November. Prince Charles and Princess Diana of Britain made a highly successful November visit to Paris.

Gabon

Central Africa
103,346 sq. mi
Pop: 1.22m.
UN, OAU, OPEC

Capital: Libreville (Pop: 350,000)
Official language: French
Religions: Christian 84% (mostly Roman Catholic), animist
Political status: Presidential republic
Head of state: Omar Bongo (since 1967)
Head of government: Léon Mébiame (since 1975)
GNP per capita: $4,250 (1983)
Currency: franc CFA (£1 = 507)

By late 1988, Gabon was set to export its own manganese for the first time. Previously, this resource was exported via the Congo. The ore was to be shipped from a new port.

Gambia

West Africa
4,127 sq. mi
Pop: 698,817
UN, OAU, CW

Capital: Banjul (Pop: 44,188)
Official language: English
Religions: Moslem 70%, Christian, animist
Political status: Republic
Head of state: Dawda Kairaba Jawara (since 1970)
GNP per capita: $170 (1984)
Currency: dalasi (£1 = 12.90)

Gambia and Senegal in October agreed to set up a free-trade zone. By late 1988, Gambia had recorded a total of 52 cases of AIDS, half of which had resulted in death.

Germany (East)

Central Europe
41,827 sq. mi
Pop: 16.6m.
UN, CMEA, Warsaw Pact

Capital: East Berlin (Pop: 1,223,309)
Official language: German
Religions: Protestant 80.5%, Roman Catholic 11%
Political status: Socialist republic
Head of state: Erich Honecker (since 1976)
Head of government: Willi Stoph (since 1976)
GNP per capita: $10,400 (1985)
Currency: GDR mark (£1 = 2.99)

East Germany's government acted quickly to stamp out all attempts at Soviet-style reforms and openness, known as "perestroika" and "glasnost". In November, Berlin banned a Soviet magazine and several Soviet films. These were deemed "too daring" by East Germany. The number of East Germans fleeing to the West rose sharply in 1988.

Germany (West)

Central Europe
96,025 sq. mi
Pop: 61m.
UN, EEC, NATO, OECD

Capital: Bonn (Pop: 290,800)
Official language: German
Religions: Protestant 49%, Roman Catholic 44.6%
Political status: Federal republic
Head of state: Richard von Weizsäcker (since 1984)
Head of government: Helmut Kohl (since 1982)
GNP per capita: $10,300 (1985)
Currency: deutsche Mark (£1 = 2.99)

A mine disaster, West Germany's worst in 26 years, claimed 51 lives in June. In August, young West German dare-devil Matthias Rust came home after spending 14 months in a Soviet prison for landing his light aircraft in Red Square. On his return, he was stripped of his pilot's licence. Also in August, a mid-air catastrophe at the U.S. base of Ramstein killed 70 people, most of them spectators attending an air show. The accident occurred when Italian Air Force jets collided during a stunt-flying display. This prompted West Germany to impose a permanent ban on all military air shows. In October, West Germany's right-wing heavyweight politician Franz Joseph Strauss died, leaving a power vacuum on the right. The political scene was rocked by a major row in November when parliamentary speaker Philip Jenninger praised Adolf Hitler and appeared to partly justify the Nazi's treatment of Jews, in a speech to commemorate the 50th. anniversary of the 1938 "Crystal Night" pogroms against the Jews. The speech caused a walkout by dozens of parliamentarians of all political persuasions. The incident came at an embarrassing moment for Chancellor Helmut Kohl.

In January, West Germany and its World War II foe, France, decided to create a joint army brigade. The force will have a total of 4,200 men based in West Germany.

Ghana

West Africa
92,010 sq. mi
Pop: 12.21m.
UN, CW, OAU, ECOWAS

Capital: Accra (Pop: 964,879)
Official language: English
Religions: Christian 52%, Moslem 13%, traditional beliefs
Political status: Republic
Head of state: Jerry John Rawlings (since 1981)
GNP per capita: $390 (1986)
Currency: cedi (£1 = 324)

Ten people, including a woman, were sentenced to death in October for the witchcraft murder and decapitation of three villagers. Campus unrest led to the three-month shut-down of two large universities.

Greece

Southeastern Europe
50,949 sq. mi
Pop: 9.97m.
UN, EEC, NATO, OECD

Capital: Athens (Pop: 1,082,126)
Official language: Greek
Religion: Greek Orthodox 98%
Political status: Democratic parliamentary republic
Head of state: Christos Sartzetakis (since 1985)
Head of government: Andreas Papandreou (since 1981)
GNP per capita: $3,300 (1985)
Currency: drachma (£1 = 239.75)

The year ended on a sour note for premier Andreas Papandreou. After undergoing heart surgery in London, he announced he was divorcing his U.S.-born wife of 37 years to marry a 34-year-old former stewardess. His socialist government also found itself embroiled in a major multi-million pound financial scandal.

Grenada

Caribbean
120 sq. mi
Pop: 88,000
UN, CW, OAS, Caricom

Capital: St George's (Pop: 4,788)
Official language: English
Religions: Roman Catholic, Anglican, Methodist
Political status: Constitutional monarchy
Head of state: Queen Elizabeth II
Head of government: Herbert Blaize (since 1985)
GNP per capita: $940 (1984)
Currency: Eastern Caribbean dollar (£1 = 4.79)

A U.S. presidential delegation led by Secretary of the Navy William Ball in October attended ceremonies held at Saint George's to mark the fifth anniversary of the U.S. military intervention in Granada. In a message, President Ronald Reagan paid homage to the 19 U.S. servicemen who died on the island in 1983, and to Grenada's economic progress.

Guatemala

Central America
42,042 sq. mi
Pop: 8.99m.
UN, OAS, Caricom

Capital: Guatemala City (Pop: 1.3m.)
Official language: Spanish
Religion: Roman Catholic
Political status: Presidential republic
Head of state: Vinicio Cerezo Arevalo (since 1986)
GNP per capita: $1,150 (1985)
Currency: quetzal (£1 = 1.77)

At least nine people died in a failed coup attempt in June at a military base, barely a month after a similar bid was put down peacefully. Continued human rights violations were reported by the Catholic Church.

Guinea

West Africa
94,926 sq. mi
Pop: 6.34m.
UN, OAU

Capital: Conakry (Pop: 705,280)
Official language: French
Religions: Moslem 69%, tribal beliefs 30%, Christian 1%
Political status: Presidential republic
Head of state: Lansana Conté (since 1984)
GNP per capita: $300 (1984)
Currency: Guinea franc (£1 = 532)

President Lansana Conté in November denied reports he had been the target of an October assassination attempt. General Conté also called for a "Basic Law" to be drafted to replace the existing constitution.

Guinea-Bissau

West Africa
13,948 sq. mi
Pop: 935,000
UN, OAU

Capital: Bissau (Pop: 109,214)
Official language: Portuguese, Crioulo
Religions: Moslem 30%, Christian 5%
Political status: Republic
Head of state: Joao Bernardo Vieira (since 1980)
GNP per capita: $180 (1983)
Currency: peso (£1 = 1,152.78)

Guinea-Bissau's most senior citizen, and one of the oldest men in the world, died in October at the ripe old age of 139. Born in 1849, he left seven widows and 14 children.

Guyana

South America
83,000 sq. mi
Pop: 812,000
UN, Caricom, CW

Capital: Georgetown (Pop: 188,000)
Official language: English
Religions: Christian 52%, Hindu 34%, Moslem 9%
Political status: Presidential republic
Head of state: Hugh Desmond Hoyte (since 1985)
Head of government: Hamilton Green (since 1985)
GNP per capita: $510 (1984)
Currency: Guyana dollar (£1 = 15.94)

The presence of at least 10,000 refugees from neighbouring Suriname continued to be a heavy strain on Guyana's economy. The refugees had fled a 1986 outbreak of fighting in the former Dutch colony.

Haiti

Caribbean
10,700 sq. mi
Pop: 5.3m.
UN, OAS

Capital: Port-au-Prince (Pop: 449,831)
Official language: French
Religions: Roman Catholic, Voodoo
Political status: Presidential republic
Head of state: Prosper Avril (since 1988)
GNP per capita: $320 (1983)
Currency: gourde (£1 = 8.87)

It was a tumultuous year for Haiti, starting with the election in January of Leslie Manigat as President. By May, violent anti-government protests spread. In June, General Henri Namphy took power. He was ousted in September by Lt. Gen. Prosper Avril. In November, the commander of one of Haiti's most feared battalions was allegedly poisoned.

Honduras

Central America
43,277 sq. mi
Pop: 4.3m.
UN, OAS

Capital: Tegucigalpa (Pop: 571,400)
Official language: Spanish
Religions: Roman Catholic
Political status: Presidential republic
Head of state: José Azcona Hoyo (since 1986)
GNP per capita: $750 (1984)
Currency: lempira (£1 = 3.54)

Honduras accused Nicaraguan forces of invading its territory in March, prompting a build-up of U.S. forces. In October, Hurricane Joan ripped through Hunduras, leaving devastation and some 15 dead.

Hungary

Central Europe
35,911 sq. mi
Pop: 10.62m.
UN, CMEA, Warsaw Pact

Capital: Budapest (Pop: 2.08m.)
Official language: Hungarian
Religions: Roman Catholic 49%, Protestant 23.5%
Political status: Socialist people's republic
Head of state: Karoly Grosz (since 1987)
Head of government: Miklos Nemeth (since 1988)
GNP per capita: $2,150 (1983)
Currency: forint (£1 = 84.54)

In May, the Communist Party's General Secretary Karoly Grosz succeeded Janos Kadar as top leader. In late November, Miklos Nemeth, a progressive young economist, was appointed Prime Minister, as the nation moved towards a more open political and economic system.

Iceland

North Atlantic
39,758 sq. mi
Pop: 244,009
UN, OECD, NATO, EFTA, NC

Capital: Reykjavik (Pop: 91,394)
Official language: Icelandic
Religion: Evangelical Lutheran
Political status: Parliamentary republic
Head of state: Vigdis Finnbogadottir (since 1980)
Head of government: Thorsteinn Palsson (since 1987)
GNP per capita: $11,410 (1985)
Currency: krona (£1 = 65.47)

A sharp downturn in the economy, partly due to falling world fish prices, led in September to calls for a freeze in wages and prices and a devaluation. In London, Miss Iceland was crowned Miss World in November.

India

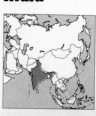

Southern Asia
1,222,713 sq. mi
Pop: 748m.
UN, CW

Capital: New Delhi (Pop: 5,714,000)
Official languages: Hindi, English
Religions: Hindu 82.7%, Moslem 11.2%,
Christian 2.6%, Sikh 1.9%, Buddhist, Jain
Political status: Federal parliamentary
republic
Head of state: R. Venkataramen (since
1987)
Head of government: Rajiv Gandhi (since
1984)
GNP per capita: $260 (1983)
Currency: rupee (£1 = 22.90)

Sikh separatist killings continued in Punjab, while India's year-old peace efforts in Sri Lanka were hampered by well-armed Tamil guerrillas. The July 1987 Indo-Sri Lanka peace accord remained bogged down. In November, premier Rajiv Gandhi kicked off a year of celebrations to mark the birth centenary of Jawaharlal Nehru, his grandfather. Two October airline disasters left some 170 dead. India's shortest man in October claimed that no one in the world could undercut his stature of just 63 centimeters (25.2 inches).

Indonesia

Southeast Asia
741,098 sq. mi
Pop: 172m.
UN, ASEAN,
OPEC

Capital: Jakarta (Pop: 6,503,449)
Official language: Bahasa Indonesian
Religion: Moslem 78%, Christian 11%,
Buddhist, Hinduist
Political status: Presidential republic
Head of state: Gen. Raden Suharto (since
1968)
GNP per capita: $510 (1986)
Currency: rupiah (£1 = 2,951)

General Suharto was re-elected for a fifth term as President, Prime Minister and Defence Minister. Two village women, attacked and buried by robbers in September, crawled out of their graves to report the crime.

Iran

Middle East
634,724 sq. mi
Pop: 49.86m.
UN, OPEC

Capital: Tehran (Pop: 6,022,078)
Official language: Farsi (Persian)
Religion: Moslem (Shi'a 96%, Sunni 3%)
Political status: Islamic republic
Head of state: Sayed Ali Khamenei (since
1981)
Head of government: Hosein Musavi-
Khamenei (since 1981)
GNP per capita: $1,690 (1986)
Currency: rial (£1 = 120.20)

In April, U.S. warships demolished two Iranian oil rigs in the Gulf in retaliation for an Iranian attack on a U.S. frigate. On July 3, a U.S. Navy cruiser shot down an Iranian jetliner in the Gulf, killing all 290 people on board, in what the White House called a "terrible tragedy". Iranian gunboats continued to attack Gulf shipping. In October, prospects for the release of three British hostages in Lebanon and two Britons held in Iran brightened following the restoration of full diplomatic ties between London and Tehran. Iran and Iraq in August implemented a cease-fire and began United Nations sponsored talks aimed at settling their eight-year conflict. Despite this, the two sides remained far apart on a troop withdrawal to international boundaries, demarcation of the frontier and navigation rights in the Shatt al-Arab, Iraq's only outlet to the sea. The exchange of prisoners of war got under way in late November, but soon hit snags. Iran and Iraq held an estimated 100,000 POWs. In October, Britain called off its Gulf naval escort patrol which had ensured the safety of vessels flying the Union Jack in the Gulf. The United States said in November it was maintaining the state of emergency declared in 1979 in its relations with Iran.

Iraq

Middle East
167,925 sq. mi
Pop: 17.09m.
UN, AL, OPEC

Capital: Baghdad (Pop: 2,183,760)
Official language: Arabic
Religions: Moslem 64%, Christian 2%
Political status: Socialist presidential
republic
Head of state: Saddam Hussein at-Takriti
(since 1979)
GNP per capita: $2,140 (1984)
Currency: Iraqi dinar (£1 = 0.53)

Some 5,000 civilians were killed by Iraqi forces in a March attack on a Kurdish village north of Baghdad. Iraq was widely accused of having used chemical weapons. In August, an estimated 130,000 Kurds fled Iraq into Turkey. In October, the U.S. Senate voted to impose sanctions on Iraq. Britain expelled two Iraqi diplomats for spying in October. Despite this, London said it would almost double its credits to Baghdad in 1989. President Saddam Hussein in November ordered his eldest son tried for the murder of a presidential guard.

Ireland

Western Europe
26,600 sq. mi
Pop: 3.54m.
UN, EEC,
OECD

Capital: Dublin (Pop: 915,115)
Official languages: Irish (Gaelic), English
Religions: mostly Roman Catholic,
Church of Ireland, Presbyterian,
Methodist
Political status: Parliamentary republic
Head of state: Patrick Hillery (since 1976)
Head of government: Charles Haughey
(since 1987)
GNP per capita: $4,040 (1985)
Currency: Irish pound (£1 = 1.12)

James Joyce's "dear dirty Dublin" celebrated its 1,000th. anniversary in style this year. In the first ever speech to the Irish Parliament by a French head of state, President François Mitterrand in February stressed France and Ireland's commitment to a unified Europe. In April, U.S. Representative Joe Kennedy met Irish premier Charles Haughey and lambasted Britain's position on Northern Ireland. Also in April, a Dublin court jailed a man for 40 years for the kidnapping of a wealthy dentist. In July, an Irish prisoner serving a life term for the murder of Britain's Lord Mountbatten in 1979 staged an unsuccessful jailbreak attempt. A major Anglo-Irish dispute erupted in November over a former Irish priest wanted by Britain for suspected terrorist links; Patrick Ryan sought refuge in Ireland after being allowed to travel from Belgium. The emigration of young people seeking work abroad resulted in Ireland's first population drop since 1961. In October, the European Court of Human Rights ruled that Irish law on homosexuality violated the right to privacy.

Israel

Near East
8,017 sq. mi
Pop: 4.33m.
UN

Capital: Jerusalem (Pop: 468,900)
Official languages: Hebrew, Arabic
Religions: Jewish 82%, Moslem 13%
Political status: Parliamentary republic
Head of state: Chaim Herzog (since 1983)
Head of government: Yitzhak Shamir
(since 1986)
GNP per capita: $6,350 (1986)
Currency: new shekel (£1 = 2.79)

Violent Palestinian protests on the Israeli-occupied territories of the West Bank and Gaza Strip continued all year, leaving more than 330 people dead and hundreds injured. Israel came under increased criticism for its handling of the uprising. The situation in the occupied territories weighed heavily on November elections in which voters refused to give an overall mandate to either of the two main parties: Premier Yitzhak Shamir's conservative Likud bloc and the Labour Party headed by the Foreign Minister Shimon Peres. The inconclusive result gave right-wing religious parties a major say in politics. In March, former Israeli nuclear expert Mordechai Vanunu was sentenced to 18 years in prison for divulging nuclear secrets to a British newspaper. In November, Israel dismissed PLO chief Yasser Arafat's declaration of an independent Palestinian state on the West Bank and Gaza as propaganda. In December, five Soviets, who had hijacked a busload of children and traded them for £1.2 million and an aircraft, surrendered after flying to Israel.

Italy

Southern Europe
116,319 sq. mi
Pop: 57.3m.
UN, EEC,
NATO, OECD

Capital: Rome (Pop: 2,815,457)
Official language: Italian
Religion: Roman Catholic
Political status: Parliamentary republic
Head of state: Francesco Cossiga (since
1985)
Head of government: Ciriaco De Mita
(since 1988)
GNP per capita: $6,096 (1984)
Currency: lira (£1 = 2,207)

Ciriaco De Mita in April formed Italy's 48th. post-war government. In Sicily, an October wave of Mafia murders left some 20 dead. In November, an inquiry into a mysterious 1980 airline disaster was opened.

Ivory Coast

West Africa
124,503 sq. mi
Pop: 10.60m.
UN, OAU

Capital: Abidjan (Pop: 1.85m.)
Official language: French
Religions: Moslem 24%, Christian 32%,
animist 44%
Political status: Presidential republic
Head of state: Félix Houphouët-Boigny
(since 1960)
GNP per capita: $720 (1983)
Currency: franc CFA (£1 = 507)

The economic crisis in Ivory Coast deepened markedly in 1988 due to a drop in world cocoa prices. The World Bank in November threatened to cut off its aid to the impoverished West Africa nation.

Jamaica

Caribbean
4,411 sq. mi
Pop: 2.3m.
UN, OAS, Cari-
com, CW

113

Capital: Kingston (Pop: 524,638)
Official language: English
Religion: mostly Protestant
Political status: Constitutional monarchy
Head of state: Queen Elizabeth II
Head of government: Edward Seaga (since 1980)
GNP per capita: $909 (1986)
Currency: Jamaican dollar (£1 = 9.56)

Hurricane Gilbert cut a huge swath of devastation through Jamaica in September, killing over 30 people and leaving 500,000 homeless. Damage stood at £4.7 billion. The U.S. and Western Europe sent disaster aid.

Japan

Northwestern Pacific Ocean
145,874 sq. mi
Pop: 121.67m.
UN, OECD

Capital: Tokyo (Pop: 8,354,000)
Official language: Japanese
Religions: Buddhist, Shintoist
Political status: Parliamentary monarchy
Head of state: Emperor Hirohito (since 1926)
Head of government: Noboru Takeshita (since 1987)
GNP per capita: $13,447 (1985)
Currency: yen (£1 = 228)

As the year drew to a close, all Japan's eyes were turned to the Imperial Palace, where aging Emperor Hirohito was fighting for his life. The prospect of his death sent shock waves through the country and millions of people followed the daily health bulletins. Crown Prince Akihito was to succeed the emperor. Prime Minister Noboru Takeshita in November celebrated the start of his second year in office. Even his critics acknowledged that he had made a good job of running the country and standing up to domestic protectionist pressures. He defused trade conflicts with the U.S. and Western Europe. Many also said he successfully tackled his responsibilities as the leader of the West's second biggest economy. In November, Mr. Takeshita pushed through the lower house of the Diet a package aimed at reforming Japan's tax system. The victory was seen as a boost to his chances for another two-year term once his first expires in October 1989. On December 7, the Nikkei stock index hit 3,009 points, the first time ever it had gone over 3,000 points. By late 1988, Japan's trade surplus stood at $95.6 billion.

Jordan

Middle East
34,443 sq. mi
Pop: 3,500,000
UN, AL

Capital: Amman (Pop: 777,500)
Official language: Arabic
Religion: Sunni Moslem 80%
Political status: Constitutional monarchy
Head of state: King Hussein II (since 1952)
Head of government: Zaid Rifai (since 1985)
GNP per capita: $1,900 (1984)
Currency: dinar (£1 = 0.599)

Jordan continued to be an active participant in the often-fragile Middle East peace process in 1988. In July, King Hussein announced that he was cutting administrative and legal links with the Israeli-occupied West Bank. The monarch met with Palestine Liberation Organization leader Yasser Arafat and Egyptian President Hosni Mubarak in October for talks focussing on future PLO-Jordanian relations. Jordan was among the first nations to recognize the Palestinian state proclaimed by Mr. Arafat in mid-November.

Kenya

Eastern Africa
224,960 sq. mi
Pop: 20.03m.
UN, CW, OAU

Capital: Nairobi (Pop: 827,800)
Official language: Kiswahili
Religions: Protestant 19%, Roman Catholic 27%, other Christian 27%, Moslem 6%, tribal beliefs 19%
Political status: Presidential republic
Head of state: Daniel arap Moi (since 1978)
GNP per capita: $280 (1985)
Currency: Kenya shilling (£1 = 1.30)

President Moi was sworn in for a third five-year term in March. In April, cattle rustlers killed 191 villagers. The government said that wildlife poachers would be shot on sight. In September, British Foreign Secretary Sir Geoffrey Howe praised Kenya's human rights record.

Kiribati

Pacific
276.9 sq. mi
Pop: 66,250
CW

Capital: Tarawa (Pop: 24,598)
Official language: English
Religions: Protestant, Roman Catholic
Political status: Presidential republic
Head of state: Ieremia Tabai (since 1979)
GNP per capita: $390 (1985)
Currency: Australian dollar (£1 = 2.46)

On July 12, the central Pacific islands of Kiribati, formerly known as the Gilbert and Ellice Islands, celebrated the ninth anniversary of their independence as a republic.

Korea (North)

Northeastern Asia
46,540 sq. mi
Pop: 20.55m.

Capital: Pyongyang (Pop: 1.28m.)
Official language: Korean
Religions: Buddhist, Chondoist, Christian
Political status: Democratic people's republic
Head of state: Kim Il Sung (since 1972)
Head of government: Li Gun Mo (since 1986)
GNP per capita: $1,180 (1985)
Currency: won (£1 = 1.65)

A well-rehearsed outpouring of revolutionary fervour swept North Korea in September as it celebrated the 40th. anniversary of its founding. In April, the country cut back its military spending to spur the economy.

Korea (South)

Northeastern Asia
38,232 sq. mi
Pop: 41.8m.

Capital: Seoul (Pop: 9,645,824)
Official language: Korean
Religions: animist, Buddhist, Confucianist, Christian
Political status: Presidential republic
Head of state: Roh Tae-Woo (since 1988)
Head of government: Lee Hyun-jae (since 1988)
GNP per capita: $2,850 (1987)
Currency: won (£1 = 1,347.38)

Chun Doo-Hwan was succeeded as President by Roh Tae-Woo in February. He was the first leader to relinquish power democratically in the history of South Korea. Mr. Chun had to apologize for abuse of power in November, saying he was ready to face punishment. The opposition captured an unprecedented combined majority of seats in April National Assembly elections. In August, Seoul successfully hosted the 1988 Olympics, which were snubbed by North Korea. In October, a woman who makes tear gas, used by police to break up anti-regime riots, became South Korea's top 1987 taxpayer.

Kuwait

Middle East
6,880 sq. mi
Pop: 1.77m.
UN, AL, OPEC, GCC

Capital: Kuwait (Pop: 60,525)
Official language: Arabic
Religion: Sunni Moslem 78%, Shia Moslem 14%, Christian 6%
Political status: Emirate
Head of state: Shaikh Jabir al-Ahmad al-Jabir al-Sabah (since 1977)
Head of government: Shaikh Saad al-Abdullah as Salim as Sabah (since 1978)
GNP per capita: $11,510 (1985)
Currency: dinar (£1 = 0.488)

Kuwait and other members of the six-nation Gulf Cooperation Council in mid-June signed a major economic cooperation pact with the EEC.

Laos

Southeast Asia
91,400 sq. mi
Pop: 3.67m.
UN

Capital: Vientiane (Pop: 377,409)
Official language: Lao
Religions: mostly Buddhist, tribal 34%
Political status: Democratic people's republic
Head of state: Phoumi Vongvichit
Head of government: Kaysone Phomvihane (since 1975)
GNP per capita: $220 (1984)
Currency: new kip (£1 = 620.73)

Soviet-backed Laos and U.S. ally Thailand signed a cease-fire in February, ending two months of fighting over a border dispute. Hundreds of Thai and Laotian soldiers died.

Lebanon

Near East
4,036 sq. mi
Pop: 3.5m.
UN, AL

Capital: Beirut (Pop: 702,000)
Official language: Arabic
Religions: Moslem (Sunni, Shiite, Druze), Christian (mostly Maronite and Greek Orthodox)
Political status: Parliamentary republic
Head of state: vacant
Head of government: vacant
GNP per capita: no reliable figures available
Currency: Lebanese pound (£1 = 712.04)

1988 was another difficult year for Lebanon, with continued hostage-taking, car-bombings, political paralysis and a spiralling economic crisis. In April, 66 people were killed in Tripoli by a massive bomb attack. Palestinian attacks into northern Israel brought repeated reprisal air raids on Palestinian camps. By year's end, more than 20 foreigners were being held hostage. Lebanon failed to elect a president to replace Amin Gemayel in September. This led to the formation of rival Christian and Moslem dominated governments.

Lesotho

Southern Africa
11,720 sq. mi
Pop: 1.63m.
UN, CW, OAU

Capital: Maseru (Pop: 109,382)
Official languages: Sesotho, English
Religions: Roman Catholic 44%, Protestant 49%
Political status: Constitutional monarchy
Head of state: King Moshoeshoe II (since 1966)
Head of government: Gen. Justin Lekhanya (since 1986)
GNP per capita: $470 (1984)
Currency: loti (£1 = 3.69)

Pope John Paul II's visit in September was marred by a hostage drama, when a group of unidentified armed men seized a bus containing pilgrims, two of whom died in a police rescue operation.

Liberia

West Africa
42,989 sq. mi
Pop: 2.5m.
UN, ECOWAS, OAU

Capital: Monrovia (Pop: 425,000)
Official language: English
Religions: Moslem 26%, Christian, traditional beliefs
Political status: Presidential republic
Head of state: Samuel Kanyon Doe (since 1980)
GNP per capita: $490 (1984)
Currency: Liberian dollar (£1 = 1.77)

President Samuel K. Doe called in November for greater international pressure against South Africa's apartheid policies. Liberia in November freed two Americans accused of plotting to overthrow Mr. Doe, who said the release was a sign of his goodwill towards U.S. President-elect George Bush. The two Americans were to have been tried for treason.

Libya

North Africa
679,358 sq. mi
Pop: 3.96m.
UN, AL, OAU, OPEC

Capital: Tripoli (Pop: 858,000)
Official language: Arabic
Religion: Sunni Moslem 97%
Political status: Socialist people's state
Head of state: Muammar Qadhafi (since 1969)
GNP per capita: $7,180 (1985)
Currency: dinar (£1 = 0.50)

In October, the U.S. accused Libya of building a chemical weapons factory. Tripoli denied the charge, saying it was willing to attend a 1989 international conference on banning chemical arms. Also in October, Libya formally ended its six-year border conflict with neighbouring Chad.

Liechtenstein

Western Europe
61.8 sq. mi
Pop: 27,400
EFTA

Capital: Vaduz (Pop: 4,606)
Official language: German
Religions: Roman Catholic 87%, Protestant 8.6%
Political status: Constitutional monarchy
Head of state: Prince Francis Joseph II (since 1938)
Head of government: Hans Brunhart (since 1978)
GNP per capita: $15,000 (1984)
Currency: Swiss franc (£1 = 2.47)

In January, free public transport was introduced throughout Lichtenstein for a twelve-month trial period. The move was aimed at reducing the level of atmospheric pollution.

Luxembourg

Western Europe
998 sq. mi
Pop: 369,500
UN, EEC, NATO, OECD

Capital: Luxembourg (Pop: 76,640)
Official languages: Luxemburgish, French, German
Religion: Roman Catholic 95%
Political status: Constitutional monarchy
Head of state: Grand Duke Jean (since 1964)
Head of government: Jacques Santer (since 1984)
GNP per capita: $12,990 (1985)
Currency: Luxembourg franc (£1 = 62.50)

A big financial scandal which was sparked off by the bankruptcy of a building firm led to a member of the Luxembourg Parliament being given a five-month suspended prison sentence in mid-October.

Madagascar

Indian Ocean
226,658 sq. mi
Pop: 10.57m.
UN, OAU

Capital: Antananarivo (Pop: 662,585)
Official languages: Malagasy, French
Religions: Christian 50%, Moslem 3%, animist 47%
Political status: Republic
Head of state: Didier Ratsiraka (since 1975)
Head of government: Victor Ramahatra
GNP per capita: $250 (1984)
Currency: Malagasy franc (£1 = 1,967)

Madagascar's President vowed in November that elections would be held in 1989, adding he would seek a third mandate. In September, the International Olympic Committee said Madagascar would be sanctioned for boycotting the 1988 Games.

Malawi

Southern Africa
36,325 sq. mi
Pop: 7.1m.
UN, CW, OAU

Capital: Lilongwe (Pop: 186,800)
Official languages: Chichewa, English
Religions: mostly Christian, Moslem 7%
Political status: Presidential republic
Head of state: H. Kamuzu Banda (since 1966)
GNP per capita: $210 (1983)
Currency: kwacha (£1 = 4.42)

Close relations with South Africa were further strengthened in 1988, with leaders of both nations saying they intended to increase cooperation. Malawi is the only African state to have diplomatic ties with Pretoria.

Malaysia

Southeast Asia
127,317 sq. mi
Pop: 16.5m.
UN, ASEAN, CW

Capital: Kuala Lumpur (Pop: 937,875)
Official language: Malay
Religions: mostly Moslem, Buddhist, Hindu, Christian
Political status: Federal constitutional monarchy
Head of state: Sultan Mahmood Iskandar (since 1984)
Head of government: Mahathir Mohamad (since 1981)
GNP per capita: $1,870 (1985)
Currency: ringgit (£1 = 4.57)

A brand-new coral island about the size of four tennis courts rose up from the sea off the Malaysian coast in May. The newcomer was called Pulau Batu Hairan, or Surprise Rock Island. In November, premier Mahathir Mohamad defused a potentially serious political crisis by offering cabinet posts to two figures who had played key roles in an April 1987 leadership struggle.

Maldives

Indian Ocean
115 sq. mi
Pop: 189,000
UN, CW

Capital: Malé (Pop: 46,334)
Official language: Divehi
Religion: Moslem
Political status: Presidential republic
Head of state: Maumoon Abdul Gayoom (since 1978)
GNP per capita: $470 (1985)
Currency: rufiyaa (£1 = 17.91)

The President, Maumoon Abdul Gayoom, began a third five-year term in November after surviving a bloody attempt to overthrow his government. Mr. Gayoom blamed "foreign terrorists" and "invading mercenaries".

Mali

West Africa
478,832 sq. mi
Pop: 8.73m.
UN, OAU

Capital: Bamako (Pop: 404,022)
Official language: French
Religions: Sunni Moslem 90%, animist 9%, Christian 1%
Political status: Presidential republic
Head of state: Moussa Traoré (since 1969)
GNP per capita: $150 (1983)
Currency: franc CFA (£1 = 507)

Mali's President, General Moussa Traoré, said at a November ceremony marking the 20th. anniversary of his rise to power that the army had seized power in 1968 to stave off political, economic and social chaos. He stressed that the main challenge for Mali now was economic rather than political problems. Also in November, a presidential decree ordered the release of some 240 prisoners.

Malta

Southern Europe
121.9 sq. mi
Pop: 343,334
UN, CW

Capital: Valletta (Pop: 9,263)
Official languages: Maltese, English
Religion: Roman Catholic
Political status: Democratic parliamentary republic
Head of state: Paul Xuereb (since 1987)
Head of government: Eddie Fenech Adami (since 1987)
GNP per capita: $3,103 (1984)
Currency: Lira Maltija (£1 = 0.576)

A Palestinian was sentenced to a 25-year jail term in November for his role in a 1985 hijack drama in which a total of 61 people were killed.

Mauritania

West Africa
398,000 sq. mi
Pop: 2.01m.
UN, AL, OAU

Capital: Nouakchott (Pop: 500,000)
Official languages: Arabic, French
Religion: Sunni Moslem 99%
Political status: Republic
Head of state: Maaouia Ould Sidi Mohamed Taya (since 1984)
GNP per capita: $450 (1985)
Currency: ouguiya (£1 = 128.42)

President Maaouia Ould Sidi Mohamed Taya said in November that his West African nation would support the struggle for the independence of Namibia. A jailed former health minister died in a Nouakchott prison in November.

Mauritius

Indian Ocean
787 sq. mi
Pop: 1.041m.
UN, CW, OAU

Capital: Port Louis (Pop: 138,482)
Official language: English
Religions: Hindu 53%, Christian 30%, Moslem 13%
Political status: Constitutional monarchy
Head of state: Queen Elizabeth II
Head of government: Anerood Jugnauth (since 1982)
GNP per capita: $1,150 (1983)
Currency: rupee (£1 = 22.50)

The former British Indian Ocean colony in March celebrated the 20th. anniversary of its independence. Several African nations criticised continued trading links between Mauritius and South Africa.

Mexico

North America
756,198 sq. mi
Pop: 76m.
UN, OAS, LAIA

Capital: Mexico City (Pop: 12,932,116)
Official language: Spanish
Religion: Roman Catholic 92.6%
Political status: Federal republic

Head of state: Carlos Salinas de Gortari (since 1988)
GNP per capita: $2,200 (1984)
Currency: peso (£1 = 4,095)

President Reagan and Mexico's outgoing President Miguel de la Madrid in February held their sixth and final summit meeting. In June, the U.S. recalled its ambassador to Mexico and expressed its anger over the freeing of a Puerto Rican nationalist wanted in the U.S. for terrorism. July presidential elections were won by Carlos Salinas de Gortari with 50.7 per cent of the vote, amid charges of fraud. President-elect George Bush met Mr. Salinas in November in a bid to smooth the troubled U.S.-Mexican relationship. In October, the U.S. said it would grant Mexico $3.5 billion to help it cope with reduced oil revenues. Mexico's massive foreign debt stood at $104 billion.

Monaco

Southern Europe
481 acres
Pop: 27,063

Capital: Monaco
Official language: French
Religion: Roman Catholic
Political status: Constitutional principality
Head of state: Prince Rainier III (since 1949)
Head of government: Jean Ausseil (since 1985)
GNP per capita: $10,000
Currency: French franc (£1 = 10.14)

As the 40th. anniversary of his reign neared, Prince Rainier of Monaco said he planned to stay in power until his son, Crown Prince Albert, was ready to take over and rule the tiny but wealthy principality.

Mongolia

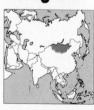

Eastern Asia
605,022 sq. mi
Pop: 1.97m.
UN, CMEA

Capital: Ulan Bator (Pop: 479,500)
Official language: Mongolian
Religion: Tibetan Buddhist Lamaism
Political status: People's republic
Head of state: Jambyn Batmunkh (since 1984)
Head of government: Dumaagiyn Sodnom (since 1984)
GNP per capita: $940 (1978)
Currency: tugrik (£1 = 5.9)

Despite the late 1987 withdrawal of one division of about 10,000 Soviet troops from Mongolia, an estimated 65,000 Soviet military personnel remained stationed there in 1988. Relations with China improved in 1988.

Morocco

North Africa
177,116 sq. mi
Pop: 23m.
UN, AL

Capital: Rabat (Pop: 841,800)
Official language: Arabic
Religions: Sunni Moslem 98%, Christian 2%
Political status: Constitutional monarchy
Head of state: Hassan II (since 1961)
Head of government: Azzeddine Laraki (since 1986)
GNP per capita: $500 (1984)
Currency: dirham (£1 = 14.10)

After a 12-year rift over the disputed Western Sahara, Morocco and Algeria resumed their diplomatic ties in May. The following month, the border between the two North African nations was reopened.

Mozambique

Southern Africa
308,642 sq. mi
Pop: 14.54m.
UN, OAU

Capital: Maputo (Pop: 882,800)
Official language: Portuguese
Religions: animist 60%, Christian 18%, Moslem 16%
Political status: People's republic
Head of state: Joaquim Alberto Chissano (since 1986)
GNP per capita: $90 (1986)
Currency: metical (£1 = 806)

Several Western nations accused the anti-government Renamo rebels of massacring hundreds of thousands of civilians. In a June move to normalise church-state relations, the government said it would return all church property nationalised after the country's independence in 1975. During a September visit, Pope John Paul II called for an end to the bloody conflict in Mozambique.

Namibia

Southern Africa
318,261 sq. mi
Pop: 1,184,000

Capital: Windhoek (Pop: 110,644)
Official languages: Afrikaans, English
Religions: Protestant, traditional beliefs
Political status: South African-controlled territory
Head of state: Louis Pienaar (since 1985)
GNP: $1.2 bil. (1985)
Currency: South African rand (£1 = 3.69)

Some 10 years after the U.N. ruled that South Africa's occupation of Namibia was illegal, independence for the mineral-rich territory at last seemed a possibility. Pretoria in November approved a regional peace plan for Namibia's independence. January 1, 1989 was set as the target date for implementing the plan.

Nauru

Pacific
8,108 sq. mi
Pop: 8,042
CW

Capital: Yaren (Pop: 4,000)
Official languages: Nauruan, English
Religions: Roman Catholic, Protestant
Political status: Republic
Head of state: Hammer DeRoburt (since 1978)
GNP per capita: $0.091 (1985)
Currency: Australian dollar (£1 = 2.46)

The tiny South Pacific island territory of Nauru, which became independent in January 1968, developed its close trade links with Australia and New Zealand in 1988.

Nepal

South Asia
56,827 sq. mi
Pop: 16.63m.
UN

Capital: Kathmandu (Pop: 235,160)
Official language: Nepali
Religions: Hindu 90%, Buddhist 5%, Moslem 3%
Political status: Constitutional monarchy
Head of state: Birendra Bir Bikram Shah Dev (since 1972)
Head of government: Marich Man Singh Shrestha (since 1986)
GNP per capita: $170 (1983)
Currency: Nepalese rupee (£1 = 37.24)

A March soccer-stadium stampede left some 75 people dead. An August earthquake killed more than 700 people. British parliamentarians in November held talks with Nepalese leaders over the future of the elite Gurkha troops in the British army.

Netherlands

Northwestern Europe
16,163 sq. mi
Pop: 14.62m.
UN, EEC, NATO, OECD

Capital: Amsterdam (Pop: 682,702)
Official language: Dutch
Religions: Roman Catholic 36%, Dutch Reformed 19%
Political status: Constitutional monarchy
Head of state: Queen Beatrix (since 1980)
Head of government: Ruud Lubbers (since 1982)
GNP per capita: $8,500 (1984)
Currency: guilder (£1 = 3.36)

Three British soldiers were killed in two May 1 attacks claimed by the Irish Republican Army. The IRA said the killings were revenge for the earlier slaying of three IRA members by British forces in Gibraltar.

New Zealand

South Pacific
103,736 sq. mi
Pop: 3.3m.
UN, CW, OECD

Capital: Wellington (Pop: 351,400)
Official language: English
Religions: Anglican, Presbyterian, Roman Catholic, Methodist
Political status: Constitutional monarchy
Head of state: Queen Elizabeth II
Head of government: David R. Lange
GNP per capita: $5,276 (1985)
Currency: New Zealand dollar (£1 = 2.66)

New Zealand in 1988 protested repeatedly and strongly against the continued French nuclear testing on the South Pacific atoll of Mururoa. Relations with the United States also remained clouded by New Zealand's firm anti-nuclear stance.

Nicaragua

Central America
49,363 sq. mi
Pop: 3.5m.
UN, OAS

Capital: Managua (Pop: 903,998)
Official language: Spanish
Religion: Roman Catholic 91%
Political status: Republic
Head of state: Daniel Ortega Saavedra (since 1984)
GNP per capita: $960 (1985)
Currency: new cordoba (£1 = 17.05)

In late March, Nicaragua released political prisoners as the first step of a cease-fire accord reached with the U.S.-backed contra rebels. President Reagan said in October he was giving up his efforts to obtain additional military aid for the contras before his term expires. In November, Managua postponed until 1990 municipal elections due in 1989. The government said it could not afford to hold the poll. Hurricane Joan hit Nicaragua in October, caused 250 deaths and disappearances and damages estimated at more than £530 million.

Niger

West Africa
458,075 sq. mi
Pop: 6.6m.
UN, OAU

Capital: Niamey (Pop: 399,100)
Official language: French
Religions: Moslem 97%, animist
Political status: Republic
Head of state: Ali Seybou (since 1987)
Head of government: Hamid Algabid (since 1983)
GNP per capita: $240 (1985)
Currency: franc CFA (£1 = 507)

President Ali Seybou stated in November that general elections would be held in late 1989, when he ends his first term in office. He did not rule out staying on for a second term, if the voters asked him to do so.

Nigeria

West Africa
356,667 sq. mi
Pop: 105m.
UN, ECOWAS, CW, OAU, OPEC

Capital: Lagos (Pop: 1,097,000)
Official language: English
Religions: Moslem 48%, Christian 34%
Political status: Federal republic
Head of state: Ibrahim Babangida (since 1985)
GNP per capita: $730 (1986)
Currency: Naira (£1 = 7.77)

Nigerian leader General Ibrahim Babangida said in October he was committed to reducing military involvement in politics as the nation moves gradually towards a return to civilian rule in 1992.

Norway

North Europe
125,049 sq. mi
Pop: 4.2m.
UN, EFTA, NATO, NC, OECD

Capital: Oslo (Pop: 451,099)
Official language: Norwegian
Religions: mostly Evangelical Lutheran, Roman Catholic
Political status: Constitutional monarchy
Head of state: King Olav V
Head of government: Gro Harlem Brundtland (since 1986)
GNP per capita: $16,400 (1986)
Currency: krone (£1 = 11.27)

Norwegian premier Gro Harlem Brundtland reshuffled her minority Labour government in June after it was defeated in a parliament vote. In September, the resort of Lillehammer, north of Oslo, was chosen for the 1994 Winter Olympic Games.

Oman

Middle East
105,000 sq. mi
Pop: 1.2m.
UN, AL, GCC

Capital: Muscat (Pop: 250,000)
Official language: Arabic
Religions: Ibadhi Moslem 75%, Sunni Moslem
Political status: Sultanate
Head of state: Qaboos bin Said (since 1970)
GNP per capita: $7,080 (1985)
Currency: Rial Omani (£1 = 0.683)

Further progress was made in 1988 towards settling a long-running border dispute with Marxist South Yemen. In mid-November, nearly 100 cases of polio were reported in Oman.

Pakistan

South Asia
307,293 sq. mi
Pop: 102.2m.
UN

Capital: Islamabad (Pop: 201,000)
Official languages: Urdu, English
Religions: Moslem 97%, Christian, Hindu
Political status: Federal Islamic republic
Head of state: Ghulam Ishaq Khan (since 1988)
Head of government: Benazir Bhutto (since 1988)
GNP per capita: $390 (1983)
Currency: rupee (£1 = 30.60)

An early April blast at a munitions depot in Islamabad killed 100 people and destroyed hundreds of tons of U.S. arms. The arms were reportedly destined for anti-Soviet Afghan rebels. In mid-April, Pakistan signed an Afghan peace accord which is to lead to the total pullout of Soviet forces from Afghanistan by February 1989. General Zia ul-Haq, Pakistan's longest-serving leader, was killed in an August plane-crash allegedly caused by sabotage. An October outburst of ethnic violence in Karachi left more than 300 dead. On December 2, Benazir Bhutto, who gave up a jet-setting life to avenge her father, overthrown in a coup by Gen. Zia in 1977 and executed in 1979, was sworn in as Prime Minister. She thus became the first woman to govern a Moslem country. Ms. Bhutto, 35, headed the first democratically-elected government since her father's ouster. She immediately announced the restoration of fundamental rights and lifted the state of emergency in force since President Zia's death.

Panama

Central America
29,768 sq. mi
Pop: 2.28m.
UN, OAS

Capital: Panama City (Pop: 386,393)
Official language: Spanish
Religions: Roman Catholic 85%, Protestant 5%, Moslem 4.5%
Political status: Presidential republic
Head of state: Manuel Solis Palma (since 1988)
GNP per capita: $2,060 (1985)
Currency: balboa (£1 = 1.77)

Relations between Panama and the United States hit rock bottom in early 1988, after the Reagan administration tried unsuccessfully in February to force out Panamanian Defence Forces chief Manuel Antonio Noriega, indicted on U.S. drug conspiracy charges in Miami. In March, Washington sent 2,000 more troops to Panama and a coup bid against General Noriega failed. Despite the crippling effects of a clampdown on Panamanian assets in the U.S. and trade with that country, General Noriega clung tenaciously to power. Alleged links between General Noriega and the U.S. intelligence services loomed large in the 1988 U.S. presidential elections.

Papua New Guinea

Pacific
170,702 sq. mi
Pop: 3.48m.
UN, CW

Capital: Port Moresby (Pop: 123,624)
Official language: English
Religions: Protestant 63%, Roman Catholic 31%, local religions
Political status: Constitutional monarchy
Head of state: Queen Elizabeth II
Head of government: Rabbie Namaliu (since 1988)
GNP per capita: $751 (1986)
Currency: kina (£1 = 1.58)

Premier Paias Wingti was ousted by opposition leader Rabbie Namaliu in July. Mr. Wingti said he would cooperate with the new government. A major September mud-slide killed 75 villagers in Morobe province.

Paraguay

South America
157,042 sq. mi
Pop: 3.79m.
UN, LAIA, OAS, LAES

Capital: Asuncion (Pop: 729,307)
Official languages: Spanish, Guarani
Religion: Roman Catholic 97%
Political status: Presidential republic
Head of state: Alfredo Stroessner (since 1954)
GNP per capita: $1,175 (1984)
Currency: guarani (£1 = 566)

President Alfredo Stroessner won his eighth five-year term in February elections marred by reports of fraud. In October, the government denied persistent rumours that President Stroessner, 75, was gravely ill.

Peru

South America
496,222 sq. mi
Pop: 20.2m.
UN, LAIA, OAS

Capital: Lima (Pop: 5,258,600)
Official languages: Spanish, Quechua
Religion: Roman Catholic over 90%
Political status: Republic
Head of state: Alan Garcia Perez (since 1985)
Head of government: Guillermo Larco Cox (since 1987)
GNP per capita: $970 (1985)
Currency: inti (£1 = 58.43)

President Alan Garcia in March unveiled a new economic policy, saying it was based on a "war footing" economy. All non-essential government spending programmes were cut back in a bid to stem runaway inflation. A nationwide wave of strikes in November forced the government to lift a controversial decree limiting salaries. Security forces continued to battle Shining Path extreme-left guerrillas. In September, archeologists discovered a major cache of 1,500-year-old artifacts at a burial site northwest of Lima.

Philippines

Southeast Asia
115,830 sq. mi
Pop: 57.36m.
UN, ASEAN

Capital: Manila (Pop: 1,630,485)
Official languages: Pilipino
Religions: Roman Catholic 83%, Protestant 9%, Moslem 5%
Political status: Republic
Head of state: Corazon C. Aquino (since 1986)
GNP per capita: $614 (1986)
Currency: peso (£1 = 36.20)

President Corazon Aquino marked the 1,000th. day of her presidency on November 21, as the Philippines faced persistent economic woes, a communist insurgency, high level corruption and threats from rightist extremists in the military. Relations

with the U.S. improved after the October signing of a pact allowing U.S. forces to continue using two huge bases in exchange for increased aid. President Reagan said he would urge his successor to launch an ambitious international plan to rehabilitate the Philippine economy from 1989. Two late 1988 typhoons killed some 700 people and caused damage estimated at over £147 million.

Poland

Eastern Europe
120,628 sq. mi
Pop: 37.6m.
UN, CMEA, Warsaw Pact

Capital: Warsaw (Pop: 1,649,000)
Official language: Polish
Religion: Roman Catholic 93%
Political status: Socialist republic
Head of state: Wojciech Jaruzelski (since 1985)
Head of government: Mieczyslaw Rakowski (since 1988)
GNP per capita: $56,420 (1985)
Currency: zloty (£1 = 313.7)

Several thousand Poles marched through the streets of Warsaw in April to commemorate the 45th. anniversary of the city's Jewish ghetto uprising. In October, Poland's new Prime Minister, 61-year-old Mieczyslaw Rakowski, who is a long-time foe of the banned Solidarity trade union, issued a stern warning that he was prepared to call in the army to prevent "social anarchy". A government decision to shut down the historic Gdansk shipyards sparked off a wave of nationwide labour unrest. Prime Minister Margaret Thatcher in November became the first British premier to visit Poland and the first Western leader to meet Solidarity chief Lech Walesa in Gdansk.

Portugal

Southwestern Europe
35,516 sq. mi
Pop: 10.29m.
UN, NATO, OECD, EEC

Capital: Lisbon (Pop: 807,937)
Official language: Portuguese
Religion: Roman Catholic 94.5%
Political status: Parliamentary republic
Head of state: Mario Soares (since 1986)
Head of government: Anibal Cavaco Silva (since 1985)
GNP per capita: $2,190 (1983)
Currency: escudo (£1 = 244.50)

A huge blaze in August burned down much of Lisbon's historic district of Baixa, which was rebuilt after a 1755 earthquake. Portugal's roads remained the most deadly in Europe, with more than 2,500 deaths in 1988.

Qatar

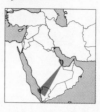

Middle East
4,415 sq. mi
Pop: 371,863
UN, AL, OPEC, GCC

Capital: Doha (Pop: 190,000)
Official language: Arabic
Religion: Moslem 95%
Political status: Emirate
Head of state: Khalifa bin Hamad Al-Thani (since 1972)
GNP per capita: $22,940 (1984)
Currency: riyal (£1 = 6.46)

Drilling began off Qatar's coast in August at a well which was reported to contain the world's largest reserves of natural gas. Drilling operations were being carried out by a large Franco-American consortium.

Romania

Southeastern Europe
91,699 sq. mi
Pop: 22.7m.
UN, CMEA, Warsaw Pact

Capital: Bucharest (Pop: 1,975,808)
Official language: Romanian
Religions: Orthodox 80%, Roman Catholic 6%
Political status: Socialist republic
Head of state: Nicolae Ceausescu (since 1967)
Head of government: Constantin Dascalescu (since 1982)
GNP per capita: $2,540 (1981)
Currency: leu (£1 = 6.25)

Apparently irked by U.S. calls for improvement in human rights policies, Romania in February said it no longer wanted preferential trading links with Washington. In September, the government watered down a controversial resettlement plan that was to have involved the levelling of thousands of small villages.

Rwanda

Central Africa
10,169 sq. mi
Pop: 6.32m.
UN, OAU

Capital: Kigali (Pop: 156,650)
Official languages: French, Kinyarwanda, Kiswhahili
Religions: Christian 68%, traditional 23%, Moslem 9%
Political status: Republic
Head of state: Juvenal Habyarimana (since 1975)
GNP per capita: $257 (1984)
Currency: Rwanda franc (£1 = 131.75)

President Juvenal Habyarimana, became in October the sole candidate for late December presidential elections. Rwanda's meagre resources were hit by the arrival of 40,000 refugees from massacres in Burundi.

St Christopher and Nevis

Caribbean
103 sq. mi
Pop: 47,000
UN, CW, OAS, Caricom

Capital: Basseterre (Pop: 14,283)
Official language: English
Religion: Protestant 76.4%, Roman Catholic 10.7%
Political status: Constitutional monarchy
Head of state: Queen Elizabeth II
Head of government: Kennedy A. Simmonds (since 1983)
GNP per capita: $820 (1983)
Currency: East Caribbean dollar (£1 = 4.79)

Saint Christopher and Nevis was spared major damage to housing and agriculture in September when Hurricane Gilbert went on a rampage through the Caribbean.

St Lucia

Caribbean
238 sq. mi
Pop: 143,600
UN, CW, OAS, Caricom

Capital: Castries (Pop: 45,763)
Official language: English
Religion: Roman Catholic 86%
Political status: Constitutional monarchy
Head of state: Queen Elizabeth II
Head of government: John Compton (since 1982)
GNP per capita: $1,105 (1985)
Currency: East Caribbean dollar (£1 = 4.79)

There was disagreement in July when Caribbean Community members, including St. Lucia, did not agree on whether to suspend Haiti's observer status with the group.

St Vincent and the Grenadines

Caribbean
150 sq. mi
Pop: 138,000
UN, CW, OAS, Caricom

Capital: Kingstown (Pop: 33,694)
Official language: English
Religions: Anglican 47%, Methodist 28%,
Roman Catholic 13%
Political status: Constitutional monarchy
Head of state: Queen Elizabeth II
Head of government: James Mitchell (since 1984)
GNP per capita: $860 (1983)
Currency: East Caribbean dollar
(£1 = 4.79)

St. Vincent in January broke its diplomatic ties with North Korea. In June, Canada granted aid to safeguard St. Vincent's forests.

San Marino

Southern Europe
24.1 sq. mi
Pop: 22,638

Capital: San Marino (Pop: 4,363)
Official language: Italian
Religion: Roman Catholic 95%
Political status: Republic
Heads of state: Two co-regents appointed every 6 months
Currency: Italian lira

The mountainous city-state of San Marino, the world's smallest republic, became the 22nd. member of the Council of Europe in late 1988.

Sao Tome and Principe

Atlantic Ocean
387 sq. mi
Pop: 113,000
UN, OAU

Capital: Sao Tome (Pop: 34,997)
Official language: Portuguese
Religion: Roman Catholic 80%
Political status: Republic
Head of state: Manuel Pinto da Costa (since 1975)
GNP: $31 mil. (1983)
Currency: dobra (£1 = 130.54)

The army crushed a coup attempt against President Manuel Pinto da Costa in March, killing two opponents of the government.

Saudi Arabia

Middle East
849,400 sq. mi
Pop: 11.52m.
UN, AL, GCC,
OPEC

Capital: Riyadh (Pop: 666,840)
Official language: Arabic
Religion: Sunni Moslem 85%, Shiite 15%
Political status: Kingdom
Head of state: King Fahd ibn Abdul Aziz (since 1982)
GNP per capita: $8,000 (1985)
Currency: rial (£1 = 6.64)

Saudi Arabia cut its diplomatic ties with Iran in April. In July, Riyadh concluded a huge arms deal with Britain including warplanes and navy vessels following U.S. refusals to supply certain weapons.

Senegal

West Africa
75,750 sq. mi
Pop: 6.7m.
UN, OAU

Capital: Dakar (Pop: 978,553)
Official language: French
Religions: Moslem 91%, Christian 6%,
animist 3%
Political status: Republic
Head of state: Abdou Diouf (since 1981)
GNP per capita: $360 (1984)
Currency: franc CFA (£1 = 507)

Following his overwhelming election victory in February, President Abdou Diouf invoked emergency powers when reports of large scale vote fraud led to widespread rioting.

Seychelles

Indian Ocean
175 sq. mi
Pop: 67,000
UN, CW, OAU

Capital: Victoria (Pop: 23,000)
Official languages: Creole, English,
French
Religion: Roman Catholic 96%
Political status: Republic
Head of state: France Albert René (since 1977)
GNP per capita: $2,320 (1984)
Currency: Seychelles rupee (£1 = 9.24)

A treasure hunt began in July to find gold and silver worth £118 million allegedly buried by 18th. century French pirate Olivier Le Vasseur.

Sierra Leone

West Africa
27,925 sq. mi
Pop: 3.67m.
UN, ECOWAS,
CW, OAU

Capital: Freetown (Pop: 554,243)
Official language: English
Religions: tribal 52%, Moslem 39%,
Christian 8%
Political status: Republic
Head of state: Joseph Saidu Momoh (since 1988)
GNP per capita: $380 (1983)
Currency: leone (£1 = 54.45)

Siaka Probyn Stevens, who ruled Sierra Leone for 17 years, died in May. His hand-picked successor, Major General Joseph Momoh, in October said that he would not tolerate anti-government "subversion".

Singapore

Southeast Asia
238.7 sq. mi
Pop: 2.59m.
UN, ASEAN,
CW

Capital: Singapore (Pop: 2,500,000)
Official languages: Chinese, Malay, Tamil,
English
Religions: Buddhist, Taoist, Moslem, Hinduist, Christian
Political status: Parliamentary republic
Head of state: Wee Kim Wee (since 1985)
Head of government: Lee Kuan Yew (since 1959)
GNP per capita: $6,630 (1986)
Currency: Singapore dollar (£1 = 3.56)

Relations with Washington soured in May after Singapore accused a U.S. diplomat of "gross interference" in its domestic affairs. In July, premier Lee Kuan Yew proposed that an international panel resolve the row. British Prime Minister Margaret Thatcher held talks with Mr. Lee in July. Singapore's leader was re-elected for an eighth term in September with 61.8 percent of the vote. He promised to resign sometime after turning 65 in late September.

Solomon Islands

Pacific
10,640 sq. mi
Pop: 270,000
UN, CW

Capital: Honiara (Pop: 26,000)
Official language: English
Religions: Protestant 76%, Roman
Catholic 19%
Political status: Constitutional monarchy
Head of state: Queen Elizabeth II
Head of government: Ezekiel Alebua (since 1988)
GNP per capita: $640 (1983)
Currency: Solomon Island dollar
(£1 = 3.59)

Ezekiel Alebua became the new Prime Minister following the resignation in late 1987 of Sir Peter Kenilorea, who was accused of accepting French aid to rebuild his own village, which had been hit by a cyclone.

Somalia

Northeastern
Africa
246,201 sq. mi
Pop: 6.11m.
UN, AL, OAU

Capital: Mogadishu (Pop: 250,000)
Official languages: Somali, Arabic
Religion: Sunni Moslem 99%
Political status: Republic
Head of state: Mohammed Siyad Barre (since 1969)
Head of government: Mohammed Ali Samater
GNP per capita: $250 (1983)
Currency: Somali shilling (£1 = 177.35)

Drought affected many regions of Somalia in 1988. The country also had to cope with the devastation caused to agriculture by hordes of locusts. Refugees from neighbouring Ethiopia continued to flood in.

South Africa

Southern Africa
433,678 sq. mi
Pop: 23.39m.
UN

Capital: Pretoria (Pop: 528,407)
Official languages: Afrikaans, English
Religion: Mainly Christian
Political status: Republic
Head of state: Pieter Botha (since 1978)
GNP per capita: $2,500 (1984)
Currency: rand (£1 = 3.69)

Although it ended on a positive note, 1988 was another difficult year for South Africa, which began its third year of emergency in June. The far-right Conservative Party won two by-elections in March. This was a setback for President Pieter Botha's limited race reforms. Pretoria defiantly told U.N. members to "do your damnedest" to try to force change in South Africa. Three anti-apartheid leaders in October left the U.S. Consulate in Johannesburg after holing up there for over a month. A controversial labour law banning "politically motivated" strikes was implemented in September. Segregated local elections held in October were marred by a low black turnout and a far-right challenge to the government. Year-long feuding between black factions in Natal left some 600 people dead. The November killing of six blacks by a white neo-Nazi led to South Africa's first ever banning of a white supremacist group. On November 22, Pretoria approved an historic plan to bring independence to Namibia and a Cuban troop pullout from Angola. In November, South Africa moved towards the freeing of veteran anti-apartheid leader Nelson Mandela, who has served 26 years of a life sentence for sabotage.

Spain

Southwestern
Europe
194,884 sq. mi
Pop: 38.9m.
UN, NATO,
EEC, OECD

Capital: Madrid (Pop: 3,188,297)
Official language: Spanish
Religion: Roman Catholic
Political status: Constitutional monarchy
Head of state: King Juan Carlos I
Head of government: Felipe Gonzalez
Marquez (since 1982)
GNP per capita: $5,198 (1986)
Currency: peseta (£1 = 202)

Anglo-Spanish ties, often troubled by a dispute over Gibraltar, took a big step forward in September when Margaret Thatcher became the first British premier to visit Spain. In December, the U.S. and Spain signed an eight-year military accord.

Sri Lanka

South Asia
25,332 sq. mi
Pop: 15.8m.
UN, CW

Capital: Colombo (Pop: 587,647)
Official language: Sinhala
Religions: Buddhist 69%, Hindu 15%,
Christian 7%, Moslem 7%
Political status: Republic
Head of state: Junius R. Jayawardene
(since 1978)
Head of government: Ranasinghe
Premadasa (since 1978)
GNP per capita: $361 (1984)
Currency: Sri Lankan rupee (£1 = 54.10)

A 1987 peace accord with India failed to end the bloodshed in Sri Lanka, which continued to be paralysed by the vicious conflict between separatist Tamil guerrillas and the Sinhalese-dominated government. More than 700 Indian troops were reported killed since the July 1987 peace pact. In September, Tamil gunmen killed a cabinet minister. Armed men belonging to a secretive Marxist group, the JVP, resurfaced in October, butchering 45 Sinhalese, mostly government employees who had defied a JVP order to stay away from work. It was the worst attack against civilians in 18 months.

Sudan

North Africa
967,500 sq. mi
Pop: 25.55m.
UN, AL, OAU

Capital: Khartoum (Pop: 476,218)
Official language: Arabic
Religions: Moslem 73%, animist 18%,
Christian 9%
Political status: Republic
Head of state: Ahmad Ali al-Mirghani
(since 1986)
Head of government: Sadiq al-Mahdi
(since 1986)
GNP per capita: $400 (1983)
Currency: Sudanese pound (£1 = 7.98)

A terrible famine continued to stalk Sudan, where more than four million people were reported to be starving. International efforts to rush relief supplies to the affected zones were hampered by the 24-year-old conflict between the predominantly Moslem north and the Christian and animist south. More than a million people have already died in the war between government forces and rebels of the Sudanese People's Liberation Army led by Col. John Garang.

Suriname

South America
63,250 sq. mi
Pop: 370,000
UN, OAS

Capital: Paramaribo (Pop: 67,905)
Official languages: Dutch, English
Religions: Moslem, Hindu, Christian
Political status: Republic
Head of state: Ramsewak Shankar (since
1988)
GNP per capita: $2,980 (1984)
Currency: Suriname guilders (£1 = 3.17)

Fighting broke out between rebels led by Ronnie Brunswijk and government troops in June, ending a truce struck in late 1987 following Suriname's first free elections after seven years of military rule.

Swaziland

Southern Africa
6,705 sq. mi
Pop: 676,049
UN, OAU, CW

Capital: Mbabane (Pop: 23,109)
Official languages: Swazi, English
Religions: Christian 77%, traditional 23%
Political status: Monarchy
Head of state: King Mswati III
Head of government: Sotja E. Dlamini
(since 1986)
GNP per capita: $730 (1984)
Currency: emalangeni (£1 = 3.69)

King Mswati III, aged 20, married the 19-year-old daughter of an Anglican priest in October. She became his fifth wife. A witch-doctor was sentenced to death in November for the ritual killing of a young boy. In October, Swaziland denounced border incursions by South African forces.

Sweden

Northern
Europe
173,731 sq. mi
Pop: 8.4m.
UN, EFTA,
OECD

Capital: Stockholm (Pop: 663,217)
Official language: Swedish
Religion: Lutheran 95%
Political status: Constitutional
monarchy
Head of state: King Carl XVI Gustaf
Head of government: Ingvar Carlsson
(since 1986)
GNP per capita: $11,977 (1985)
Currency: Swedish krona (£1 = 10.62)

The fate of farm animals became a hot issue as the government approved a "bill of rights" for barnyard beasts. In April, the U.S. and Sweden marked the 350th. anniversary of the arrival of Swedes in America.

Switzerland

Western Europe
15,943 sq. mi
Pop: 6.5m.
EFTA, OECD

Capital: Bern (Pop: 301,100)
Official languages: German, French,
Italian, Romansh
Religions: Roman Catholic 47.6%,
Protestant 44.3%
Political status: Federal state
Head of state: Otto Stich (since 1988)
GNP per capita: $14,030 (1985)
Currency: franc (£1 = 2.47)

Britain's Prince Charles escaped badly shaken but unhurt in March when an Alpine avalanche buried one of his closest friends. In mid-November, a Swiss national was taken hostage in Lebanon.

Syria

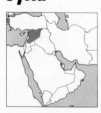

Middle East
71,498 sq. mi
Pop: 10.96m.
UN, AL

Capital: Damascus (Pop: 1,251,028)
Official language: Arabic
Religions: Sunni Moslem 90%
Political status: Republic
Head of state: Hafez al-Assad (since 1971)
Head of government: Mahmoud Zubi
(1987)
GNP per capita: $2,000 (1984)
Currency: Syrian pound (£1 = 53.21)

Syria continued to play a major military and political role in strife-torn Lebanon, as pro- and anti-Syrians clashed in Beirut. Syria's influence over events in Lebanon contributed to a political stalemate there following Lebanon's failure to elect a president in September.

Taiwan

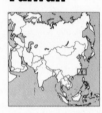

East Asia
13,969 sq. mi
Pop: 19.5m.

Capital: Taipei (Pop: 2.56m.)
Official language: Chinese
Religions: Buddhist, Taoist, Christian
Political status: Republic
Head of state: Lee Teng-hui (since 1988)
Head of government: Yu Kuo-hwa (since
1984)
GNP per capita: $3,748 (1986)
Currency: New Taiwan dollar (£1 = 50.78)

A wind of change swept through the ruling Kuomintang leadership in July, reflecting an urge for reform and greater democratisation. Relations with mainland China continued to improve. In September, Taipei authorised direct trade with China. For the first time since 1949, a Taiwan trade delegation visited Moscow in October. U.S.-Taiwan trade tensions heightened after Washington enacted trade restrictions in August.

Tanzania

Eastern Africa
364,886 sq. mi
Pop: 23.2m.
UN, CW, OAU

Capital: Dodoma (Pop: 47,703)
Official languages: Kiswahili, English
Religions: Moslem 33%, Christian 40%
Political status: Republic
Head of state: Ndugu Ali Hassan Mwinyi
(since 1985)
Head of government: Joseph S. Warioba
(since 1985)
GNP per capita: $210 (1984)
Currency: Tanzanian shilling (£1 = 163.10)

Tanzania finally reached agreement with the International Monetary Fund in November after months of hard bargaining. This meant that the IMF would back the Tanzanian government's austerity measures.

Thailand

Southeast Asia
198,456 sq. mi
Pop: 52.5m.
UN, ASEAN

Capital: Bangkok (Pop: 5,446,708)
Official language: Thai
Religions: Buddhist 95%, Moslem 4%
Political status: Constitutional monarchy
Head of state: King Bhumibol Adulyadej (since 1946)
Head of government: Prem Tinasulanonda (since 1980)
GNP per capita: $720 (1985)
Currency: baht (£1 = 44.30)

A Chicago, Illinois, museum in November returned a 1,000-year-old sandstone temple carving to Thailand, thus ending a lengthy dispute between Bangkok and Washington. Thai officials said the artifact was stolen by U.S. soldiers during the Indochina War in the 1960s. Late November flooding and mudslides left an estimated 1,000 dead, mainly in a province south of Bangkok. The government appealed for international assistance, saying the disaster was among the worst natural calamities Thailand had ever endured.

Togo

West Africa
21,925 sq. mi
Pop: 3.16m.
UN, ECOWAS, OAU

Capital: Lome (Pop: 366,476)
Official language: French
Religions: animist 46%, Christian 37%, Moslem 17%
Political status: Republic
Head of state: Gnassingbe Eyadema (since 1967)
GNP per capita: $280 (1983)
Currency: franc CFA (£1 = 507)

The West African nation on September 23 marked the second anniversary of the attempted overthrow of Gen. Gnassingbe Eyadema's regime, allegedly carried out by commandos from nearby Ghana.

Tonga

South Pacific
289 sq. mi
Pop: 94,535
CW

Capital: Nuku'alofa (Pop: 28,899)
Official languages: Tongan, English
Religions: Christian 90%
Political status: Constitutional monarchy
Head of state: King Taufa'ahau Tupou IV (since 1965)
Head of government: Prince Fatafehi Tu'pelehake (since 1965)
GNP per capita: $580 (1986)
Currency: pa'anga (£1 = 2.46)

The tiny South Pacific Kingdom of Tonga was granted a low-interest loan of £1.4 million by the United Nations International Agricultural Development Fund in July. The aid was for Tonga's fishing industry.

Trinidad and Tobago

Caribbean
1,978 sq. mi
Pop: 1.22m.
UN, Caricom, CW, OAS

Capital: Port-of-Spain (Pop: 58,400)
Official language: English
Religions: Christian 48.6%, Hindu 25%, Moslem 5.9%
Political status: Republic
Head of state: Noor Hassanali (since 1986)
Head of government: Arthur Robinson (since 1986)
GNP per capita: $6,360 (1985)
Currency: Trinidad and Tobago dollar (£1 = 6.38)

Faced with a worsening economic situation, the government in November dismissed 25,000 of the 60,000 government employees. This move came after an August devaluation of the currency by 15 percent.

Tunisia

North Africa
59,664 sq. mi
Pop: 7.32m.
UN, AL, OAU

Capital: Tunis (Pop: 596,654)
Official language: Arabic
Religion: mainly Moslem
Political status: Republic
Head of state: Zine el Abidine Ben Ali (since 1987)
Head of government: Hedi Baccouche (since 1987)
GNP per capita: 1,250 (1985)
Currency: dinar (£1 = 1.45)

Abu Jihad, the Palestine Liberation Organization's second in command, was assassinated in Tunis in April. The killing was allegedly carried out by Israeli commandos. In November, President Zine el Abidine Ben Ali said general elections would be held in 1989 rather than in 1991.

Turkey

Southeastern Europe
300,947 sq. mi
Pop: 50.67m.
UN, NATO, OECD

Capital: Ankara (Pop: 2,251,533)
Official language: Turkish
Religion: Moslem 98,2%
Political status: Republic
Head of state: Kenan Evren (since 1980)
Head of government: Turgut Ozal (since 1983)
GNP per capita: $1,020 (1986)
Currency: Turkish lira (£1 = 2,076)

In February, Turkey became the first nation to ratify the European Convention on torture. This came a month after a U.N. body put Turkey on a blacklist of countries practising torture. Prime Minister Turgut Ozal escaped virtually unharmed from a spectacular June assassination bid in which 13 people were injured. Mr. Ozal vowed to stay on as premier in September despite nearly 65 percent of voters rejecting constitutional reforms proposed by his government. He had earlier promised to resign if the vote went against him. A June landslide killed 63 people. In August, an estimated 130,000 Kurds fleeing from Iraqi air strikes on their camps streamed across the border into Turkey. Sheltering and feeding the refugees posed a major problem.

Tuvalu

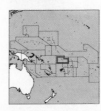

South Pacific
9.5 sq. mi
Pop: 8,229
CW

Capital: Funafuti (Pop: 2,620)
Official languages: Tuvaluan, English
Religion: Protestant
Political status: Constitutional monarchy
Head of state: Queen Elizabeth II
Head of government: Tomasi Puapua (since 1981)
GNP per capita: $500 (1984)
Currency: Australian dollar

The former British Protectorate of Tuvalu celebrated the 10th. anniversary of its independence on October 1. Money sent home by Tuvaluans working abroad remained among the islands' chief sources of income.

Uganda

Eastern Africa
91,343 sq. mi
Pop: 16.79m.
UN, CW, OAU

Capital: Kampala (Pop: 458,423)
Official languages: English, Kiswahili
Religions: Christian 62%, Moslem 6%
Political status: Republic
Head of state: Yoweri Museveni (since 1986)
Head of government: Samson Kisekka (since 1986)
GNP per capita: $230 (1984)
Currency: Uganda shilling (£1 = 106.08)

Ugandans celebrated the 26th. anniversary of independence from Britain in October amid political uncertainty and a continued rebel insurgency in the north. The government sought to rebuild the country's wrecked infrastructure. British, Italian and Chinese firms did brisk business rebuilding roads.

Union of Soviet Socialist Republics

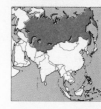

Eurasia
8,649,496 sq. mi
Pop: 284.5m.
UN, CMEA, Warsaw Pact

Capital: Moscow (Pop: 8,715,000)
Official language: Russian
Religions: Christian, Moslem, Jewish, Buddhist
Political status: Federal union
Head of state: Mikhail Gorbachev (since 1988)
Head of government: Nicolai Ryzhkov (since 1985)
Head of Communist Party: Mikhail Gorbachev (since 1985)
GNP per capita: $6,000 (1985)
Currency: ruble (£1 = 1.06)

The year ended in tragedy, when a devastating December earthquake hit Armenia, killing tens of thousands of people. The extent of the disaster was such that President Mikhail Gorbachev had to cut short a visit to New York and cancel trips to Britain and Cuba. It was not all smooth sailing for Mr. Gorbachev, despite a string of successes at home and abroad. On the political front, he consolidated his hold on the reins of power, pushing his main critics and rivals to the sidelines and adding the title of President to his powerful post as General Secretary of the Communist Party in October. Hard-line opponents of Mr. Gorbachev's reform policies of "perestroika" and "glasnost" were replaced by reform-minded officials. The wind of change also blew through the economy: waste, a top-heavy bureaucracy, fraud and chronic inefficiency were targeted by the authorities. There was progress on the human rights front with the freeing of a number of political prisoners. Soviet space technology took a big step forward with the November maiden flight of the shuttle Buran (Snowstorm).

On the international front, the Soviet Union won acclaim for the April signing of a peace accord in Afghanistan. Moscow agreed to withdraw all its troops from that country by February 1989. Mr. Gorbachev travelled widely to the West and the Third World. In December, he held his final meeting with outgoing President Ronald Reagan. The improvement of relations with Washington was marred by a dispute over alleged Soviet bugging of the U.S. Embassy in Moscow.

However, regional nationalism and ethnic strife, which spread from the Baltic to the Caucasus, became a major problem. Year-long tension and clashes between Armenians and Azerbaijanis left dozens dead and forced Mr. Gorbachev to send in the army to try to restore calm in the disputed Nagorny Karabakh region. The Kremlin's authority was defied in the Baltic republics of Latvia, Estonia and Lithuania, where demands for greater autonomy reached a crescendo in November.

United Arab Emirates

Middle East
32,300 sq. mi
Pop: 1.77m.
UN, AL, GCC, OPEC

Capital: Abu Dhabi (Pop: 670,125)
Official language: Arabic
Religion: Moslem 90%
Political status: Federation of emirates
Head of state: Sheikh Zayed bin Sultan Al Nahyan (since 1971)
Head of government: Sheikh Rashid bin Said al-Maktoum (since 1979)
GNP per capita: $19,270 (1985)
Currency: dirham (£1 = 6.50)

The world-wide drop in oil prices seriously affected the United Arab Emirates in 1988, leading the Gulf state to impose budgetary restrictions in a bid to cut down the growing £1.8 billion deficit.

United Kingdom

Northwestern Europe
94,226 sq. mi
Pop: 55,78m.
UN, CW, EEC, NATO, OECD

Capital: London (Pop: 6,800,000)
Official language: English
Religions: Church of England, Roman Catholic
Political status: Constitutional monarchy
Head of state: Queen Elizabeth II
Head of government: Margaret Thatcher (since 1979)
GNP per capita: $7,860 (1985)
Currency: pound sterling

The year began with Margaret Thatcher becoming the longest continuously-serving peace-time prime minister this century. Despite increasing economic woes, which saw the euphoria of a tax-cutting budget in March fade as balance of payments debts and interest rates rose, her Tory party retained its lead over other parties. The government announced further moves in its privatisation programme. Radical changes in education and housing were also passed as Conservative dominance was helped by disarray in opposition ranks. Labour's Neil Kinnock withstood a leadership challenge, but his party was split over defence. The rupture in the old Alliance became permanent with the Social and Liberal Democrats gaining a new name (Democrats) and new leader (ex-commando Paddy Ashdown) to leave David Owen heading the SDP with only three MPs. The political shock of the year was the Scottish Nationalist victory in November at the Labour stronghold of Govan, Glasgow.

Mrs. Thatcher spent much of the year on the world stage, maintaining her old friendship with President Reagan and cultivating her newer one with President Gorbachev. Mrs. Thatcher emerged as a trenchant critic of moves to greater European unity and lambasted the governments of Belgium and Ireland for their handling of the extradition case of former priest, Patrick Ryan. Northern Ireland witnessed a new upsurge in violence. Horrific killings at two Belfast cemeteries followed the shooting by the SAS of an IRA bomb squad in Gibraltar in March. British servicemen were among the victims as the IRA stepped up its campaign of violence during the summer, but so were innocent casualties of "the troubles".

The disaster of the year occurred in July when an explosion on the Piper Alpha oil rig left 165 people dead. This led to calls for stricter safety standards. A December 12 rush-hour train crash left at least thirty people dead and more than 100 injured on the outskirts of London. It was the worst accident involving British Rail in more than two decades.

United States

North America
3,539,289 sq. mi
Pop: 238.7m.
UN, NATO, OAS, OECD

Capital: Washington D.C. (Pop: 638,333)
Official language: English
Religions: Protestant 56%, Catholic 36.7%, Jewish
Political status: Federal republic
Head of state: Ronald Reagan (since 1981)
GNP per capita: $16,710 (1986)
Currency: dollar (£1 = 1.7)

The race to succeed Ronald Reagan dominated the political year with George Bush seeing off the Republican challenge of Robert Dole and Michael Dukakis emerging from the Democratic pack to defeat the spirited campaign of Jesse Jackson. As Mr. Reagan entered the final stretch of his eight years in office, he won Senate approval in May for the historic December 1987 U.S.-Soviet treaty on the scrapping of all medium-range nuclear missiles. It was the first major superpower arms treaty to win Senate approval since 1972 and contributed to the success of Mr. Reagan's visit to Moscow in early June. However, continued work on the futuristic and costly "Star Wars" project caused new tension with the Kremlin. In November, the Pentagon unveiled its B-2 "Stealth" bomber designed to streak unnoticed past enemy radar. A major bribes and fraud scandal rocked the Defence Department in July, leading to suspension of payments on a billion dollars worth of defence contracts.

Relations between the Reagan administration and the U.N. had their ups and downs in 1988. In September, Mr. Reagan ordered the payment of nearly £306 million in current and past dues to the cash-strapped U.N. But in November, a U.S. decision to bar PLO chief Yasser Arafat from entering New York to address the U.N. brought international condemnation.

October marked the first anniversary of Wall Street's cataclysmic "Black Monday". Although the situation that prompted the record 508-point drop in the Dow Jones index receded in 1988, financial markets were still awaiting the return of the small investor.

The U.S. roared back into space in September as the shuttle Discovery completed the first U.S. manned space mission since the Challenger disaster 32 months earlier.

President-elect George Bush, who was to take office on January 20, 1989, faced tough challenges. Among the major hurdles confronting him are the gargantuan national debt, a stubborn budget deficit, continued strife in Central America, trade tensions with Asia, a deadlocked Middle East peace process and rapidly changing relations with Soviet leader Mikhail Gorbachev.

Uruguay

South America
72,172 sq. mi
Pop: 2.95m.
UN, LAIA, OAS

Capital: Montevideo (Pop: 1,237,227)
Official language: Spanish
Religion: Roman Catholic 66%
Political status: Republic
Head of state: Julio Maria Sanguinetti (since 1985)
GNP per capita: $1,800 (1984)
Currency: Nuevo Peso (£1 = 534.69)

A Montevideo cinema showing the controversial film "The Last Temptation of Christ" was hit by a November arson attack. President Sanguinetti in November approved an anti-inflation plan. Police nabbed eight people for a baby-selling racket.

Vanuatu

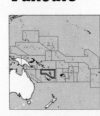

South Pacific
5,700 sq. mi
Pop: 141,000
UN, CW

Capital: Vila (Pop: 15,000)
Official languages: Bislama, English, French
Religion: Christian 80%
Political status: Republic
Head of state: Ati Sokomanu (since 1980)
Head of government: Walter Lini (since 1980)
GNP per capita: $350 (1981)
Currency: Vatu (£1 = 183)

Vanuatu in 1988 headed towards a reconciliation with its former colonial power, France, after years of discord over the issue of independence for the neighbouring French South Pacific territory of New Caledonia.

Vatican City

Southern Europe
108.7 acres
Pop: 1,000

Capital: Vatican City
Official languages: Italian, Latin
Religion: Catholic
Head of Roman Catholic Church: Pope John Paul II (since 1978)
Secretary of State: Cardinal Agostino Casaroli (since 1979)
Currency: lira (£1 = 2,207)

The Vatican in June excommunicated renegade French Archbishop Marcel Lefebvre for violating church rites. This marked the first schism in the Roman Catholic Church in more than a century.

Venezuela

South America
352,143 sq. mi
Pop: 17.32m.
UN, LAIA, OAS, OPEC

Capital: Caracas (Pop: 1,816,901)
Official language: Spanish
Religion: Roman Catholic
Political status: Republic
Head of state: Jaime Lusinchi (since 1984)
GNP per capita: $2,680 (1985)
Currency: bolivar (£1 = 51.08)

Ruling party candidate Carlos Andres Perez, who was Venezuela's president from 1974 to 1979, won an easy victory in December 4 elections, defeating his rival Eduardo Fernandez. Mr. Perez will succeed President Lusinchi on February 2, 1989.

Vietnam

Southeast Asia
127,245 sq. mi
Pop: 61.95m.
UN, CMEA

Capital: Hanoi (Pop: 2,600,000)
Official language: Vietnamese
Religions: Buddhist, Taoist
Political status: Socialist republic
Head of state: Vo Chi Cong (since 1987)

Head of government: Du Muoi (since 1988)
GNP per capita: $300 (1984)
Currency: dong (£1 = 653)

Vietnam in May pledged to withdraw 50,000 of its estimated 120,000 troops from Cambodia by the end of 1988. Relations with the U.S. improved following a July accord for former Vietnamese prisoners to emigrate to the United States. Great progress was made this year on the issue of U.S. servicemen still believed missing in Vietnam. Fierce November typhoons caused major damage.

Western Samoa

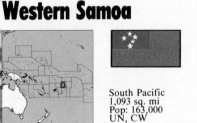

South Pacific
1,093 sq. mi
Pop: 163,000
UN, CW

Capital: Apia (Pop: 33,170)
Official languages: Samoan, English
Religions: Congregationalist 47%, Roman Catholic 22%, Methodist 16%
Political status: Constitutional monarchy
Head of state: King Malietoa Tanumafili II
Head of government: Tofilau Eti Alesana (since 1988)
GNP per capita: $770 (1985)
Currency: tala (£1 = 3.53)

February general elections resulted in the defeat of Va'ai Kolone. The new premier, Tofilau Eti Alesana, head of the Human Rights Protection Party which has been ousted in December 1985, took office in April.

Yemen (North)

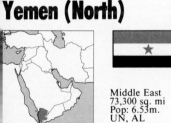

Middle East
73,300 sq. mi
Pop: 6.53m.
UN, AL

Capital: San'a (Pop: 277,817)
Official language: Arabic
Religion: Moslem (Sunni 39%, Shi'a 59%)
Political status: Republic
Head of state: Ali Abdallah Saleh (since 1978)
Head of government: Abdel Aziz Abdel Ghani (since 1983)
GNP per capita: $510 (1983)
Currency: riyal (£1 = 18.20)

North Yemen's leader, Colonel Ali Abdallah Saleh, accepted a third term as head of state on July 17, soon after submitting his resignation and asking the Consultative Assembly to choose a new president.

Yemen (South)

Middle East
130,065 sq. mi
Pop: 2.3m.
UN, AL

Capital: Aden (Pop: 318,000)
Official language: Arabic
Religions: mostly Moslem, Christian, Hindu
Political status: People's democratic republic
Head of state: Haidar al-Attas (since 1986)
Head of government: Yasin Sa'id Nu'man (since 1986)
GNP per capita: $500 (1985)
Currency: dinar (£1 = 0.608)

In May, South Yemen's government marked the 25th. anniversary of its revolution, as it sought to solidify its legitimacy by improving ties with its Horn of Africa neighbours.

Yugoslavia

Southern Europe
96,835 sq. mi
Pop: 23.27m.
UN

Capital: Belgrade (Pop: 1,470,073)
Official languages: Serbo-Croat, Macedonian, Slovene
Religions: Orthodox 41%, Roman Catholic 32%, Moslem 12%
Political status: Federal socialist republic
Head of state: Lazar Mojsov (since May 1987)
Head of government: Branko Mikulic (since 1986)
GNP per capita: $5,600 (1985)
Currency: dinar (£1 = 2,387)

Nearly 40 years after Yugoslavia was kicked out of the Socialist bloc by Moscow, Soviet leader Mikhail Gorbachev in March visited Belgrade, ending the ideological rift. A wave of often-violent Serbian nationalism left the country facing its worst crisis since Marshal Josip Broz Tito's death in 1980. Yugoslavia's eight million Serbs, led by Serbian Communist Party chief Slobodan Milosevic, demonstrated repeatedly to back their demands for greater control over the autonomous provinces of Kosovo and Vojvodina. The ethnic unrest came on top of a disastrous economic situation, with inflation reaching 250 percent and high unemployment.

Zaire

Central Africa
905,365 sq. mi
Pop: 31.78m.
UN, OAU

Capital: Kinshasa (Pop: 2,653,558)
Official language: French
Religions: mostly Roman Catholic, Protestant, Moslem
Political status: Presidential republic
Head of state: Marshal Mobutu Sésé Séko (since 1965)
Head of government: Mabi Mulumba (since 1987)
GNP per capita: $160 (1983)
Currency: zaïre (£1 = 246.20)

Pope John Paul II in April warned the bishops of Zaire against what he said was a rising trend to polygamy in their country. He urged Zairians to reject polygamy, adding this was harmful to Christian marriages.

Zambia

Southern Africa
290,586 sq. mi
Pop: 7.12m.
UN, CW, OAU

Capital : Lusaka (Pop: 538,469)
Official language: English
Religions: Christian 66%, Moslem
Political status: Republic
Head of state: Kenneth David Kaunda (since 1964)
Head of government: K.S.K. Musokotwane (since 1985)
GNP per capita: $410 (1984)
Currency: Kwacha (£1 = 13.80)

Zambians faced five more years of stiff belt-tightening after President Kenneth Kaunda was sworn in for his sixth term of office in October. Mr. Kaunda has led Zambia since its 1964 independence from Britain.

Zimbabwe

Southern Africa
150,699 sq. mi
Pop: 8.64m.
UN, CW, OAU

Capital: Harare (Pop: 656,100)
Official language: English
Religions: mostly Anglican and Roman Catholic
Political status: Republic
Head of state: Robert G. Mugabe (since 1987)
GNP per capita: $780 (1984)
Currency: Zimbabwe dollar (£1 = 3.08)

Zimbabwe President Robert Mugabe in April declared an amnesty for all the country's dissident rebels in a bid to further strengthen the merger of the opposition Zimbabwe African Peoples Union, led by rival politician Joshua Nkomo, into his ruling Zimbabwe African National Union. This brought new hope for an end to years of anti-government violence.

Abbreviations		
AL	Arab League	
ANZUS	Australia, New-Zealand, U.S.	
ASEAN	Association of South East Asian Nations	
Caricom	Caribbean Community and Common Market	
CFA	African Financial Community currency	
CMEA	(or Comecon) Council for Mutual Economic Assistance	
CW	The Commonwealth	
ECOWAS	Economic Community of West African States	
EEC	European Economic Community	
EFTA	European Free Trade Association	
GCC	Gulf Cooperation Council	
LAES	Latin American Economic System	
LAIA	Latin American Integration Association	
NATO	North Atlantic Treaty Organization	
NC	Nordic Council	
OAS	Organization of American States	
OAU	Organization of African Unity	
OECD	Organization for Economic Cooperation and Development	
OPEC	Organization of Petroleum Exporting Countries	
UN	United Nations	
WP	Warsaw Pact	

General Index

Photo Credit Index

128